D0274904

LONDON'S UNDERGROUND

LONDON'S UNDERGROUND

10th Edition

JOHN GLOVER

388.428

HARTLEPOOL BOROUGH LIBRARIES

HC 5/04

1192341

Ian Allan

PUBLISHING

Front cover: **Advertising liveries were seen on a few trains in the second half of the 1990s. Perhaps the best known was the C69-stock set which was finished in a Yellow Pages all-over colour scheme in 1998/9. It is seen here liberated from the Circle Line (although still with that line's route indicator), working the Chesham-bound branch shuttle on 17 May 1998. This is the long section of the branch which, on leaving Chalfont & Latimer, more or less parallels the main line to Amersham for some distance before swinging away to the north.** *R. L. Sewell*

Back cover (1): **Hounslow East station was reconstructed in 2002/3 with new station buildings. The line here is above ground level and crosses Kingsley Road (foreground) on a bridge. The new station entrance and ticket office is on the westbound side of the line. The striking building is seen here with most of the major works complete on 22 March 2003.** *Author*

Back cover (2): **A pair of 1938-stock trains pass at Finchley Central on 22 August 1967. The date is the centenary of the opening of the Edgware, Highgate & London Railway, which later became part of the Great Northern and its successor the LNER. Since 1940 it has been part of the Northern Line. The approaching train is for High Barnet, a branch which was opened in 1872. The 1938 stock monopolised Northern Line operations for over 30 years.** *Author*

Back cover (3): **The 1992 stock for the Central Line disgraced itself on 25 January 2003 when a traction motor became detached and dropped onto the line. Derailment followed, as the westbound train was approaching Chancery Lane. In happier days, a train of this stock arrives at West Ruislip on 15 March 1997. The signalbox in the background is used for the parallel National Railways route and has no involvement with the Underground.** *Author*

Back cover (4): **The Jubilee Line Extension is seen with a Stratford-bound train on 29 September 2001. The 1996-stock train is running alongside the North London line of Network Rail but is kept apart from it by a substantial barrier. This is the view looking northwards towards the beginnings of Stratford Market depot.** *Author*

Above: **Boston Manor station of 1934 sees a westbound Piccadilly Line train of refurbished 1973 stock arriving on 22 March 2003. The 'Underground' feel of the architecture, with its tower, is unmistakeable** *Author*

Half title: **The original Metropolitan Railway platforms at Baker Street station were generally refurbished and relit as part of a plan to restore their general appearance similar to that when new. The shafts in the picture originally led to daylight, but this has been simulated electrically.** *Thorn EMI Lighting Ltd*

Title page: **The newest part of the Underground is the Jubilee Line, which opened throughout to Stratford in late 1999.** *Author*

First published 2003

ISBN 0 7110 2935 0

All rights reserved. No part of this book may be reproduced or transmitted in any form or by any means, electronic or mechanical, including photocopying, recording or by any information storage and retrieval system, without permission from the Publisher in writing.

© Ian Allan Publishing Ltd 2003

Published by Ian Allan Publishing

an imprint of Ian Allan Publishing Ltd,
Riverdene Business Park, Molesey Road,
Hersham, Surrey KT12 4RG
Printed by Ian Allan Printing Ltd,
Riverdene Business Park, Molesey Road,
Hersham, Surrey KT12 4RG

Code: 0311/B2

Acknowledgements

So many people have helped in one way or another with the preparation of this book that it is almost invidious to single out some of them. However, I should like to mention especially Bob Bayman, the late Jack Gaywood, David Hartland and Susan Mayne, and the late Henry Howson who wrote the early editions. The responsibility for the contents is however mine alone. I am grateful to my wife, Ann, who has done her very best to encourage me to get the work finished; thanks also to Ian Allan Publishing for their efforts to make this book a success.

Contents

Introduction

What do we mean by a metropolitan or an underground railway? The following definition was coined by Michael Robbins in 1981 for the International Union of Public Transport:

'A metropolitan railway is one designed to provide a system for the carriage of large numbers of passengers within a city area by means of railed vehicles under external control, within space which is wholly or partly in tunnel and is completely devoted to their use.'

To which was later added:

'A transport system using its own reserved infrastructure to handle traffic in excess of 10,000 people per hour, based largely on the railway technology currently available or in course of development.'

URBAN RAILWAYS ARE, ESSENTIALLY, A HIGH-DENSITY OPERATION

This, the 10th edition of one of the first histories of London Underground, comes at a time when change is once again under way. When the book first appeared in 1951, the Underground had just been nationalised. Since then, it has been municipalised, renationalised, and then municipalised again. Over that period, the Underground has also seen an enormous growth in passenger numbers, though these have included substantial downward movements within that overall trend. There have also been some relatively modest additions to the system, and a few minor closures.

When did it all start? In 1863 the first element of the Underground system was born into an era of the horse bus and the hansom cab, of steam railways…and traffic congestion. The system expanded slowly until the turn of the 19th century, when the advent of electric traction suddenly offered new horizons. There followed a frenzied period of construction. This was private capital being employed for private gain, even if the profits turned out to be somewhat illusory. Criss-crossing of the central area by tube railways was completed in 1907, after which the promoters concentrated on extensions into what became the suburbs. Later, tunnels were enlarged and station platforms lengthened to cope with the growing traffic.

The deep-level 'tubes' vastly enhanced the travel opportunities in the built-up area, but by pushing out beyond it were also instrumental in the creation and nurturing of suburban London.

The Underground had a powerful effect on land use patterns and development, but its own evolution from the 1920s onwards was dependent on at least some support from public funds. Perhaps the long drawn out postwar hiatus in the 1950s was due to lack of agreement as to what the Underground was there to achieve. It was a period of stagnation, interrupted by the construction of the Victoria Line in the 1960s and, later, the Piccadilly Line Extension to Heathrow and the Jubilee Line.

Over the 140-year period since the first train ran on the Metropolitan Railway, there have also been enormous technical advances.

The Underground is in no sense a minor railway; in recent years roundly equal numbers of passenger journeys have been made on London Underground and the whole of the National Rail network.

Below: **The impressive Canada Water station, combined with a bus station, was opened in 1999.** *Author*

Change is an essential part of progress, but the rate of change for London Underground has surely quickened. In the last four years, the following major events have occurred:
- the completion of the Jubilee Line extension to Stratford
- the signing of various Public Private Partnership (PPP) contracts, including those for the care of and improvement in the infrastructure
- the consequential restructuring of London Underground Ltd as a railway operating company
- a substantial growth in patronage
- the setting up of Transport *for* London, to which the intended transfer of the Underground was heavily delayed
- a highly disruptive accident at Chancery Lane on the Central Line
- a relatively turbulent period for both political and labour relations
- two derailments, in quick succession, at Barons Court and Camden Town.

As the reader will find in the following pages, this is principally a record of the Underground's development, concentrating on the growth of a whole system of lines from small beginnings. Its creation has been an outstanding achievement, notwithstanding the criticisms which may fairly be made.

Perhaps the most remarkable aspect is that the Underground works today as well as it does; the credit for this lies almost entirely with the management and the staff of all grades, whose collective business it is to run the railway.

CHAPTER ONE

Steam Beneath the Streets

> 'The success with which this new line is working ...[has]...infinitely surpassed the expectations of its promoters.'
>
> *Illustrated London News, 23 January 1863*

London is a long-established city. The site was originally selected way back in Roman times, as it offered good drinking water and suitable locations at which to construct quays. Fifty km or so up from the Thames Estuary, London offered a degree of inland penetration by waterborne transport, which was far preferable to the muddy tracks on land which were, initially, the only alternatives for the occupying armies.

The River Thames thus became a major highway, and also a divider; hence London's axis has always been east-west. This influenced the detailed layout, but London was able to develop in all directions unlike, say, Liverpool, bounded by the Irish Sea and the River Mersey. All principal streets, such as the Strand and Piccadilly, run broadly parallel to the river. Industry was situated to the east, so that the prevailing westerly winds carried the resulting smoke away from the city; as a result the west end became 'superior'. On the south bank, the alluvial deposits delayed the building of roads. Thus, the north bank with its better natural drainage was developed first, and it has always retained its pre-eminence in commercial, business, court and governmental terms.

In 1500 London's population was 75,000, considerably smaller than that of Paris or the Mediterranean centres. In the 17th century it grew from 200,000 to 575,000 and by 1800 it had topped the million mark. Growth accelerated, and by 1900 it was over six million. It is about seven million today.

This was made possible by the agricultural and industrial revolutions, and the expansion of foreign trade. It was reflected in the traffic both on the river and in the street. Street improvements, slum clearance and more bridges across the Thames went hand in hand. Following the end of the Napoleonic wars in 1815, the need for the enhancement of street facilities became ever more pressing; London continued to spread outwards beyond the previously built-up area.

There was money to be made out of transporting people, and in 1829 George Shillibeer used horse buses for the first successful route between Marylebone, King's Cross, Old Street and Bank. A fixed timetable was operated with no pre-booking, both novelties in comparison with the hackney cabs. However, horse buses were expensive, and most suburban dwellers from Camden or Camberwell walked to work.

FIRST RAILWAYS ESTABLISHED

The first main-line railways built for local traffic were the London & Greenwich, opened 1836-8, and the London & Blackwall, opened from 1840. They were orientated towards passenger traffic, as were subsequent lines constructed to the south and east of the city. They thus contrasted with the main-line railways in north and west London where short-distance traffic was discouraged by having few local stations and fewer trains. This led to the uneven development of the urban railway system, and later this provided business expansion opportunities for what became the Underground.

But why did those main-line railways stop at the edge of the central area? In the mid-1840s the promotional boom surrounding railway building became intense. This nationwide phenomenon of the 'railway mania' was so strong that there were genuine fears that the capital would be over-run with railways.

This led to the setting up of a Royal Commission, which reported in 1846. The Commission recommended that the main-line railways be excluded from central London, which resulted in their terminals being sited along the New Road (today's Euston Road) and its continuation along City Road to the east, and Marylebone Road to the west. In the south the barrier was to be the river.

With some exceptions (especially Charing Cross) that decision stood. The railways were thus not going to be allowed to contribute to solving central London's by now chronic traffic problems. Rather, they would henceforth be adding to it, by disgorging passengers onto the road system at what were then the outskirts. Even so, had they been given the go-ahead to approach the heart of London more closely, it is an open question as to what extent they would have done so. The costs of property acquisition and demolition, or tunnelling, would have been relatively enormous, to say nothing of the investments represented by their existing termini which would then have become redundant.

CONGESTION

In 1855 a Parliamentary Select Committee had been set up to consider how to combat road congestion. It was estimated that over 750,000 people were entering London every day, whether by main-line railway or by road, and the streets were being blocked by a variety of horse-drawn and iron-tyred vehicles. A mixture of omnibuses, coaches, hackney carriages, drays and others, they were all making an enormous noise on the cobbled roads. Also, it wasn't so much exhaust fumes that caused problems, but cleaning up the dung and disposing of it that was a major operation. It was also most unpleasant under foot, especially in bad weather. With frayed nerves and tempers, Londoners looked around for alleviation, and the Press were vocal in their denunciation of the 'scandalous state of London's transport facilities'.

Grandiose and, one fears, ultimately impractical ideas were abundant. One of the most ambitious was the construction of a tile-lined glass arcade encircling central London. There would have been a street above and a railway below; trains on no less than four tracks would be powered by atmospheric pressure. This came from Sir Joseph Paxton of Crystal Palace fame, and was to have been titled the 'Great Victorian Way'. The Committee, though, seem to have had their feet firmly on the ground, and their recommendations included the removal of river bridge tolls, and the linking of street improvements with underground railway building.

Some advance in road passenger transport was afforded by the formation of the Paris-based London General Omnibus Co in 1856. This led to a shake-out of the multiplicity of horse-bus operators competing one with another, and to an altogether more orderly situation. Somewhat later, from 1870 onwards, the development in earnest of the rival horse tram offered the prospect of a cheaper operation, as the use of rails allowed the haulage of greater loads. In addition, all horse transport was given a boost through the importation of cheaper grain from abroad. But by then there was a new phenomenon in London, in the form of the Metropolitan Railway.

THE METROPOLITAN

In his evidence to the Royal Commission, Charles Pearson, solicitor to the City of London, had presented his proposals for his Arcade Railway & Central City Terminus Co. 'Ingenious' said the Commission, and left it at that. But Pearson was undoubtedly right in his

Above: **C. W. Clark's station for the Metropolitan Railway at Paddington, Praed Street, seen here on 25 July 1946. The range of goods sold in the various commercial outlets has changed considerably since then.** *Great Western Railway*

Right: **Farringdon is still a graceful station, seen here in June 2003, looking east with a C-stock train approaching. Behind the photographer, the curve reverses.** *Author*

championing the cause of railways as a means of offering relief to London's streets. Pearson also had social reforming instincts, and another of his aims was to clear the slums from the valley of the River Fleet and relocate their luckless dwellers in new suburbs built for the purpose. From there they would be able to travel cheaply to work by rail, using the special low workmen's fares which he had long since advocated.

It is thus of no surprise to find him as a leading light in the promotion of the Metropolitan. The first authoritative notice of the enterprise which founded the Metropolitan Railway was to '... encircle the Metropolis with a tunnel to be in communication with all the railway termini, without forcing the public to traverse the streets in order to arrive at their destination'.

With the help of John Stevens, Architect and Surveyor to the City (Western Section), Pearson evolved a plan for a steam-operated underground railway to run the 5.88km between Farringdon Street and Bishop's Road, Paddington. This was to follow Farringdon Road and King's Cross Road to King's Cross, and then run more or less beneath the course of Euston Road, Marylebone Road and Praed Street to Paddington. Thus it would serve as a link between three main-line railway termini: the Great Western at Paddington, the London & North Western at Euston, and the Great Northern at King's Cross. It did in fact eventually

serve St Pancras as well when that station was completed in 1868; prior to this Midland Railway trains had used the Great Northern's premises at King's Cross via a now long-defunct connection between Bedford and Hitchin.

Farringdon Street was chosen as the site for the eastern terminus, principally because the City Cattle Market, then occupying the site, was about to be moved to Copenhagen Fields, Islington. The Act of Parliament obtained by the North Metropolitan Railway Company in 1853, however, only authorised the construction of the section between Edgware Road and Battle Bridge. Here, it is said, Queen Boadicea routed the Roman legions before 'putting London to fire and the sword'. Battle Bridge became the more prosaic King's Cross when, in 1830, a tall octagonal building surmounted by a statue of King George IV was erected. Although

demolished only 15 years later, the name stuck. Further Acts were thus necessary for the construction of the original line.

CONSTRUCTION

Work began in 1860, and it was always envisaged as being a complex task. Although the construction of bored tunnels had been well practised by the canals and main-line railways, this was something new. The method of digging a trench for the trains and then roofing it over became known as 'cut and cover' construction. Finding and diverting sewers, gas and water mains and drains was followed by the excavation of vast chasms in the streets 9m wide and 7.5m deep or more, to be lined with brickwork and roofed over, followed finally by the re-laying of the streets for surface traffic. Although the method minimised interference with private property and avoided the need for its purchase as the law then required, the effects on the road traffic in the vicinity must have been disastrous. Generally, damage to buildings was minimal, although owners were not slow in claiming for any structural defects which could possibly have been caused by 'the digging of an enormous ditch' in front of their properties.

There was a severe setback in June 1862, when the River Fleet, which had been diverted into a ditch alongside the railway, burst. This flooded the workings to a depth of 3m between Farringdon and King's Cross. The opening was put back to the following year, partly as a result of this mishap, but also because of the need for signalling alterations to satisfy the Board of Trade.

The *Illustrated London News* sought to reassure its readers on how the operation would be conducted as early as 1860. 'It is intended to run light trains at short intervals, and calling at perhaps alternate stations. All risk of collision will be avoided by telegraphing the arrival and departure of each train from station to station, so that there will always be an interval of at least one station between the trains.'

ATMOSPHERIC, FIRELESS OR STEAM?

The means of traction was debated while the Bill was in Parliament. John Fowler, the engineer, was said to have envisaged at first that trains should be blown through an airtight tunnel using giant compressors at each terminus. Such a system was being used on a mail-carrying narrow gauge railway in the City, but as with Brunel's atmospheric railway in South Devon before it, the difficulties of maintaining a satisfactory seal proved insurmountable. Thus Fowler opted for a fireless locomotive, to be recharged with high pressure steam at each terminus, and assisted with a firebrick heater on the locomotive itself to maintain a working pressure. Regrettably, although having the desired effect in getting the Bill enacted, the technical problems proved to be altogether too much. A prototype was constructed by Robert Stephenson, but it languished in the sheds after being christened 'Fowler's Ghost'. Therefore, the Metropolitan opened for traffic on 10 January 1863 using conventional steam locomotives.

It had been a considerable feat to obtain finance for such a novel undertaking, the costs of its construction inevitably being huge in comparison with its length. But an even greater potential hurdle must have been the attitude of the public to being hauled through glorified sewers by smoke-belching monsters. Pearson had been indefatigable in his promotion of the project, and it is sad to record that he died in 1862, too soon to see the realisation of his ambitions.

OPENING

Much interest had been created by the very visible construction methods, and private viewing days were laid on for Mr and Mrs Gladstone and other notables, who rode through the newly built tunnels in decidedly unstatesmanlike open wagons. On 9 January 1863, less than three remarkable years after construction had started, the formal opening was celebrated by a banquet held at Farringdon Street. Special trains were heralded by music from a band as they approached the station.

Despite a sceptical Press, the Metropolitan was well patronised from the start. With fares of up to 9d (3.75p) for a First-class return, as much as £850 was taken on the first day. Patronage was 9,500,000 in the first year and 12,000,000 in the second. It did not look back.

From the start of public services proper on 10 January, closed carriages were used. This original section of the Metropolitan was laid to mixed gauge, both standard at 4ft 8½in (1,435mm) and the Great Western's broad gauge of 7ft 0¼in (2,140mm). At first, the GWR supplied the motive power, rolling stock and personnel. Twenty-two coke-burning 2-4-0Ts of Gooch design were fitted with condensing apparatus, whereby nuisance from atmospheric pollution was to be attenuated. They were named after insects, foreign rulers and flowers, in typical Great Western fashion, with names like *Gnat*, *Kaiser* and *Violet*. These were complemented by 45 eight-wheeled coaches of various origins, but all were lit by coal gas as were the stations.

The Great Western proved to be an uncertain partner for the Metropolitan. The Metropolitan management were anxious to increase service frequency from the basic four trains an hour to cope with a traffic running at 27,000 journeys daily, but the cautious Great Western objected to the effect of the additional working costs. Perhaps the arrangement did not allow them to share in the additional revenue? Only two months after opening, payments were being withheld; then, outraged at not receiving an allotment of shares in the Moorgate Street extension, the GWR used this as a lever to bring the Metropolitan to heel.

Or so it hoped. Late in July 1863, Paddington issued an ultimatum that the GWR would cease all operations from 30 September, a date then advanced to 11 August. Furthermore, it would not sell the locomotives and rolling stock to the Metropolitan for that company to run the service itself.

Both the Great Western and the City of London Corporation had put up substantial sums for the Metropolitan, the GWR seeing advantage in the access to the City which it otherwise had no hope of reaching. The Corporation wanted the removal of carts from the streets. Both it and the GWR were thus keen to see rail access to the new market at Smithfield.

Fortunately for the Metropolitan, the company had also seen fit to enter into arrangements with the Great Northern. As a result, physical connections had been provided to that company's lines. Hence it was to the Great Northern that the Metropolitan turned in their hour of need. It transpired that the Great Northern was not averse to scoring a few points off Paddington. By a superhuman effort in concert with the London & North Western, the GNR managed to assemble sufficient rolling stock to work the services from 11 August using the standard gauge, which had so fortuitously been provided.

With scratch crews unfamiliar with the line, service quality went downhill rapidly. On the first day alone, six trains were derailed due to misalignment of the hitherto unused standard gauge rails, but order was soon restored. (One can only imagine the effects of such an occurrence today!) The arrangement could only be a stopgap, and the Metropolitan hurriedly ordered locomotives and coaches of their own.

LOCOMOTIVES

The Metropolitan's locomotives were outside-cylindered 4-4-0Ts built by Beyer, Peacock & Co of Manchester and were an adapted version of a design supplied for export to Spain. There was no cab roof, only a cab plate, which on later versions carried a top lip which was bent back

Below: **The Metropolitan's early Class A locomotives from Beyer Peacock had little to protect the crew from anything that the weather or the locomotive itself might throw at them. This is No 10 in a location not identified but which is probably Neasden Works.** *IAL*

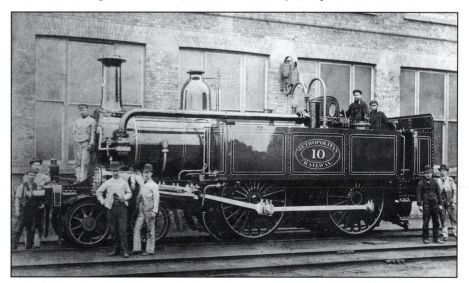

to afford a little more protection for the crew. When delivered, the engines were painted a bright green, with the typical Beyer Peacock fittings of polished brass domes and numbers on the copper-capped chimneys. Each weighed just over 42 tons. The first order for 18 of the 'A' class, all of which bore classical names such as *Apollo*, *Daphne* or *Aurora*, was later expanded

Left: **The 'F' class 0-6-2T locomotives were built for the Metropolitan by the Yorkshire Engine Co in 1901. No 90 lasted until 1957, when it was withdrawn as No L49.** *IAL*

Centre left: **The 'E' class 0-4-4Ts were built for the Metropolitan by Hawthorne Leslie at the end of the 19th century. No 81, later L48, is seen in this undated photograph with a Neasden destination board on the buffer-beam. Although the company's coat of arms is carried on the front sandbox, the side tanks look somewhat bare. The last of this class of seven locomotives, No 1/L44, survives in preservation at the Buckinghamshire Railway Centre.** *IAL*

Below: **Later, the 'A' class was superseded by the 'B' class, but they were still broadly similar. Where the smartly turned-out No 48 differed was in the extent of its cab, and other locomotives were gradually upgraded. The prominence of the condensing pipes designed to remove environmental nuisances will also be noted.** *F. Moore*

Below right: **Shunting is the traditional preserve of small tank engines, and the Metropolitan acquired two 0-6-0STs from Peckett & Sons of Bristol. This is No 101, later L53, which clocked up 63 years of service with the company and its successors, from 1897 to 1960. Most of that time was spent in the vicinity of Neasden.** *IAL*

to 44 over several batches delivered from 1864 to 1870. The improved 'B' class followed and ran to 22 locomotives between 1879 and 1885. The Metropolitan replaced the green livery with a colour described as 'slightly darker than Midland Railway red' from 1885.

This outstandingly successful class was further multiplied for the Metropolitan District Railway, which we have yet to meet. This company secured 54 locomotives, representing a build of 120 in all. The principal (and important) difference was the Metropolitan's use of the automatic vacuum brake, having first experimented with the Clark & Webb chain brake, whereas the District used the incompatible Westinghouse air system. The Metropolitan District used these locomotives exclusively up until the end of steam traction in 1905, but the Metropolitan went on to purchase and build a number of other types of tank engines for general work.

VENTILATION

One of the biggest problems confronting the engineers of the underground steam railways was to provide and maintain a supply of breathable air in tunnels and stations. The

Above: **The conditions on the footplate, in tunnels, may be left to the imagination. This is Beyer Peacock 4-4-0T No 23 of the Metropolitan Railway.** *Author*

Metropolitan engines burned coke, which is clean but gives off poisonous fumes, and after abortive trials with additional ventilation at the stations, the railway went over to coal. This had the immediate result of an extremely smoky atmosphere. It reached its worst at Gower Street (today's Euston Square). As a remedy, certain openings originally provided in the covered way at King's Cross and elsewhere for lighting purposes were adapted as smoke vents, and finally 'blow holes' were bored all along the route between King's Cross and Edgware Road. They were covered by gratings in the roadways above, and were prone to sudden belchings of steamy vapour which startled the passing horses.

The locomotives were fitted with condensing gear, which gave the driver a means of diverting exhaust steam from the chimney outlet into the water tanks, where the steam condensed, leaving the tunnels more or less clear of smoke and vapour. The trouble was that the blast on the fire

was also much reduced, and the power of the engine correspondingly impaired, whereas to maintain schedules between closely spaced stations needed a pretty lively engine. By rule the driver would operate his condensing lever on approaching a tunnel section, and restore the chimney exhaust wherever the line was not enclosed. From the sulphurous state of the tunnels, which some passengers found actively nauseating, it seems that the rule was not always obeyed. Matters were bearable initially, but conditions worsened as service frequency increased, and niceties such as the replacement of the warmed condensing water with cold at the end of each journey were abandoned.

COACHING STOCK

The first of the new coaches was delivered by the Ashbury Railway Carriage Co on 1 October 1863. They were finished externally in varnished teak, stippled brown. First-class accommodation was distinguished by being painted white above the waist, and was fitted with carpets, mirrors and well-upholstered seats. No doubt this offset to some extent the discomfort caused by penetrating smoke in such confined spaces. Furnishings decreased in elegance according to the class, as did the space allotted per person, and one imagines that the Third-class passenger was usually glad to resurface, somewhat stiff after a ride during which all the windows had to be kept closed. It seems a little incongruous that after all this there should have been a 'No Smoking' rule applied impartially across all three classes, although this was later rescinded.

For the locomotive crews, the experience of driving underground steam locomotives, even with rather more openings to the sky than remain today, was not pleasant.

'In the summer you could hardly breathe going through the tunnels, it was so hot. It was enough to boil you on the footplate. You took your jacket off and stripped down to your shirt. There was a terrific wind and smoke going through the tunnels ... I'd shovel about two hundredweight [102kg] in a day's work: it was a dirty, hot, sweaty job, but we had to put up with it.'

This was George Spiller, in the early years of the 20th century. Nevertheless, the locomotives performed a grand job, and it is pleasing to relate that one of the 66 constructed for the Metropolitan, No 23, has survived, to find a permanent resting place in London's Transport Museum.

The broad gauge trains had disappeared for good from central London, and their rails were totally removed by 1873. It allowed station platforms to be widened and this is why, even today, some of the tunnel mouths appear to be rather wider than necessary.

TRAFFIC

The Metropolitan was run first and foremost as a passenger railway, and carried 9½ million passengers in its first year, a figure which rose to

Above: **No 23 is seen in London Transport days with a train made up of open wagons. This locomotive was kept on the books until it was withdrawn in 1948. It was then 'back-restored' to 1903 condition, in which it lost the cab, seen here to good advantage. Today, it resides on the first floor of London's Transport Museum in Covent Garden.** *Author's collection*

Right: **Price competition on the Underground? Whatever next? The Metropolitan extols its services. Buying a ticket then involved knowing on which company's services you were going to travel.** *Author*

28 million by 1868. Workmen's trains were introduced at a fare of 1d (0.4p) per single journey, but the line remained peripheral to central London. Even so, it was outstandingly successful in revenue yield per route km in comparison with its contemporaries, as the table below shows:

Passenger Receipts per route km per week		
Railway	*Route km*	*Revenue/route km*
London & North Western	2,050	£25.55
Great Western	2,042	£17.36
Great Eastern	1,083	£13.76
London & South Western	788	£21.36
South Eastern	492	£33.17
London, Chatham & Dover	135	£49.48
London, Tilbury & Southend	68	£17.68
Metropolitan	6	£447.62

METROPOLITAN DISTRICT

Once the business is established, attitudes change. Murky and grimy the Metropolitan may

have been, but that did not deter the good people of west London from pressing for their own equivalent. At least the journey could be accomplished in the warm and dry, and more quickly than along the streets. A few years after the opening of the Metropolitan, the Metropolitan District started operations with an

east to west route running through the heart of the capital. This was an entirely separate company despite the similarity of name. In the years to the end of the 19th century, each line was to carry out a programme of extension with the same object in view: to bring the suburbs and the underdeveloped country beyond into direct rail communication with central London.

The first section of the Metropolitan District Railway opened in 1868 between South Kensington and Westminster, a distance of 3.75km. Construction was not without difficulty:

the Westbourne River had to be contained and carried over Sloane Square station in a conduit, and the company had to take special precautions to ensure that Westminster Abbey did not vanish into the 'cut and cover' construction. History often has a knack of repeating itself, with the construction of the Jubilee Line Extension being blamed in recent times for slight movements in Big Ben's clock tower.

Concurrent developments saw what became known as the Inner Circle begin to take shape. The Metropolitan extended from a junction west of Edgware Road, with a new line turning south through Notting Hill Gate to meet the Metropolitan District in an end-on junction at South Kensington. Environmental objections overcame the original intention to run across Kensington Gardens and Hyde Park on the surface, and the present route was selected instead. Here too, the sensibilities of the area's residents were involved, and in Leinster Gardens, Bayswater, the railway was forced to build a dummy pair of houses, Nos 23 and 24. Although identical to the adjacent houses, they are merely façades 1.5m thick, complete with false windows and front doors (minus letter boxes). Their purpose was to fill what would otherwise have been an ugly gap in the uniform, dignified, frontage of the row of buildings, for at this point the Metropolitan Railway passes beneath.

For the first two and a half years, the whole line through to Westminster was worked by Metropolitan stock, under an agreement between the two companies, but in the meantime, the District (as it quickly became known in popular parlance) extended its lines eastward under Victoria Embankment to

Blackfriars. Bearing in mind the smoke problem, the later District Railway engineers built their line in open cutting wherever possible and avoided much of the nuisance. This was not practicable along the Embankment and City sections, and here ventilators proved essential and unduly costly, because of the need for camouflage. In the neighbourhood of Temple Gardens all surface evidence of an underground railway was frowned upon, excepting Temple station itself, and the pump house chimney stack there had to be carried horizontally right along the station wall and up the side of a neighbouring building. Here it was decently screened by the wall and could smoke without giving offence. The Embankment and this portion of the District were built together, the railway opening in May 1870, and the road six weeks later.

Top: **The Metropolitan District Railway Beyer Peacock-built 4-4-0Ts were similar to the build for the Metropolitan. This is No 4 of the first, 1871 batch. Out of a total fleet of 34, all but six had been sold off by 1907. The closeness to each other of the coaching-stock bodies will be noted; by keeping them short, their relative movements on curved track will be minimised.** *Author's collection*

Above: **Another view of District Railway No 4, here carrying a Wimbledon destination board, with a nine-coach load of non-bogie vehicles. It may be approaching that terminus on its journey over the London & South Western Railway.** *Author's collection*

In the meantime, extension westward was contemplated. Projection to West Brompton over the District's own tracks took place in 1869, although the purpose, which was to connect physically with the West London Extension

Above: **A District Railway train is seen arriving at Charing Cross station in 1895 (now Embankment). It too has a high overall roof, and a large number of posters covering the walls. This was to be something to which Frank Pick turned his attention.** *Author's collection*

Right: **The Metropolitan and the District companies were always at each other's throats, and in this picture the District seems to be getting in front. This is merely a scene in London's Transport Museum, but it is a theme which crops up several times in the history of the Underground.** *Author*

Railway, was never fulfilled. Kensington still lay on the western outskirts, and beyond was practically open country, with places like Hammersmith and Chiswick still villages but growing rapidly. Extension became a fruitful proposition, with District trains reaching Hammersmith in 1874.

IN SEARCH OF PROSPERITY

The suburbs were seen as the key to prosperity, and the District pressed on westwards. The West Brompton stub was pushed south to Putney Bridge in 1880, while arrangements were made to work the independently sponsored Hounslow branch from Acton Town in 1883. The District's last westward extension in the 19th century was over the Thames at Putney in 1889, to join up with a London & South Western Railway anxious to preserve 'its' territory, and on to Wimbledon.

Meanwhile, the Metropolitan had been driving steadily east and west, with its ends both pointing towards the Thames, while an eastern extension to Moorgate was opened in 1865. In the west, a railway between Hammersmith Broadway and Bishop's Road (Paddington) was opened in 1864 by the independent Hammersmith & City Railway, which made working arrangements with both the Metropolitan and the Great Western. Somewhat unwisely, the GWR had allowed this railway to cross its main line on the level; a diveunder was subsequently constructed between Royal Oak and Westbourne Park, which was opened in 1878. A service was also provided from Latimer Road to Kensington (Olympia), then known as Addison Road, on the West London Railway. It was worked by portions detached from Hammersmith trains and ultimately gave access to the District at Earl's Court. As from 1872, after the District had struggled eastwards as far as Mansion House, it became part of the meandering 'Outer Circle' worked by the LNWR between there and Broad Street via Addison Road and Willesden.

By a connection at Grove Road Junction, Hammersmith, the Metropolitan gained access to Richmond from 1877, with a branch leaving this line at Turnham Green and continuing to Ealing Broadway (1879). This link was between the present Hammersmith & City line north of its Hammersmith terminus, and the LSWR line, the remains of which can be seen to the west of Hammersmith D&P station descending between the eastbound District and Piccadilly Line tracks.

The District's arrangements with the Metropolitan for that company to operate its trains meant that, in return, the Metropolitan received 55% of the receipts. However, this proportion was tied to a given service level, and if the District wanted more trains (as it did), it had to pay out more to the Metropolitan. Hoping to escape from what it considered to be an excessive outpayment to the other company, the District determined to work its own trains, and gave notice to that effect. It thus built for itself a depot at West Brompton, now known as the Engineers' Depot at Lillie Bridge. Additionally, use of the Metropolitan's facilities would be avoided wherever possible, and to this end the District created its own separate running lines westwards from South Kensington. The upshot was a prolonged 'who does what' battle on the 1872 Circle service between Mansion House and Moorgate; eventually the Metropolitan agreed that it would accept District trains and provide half the Circle service on Metropolitan metals.

The District also worked its own lines. Although a solution had been found, further altercations followed on matters such as the division of receipts for bookings to the South Kensington exhibitions held annually on what is now the Imperial Institute site, and of which the 'Exhibition Subway' is a tangible reminder. The quarrels enriched nobody.

Decent rolling stock was also provide by the District. This company too used coal gas lighting, but rather than copying the Metropolitan system of carrying gas in long rubber bags in a clerestory on the carriage roofs, the District pioneered a distinct improvement in 1878 by substituting oil-gas compressed into wrought-iron cylinders hung below the carriages. The gas was produced at Lillie Bridge depot and transported at night in mobile containers to various points on the system, where the carriage cylinders could be recharged. The use of compressed oil-gas later became general in Britain.

While all this was going on, the Metropolitan began its long excursions into north west London and the land beyond, a journey that was to take it eventually to Verney Junction in deepest Buckinghamshire and over 80km from Baker Street. The promoters of the Aylesbury & Buckingham Railway could hardly have imagined that their railway, remote and unconnected with the London Underground system as it was, would one day become part of that distant and greater whole. Yet both the Aylesbury & Buckingham and the independent St John's Wood Railway which built a single line from Baker Street to Swiss Cottage were opened in 1868.

The Swiss Cottage appendage was forced to operate as a shuttle, the Metropolitan refusing use of the Baker Street Junction to enable trains to be projected towards the City. A passing loop had been provided at St John's Wood, and pilotmen were employed for the two sections each side of the loop to act as the authority to proceed. One wore a red cap and the other blue, and St John's Wood became noted for a spectator sport. Here, each man changed over to the other's train, which he had to pilot to his original starting point, and seconds counted. On drawing level with the train waiting at the opposite platform face, the incoming pilotman would leap nimbly off the moving locomotive and join the outgoing footplate. The more prosaic wooden token, held by the guard rather than the driver, soon replaced the human one.

Five six-wheeled tank locomotives were built for this service by the Worcester Engine Co to cope with the steep gradients, but they turned out to be overpowered and were replaced by the standard 4-4-0Ts.

THE WIDENED LINES

Meanwhile, the prospect of trains from the Great Northern and elsewhere converging on its tracks and disrupting its traffic had been

Above: **The advertising on the outside of Gloucester Road station was still fully visible as late as 30 July 1955, when this photograph was taken. Such locations do not immediately identify themselves in one's mind with the Metropolitan nowadays, but such was the effect of 19th century railway politics.** *IAL*

exercising the Metropolitan, and it was decided to construct a second pair of tracks between King's Cross and Moorgate. East of King's Cross, the 'Widened Lines' dipped down through a second Clerkenwell Tunnel, passing beneath the Metropolitan which was carried above them on the 'Ray Street Gridiron'. This was a remarkable skew bridge of wrought iron which also acted as a strut between the walls of the deep cutting. When all work was complete in 1869, a cross-London route was in place serving the Great Western, the Midland (via a connection to its new main line north of St Pancras) and the London, Chatham & Dover (by a spur to Farringdon from Blackfriars), as well as the Great Northern. All were thus enabled to reach the Smithfield meat market. The Midland got its trains from Bedford to Moorgate in July 1868, nearly three months before St Pancras was ready.

The Metropolitan reached east to the Great Eastern at Liverpool Street in 1875, making connections with the main line as well as building its own station. Ironically, in view of the constructional and subsequent operational complexities which ensued for the GER's Liverpool Street terminus, the connecting tunnel saw next to no use; the extension of Metropolitan services to Walthamstow (or anywhere else) over Great Eastern metals was not to be. A century later, the disused tunnel housed the BR Staff Dining Club, but it is now buried in the Broadgate development. The terminus at Aldgate was reached in 1876.

For the time being, that was it, as far as the Inner Circle was concerned.

COMPLETING THE CIRCLE

The principal problem was that the Metropolitan was now under the control of the redoubtable Sir Edward Watkin, while the

signs of improving, especially as the financial results of the completion of the Circle project were disappointing. But there were fundamental difficulties in running a railway without a terminus: how would locomotives be coaled and watered, and the carriages 'gassed'?

The practical solution was the imposition of a two-minute stop at Aldgate for all trains to have the condensing water changed, with locomotives removed for servicing at South Kensington (Metropolitan) or High Street Kensington (District). The locomotives were then reattached to the following trains. The problem of how to recover from delays without the benefit of a terminal layover was tackled in part by an examination of the cause. Most trains using the Circle tracks originated and terminated on the many branches which radiated from that core, using it as a kind of overgrown carousel, and the system in the early days was overstretched. Eventually, a compromise of six Circle trains an hour instead of the eight intended enabled a workable result to be achieved. During busy parts of the day, the Metropolitan still managed to run an extra 13 trains an hour of its own along the northern side, a quite remarkable feat in the age of steam.

Above: **Today, Barbican station is shorn of its roof, although the supports can still be seen high on the walls if one looks closely. An A-stock train for Aldgate approaches.** *Author*

neighbouring District which had generally been considered a natural business partner and likely to fall under the same ownership, was headed by James Staat Forbes. With conflicting railway interests in Kent, these two men were personal enemies; what price therefore the construction of an inordinately expensive piece of linking railway under the City between Aldgate and Mansion House, 1.82km long, which could be worked satisfactorily only in close co-operation?

Even without Watkin, relationships between the companies had been strained. Yet the public clamour for completion of the Inner Circle could not be resisted indefinitely. The necessary parliamentary powers were in existence, and eventually the City Lines and Extensions Act received Royal Assent in 1879. Mindful of the disruption that 'cut and cover' construction could cause, it was stipulated in the Act that during construction the streets must be kept open for road traffic from 6am to 6pm. Consequently, the excavations had to be covered with a timber roof as they advanced. Eventually, work proceeded at 6m a night with completion achieved on 6 October 1884. It should perhaps be stressed that the Circle (or Inner Circle) has never been more than a marketing name for a service; there was never a Circle Railway Co.

Operation of the Circle was not straightforward. To make sure that the intentions of the legislators were carried out, the Act had laid statutory obligations on the companies to maintain the Circle Line service once it had been established. This was perhaps wise, as the ability of the two companies to agree showed no

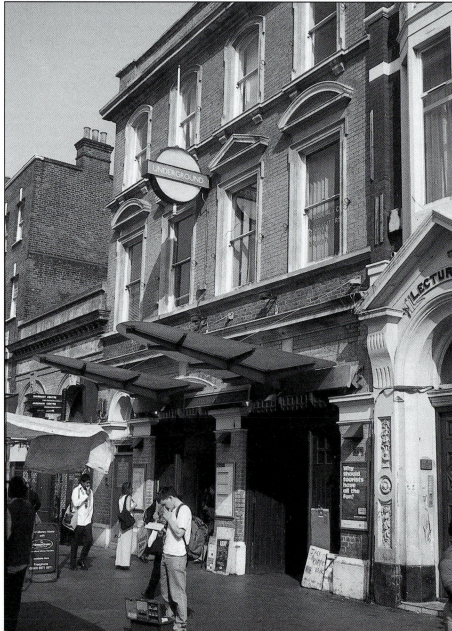

Other than the problems related to the use of steam traction, the same limitations remain today. Circle Line trains are sometimes thought to be infrequent, but you can't run more than about 8tph (trains per hour) without disadvantages of this nature.

EAST LONDON LINE

The City Lines and Extensions Act had also authorised both companies to extend eastwards and link with the East London Railway and its outlets to the south; the District also built its own eastern terminal at Whitechapel. The East London company had bought the Thames Tunnel, which was then in use as a pedestrian subway, in 1865. They converted it to railway use and arranged with the London, Brighton & South Coast Railway to operate a service from New Cross to Wapping from 1869. Connections to the South Eastern and Great Eastern companies followed, the latter via Whitechapel and Bishopsgate Junction to Liverpool Street main line. The present Shoreditch, at which trains from New Cross/New Cross Gate terminate, is all that remains at the northern end, and rail connections to the south have long been severed.

A curve at St Mary's Whitechapel linked in the Underground railways from 1884, and from that time the Metropolitan and the District provided the local services under a working agreement. The main-line companies all worked freight trains through the tunnel, and a passenger service went through to Liverpool Street. It was said that Forbes, Chairman of the District, envisaged trains starting at New Cross and, having reached Aldgate East, running round the Circle in each direction alternately, and back to New Cross! It was no wonder that the operating managers of the day had difficulties.

METROPOLITAN MAIN LINE

If the completion of the Inner Circle was something that had to be virtually forced out of the companies, the same could not be said for the Metropolitan's bid for main-line status. Sir Edward Watkin, Chairman from 1872 to 1894, also controlled the Manchester, Sheffield & Lincolnshire, the East London and South Eastern Railways, as well as having Channel Tunnel interests. It was not therefore altogether surprising to find him championing the Metropolitan as part of a great trunk railway from the Midlands and the North, across London to Dover, and thence to the Continent. The shareholders found that the short urban railway in which they had placed their savings was now intent on greater things. No matter; by 1879 the Swiss Cottage appendage was extended to Willesden Green, and less than a year later to Harrow-on-the-Hill. At Neasden, a

Left: **The original District Railway station at Whitechapel of 1879 was rebuilt on the same site in 1902. It is cramped, but full of interesting passageways! It does however present an early façade to the street, complete with the later addition of wings.** *Author*

site was earmarked for workshops to replace what must have been desperately cramped facilities at Edgware Road. The single-track tunnel section from Baker Street to Finchley Road was doubled in 1882.

Pausing for breath, briefly, at Harrow, it was not until 1885 that Watkin got his railway to Pinner, followed by extension to Rickmansworth in 1887. By now, the Metropolitan had a main line 28km in length, which amounted to a very long country tail to wag the urban dog. From Rickmansworth began the unremitting climb for steam traction into the Chilterns at a ruling gradient of 1 in 105. Although Aylesbury was the traffic objective and the company had the necessary powers to build the line, finance could not be raised and the railway was instead diverted to Chesham (41km from Baker Street). Here, the grateful inhabitants presented the Metropolitan Railway with the land required for the last 800m into the terminus to enable a town-centre site to be found for the station; Chesham was reached in 1889. Would that communities elsewhere had also taken such a positive approach!

Finally, the section from Chalfont & Latimer, which became the branch junction, to Amersham (38km) and Aylesbury (61km) was completed in 1892. From Aylesbury, further possibilities arose. For this was the starting point of the Aylesbury & Buckingham line, which to Quainton Road provided a natural extension of the Metropolitan before turning north to Verney Junction on the Oxford-Bletchley railway. The A&BR's single line was promptly taken over by the Metropolitan, and doubled. The stage was now set for what was shortly to be renamed the Great Central Railway, formerly the Manchester, Sheffield & Lincolnshire, to press south and gain running powers over what were now Metropolitan tracks from Quainton Road. This was duly agreed, although separate running lines for Marylebone trains were constructed south from Harrow-on-the-Hill. This work was completed in 1899, and a relic can be seen today in the mileposts; those of 197 miles (317km) and upwards south of Harrow. These represent the distance from Manchester, by a route which in substantial part no longer exists.

WOTTON TRAMWAY

There remained the oddity of the Wotton Tramway, or the Brill branch, and a more unlikely concern to have become part of London Transport in 1933 can hardly be imagined. It started life as a private single-track railway owned by the Duke of Buckingham, and was constructed to carry staff and goods between Quainton Road station and the Duke's estate at Wotton. The line was 10.5km long, with intermediate stations at Waddesdon, Westcott, Wotton, Church Siding and Wood Siding; trains took all of 1½ hours for the journey, including stops. Construction started in 1870; the first section from Quainton Road to Wotton was brought into use on 1 April 1871, and the whole line completed to Brill by the summer of 1872.

The first locomotives were a pair of thoroughly unconventional Aveling & Porter 0-4-0 geared machines, supplied at a cost of £400 each. Each 10-tonne locomotive had a single overslung cylinder, 197mm x 254mm (7¾ in x 10in), connected through a countershaft and pinion to further pinions on the axles. Their maximum speed was about 13km/h.

Operation was at first contracted out, while maintenance work was undertaken by the Duke's staff. Signalling was primitive, but only one engine was in use at a time. The operating regulations were notably strict, and a Rule Book was published in 1873. This contained a list of fines which might be levied on staff for misdemeanours. Thus, 'If the train be late at Quainton Junction, in consequence of a late Start, the fault of the driver in not having his engine ready, a fine of Half a day's Pay to be imposed.'

On the death of the Duke in 1894, the tramway passed as part of the estate to Earl Temple, and in that year the working of the line was taken over by the Oxford & Aylesbury Tramroad Co. This company set about improving the line, replacing the original light rails laid on longitudinal sleepers with flat-bottomed rails spiked direct to transverse sleepers. The rolling stock was also replaced, and the two original locomotives sold to the Nether Heyford brickworks, near Weedon, Northamptonshire.

Not wishing to miss any expansion potential in the area, the Metropolitan was pleased to work the railway and purchase the rolling stock when approached. The company assumed control on 1 December 1899. The Metropolitan had already provided a new coach, which was much higher off the ground than the original offerings. Station platforms were raised, but to avoid the expense of complete rebuilding they were altered at one end only, retaining the 1894 tramroad buildings at the old level.

THE FUTURE IS ELECTRIC

By the mid-1890s, trams in London were conveying 280 million passengers per year. Horse buses were still supreme in central London, from which trams were excluded. There were around 10,000 (mostly) hansom cabs in use. At the end of the 19th century, steam operation on the Metropolitan and Metropolitan District Railways had nearly reached its zenith.

In a joint venture with the London, Tilbury & Southend Railway, the Whitechapel & Bow extension of the District line, with services to Barking and Upminster, remained to be completed. Services began in 1902, but operations beyond East Ham were not really established for another 30 years.

The Uxbridge branch of the Metropolitan from Harrow-on-the-Hill was completed and steam trains began to work that line in 1904. This was a temporary expedient only as they were replaced by electric traction within six months.

Appendices I and II show the growth of the system, and the opening dates of various sections of the Underground.

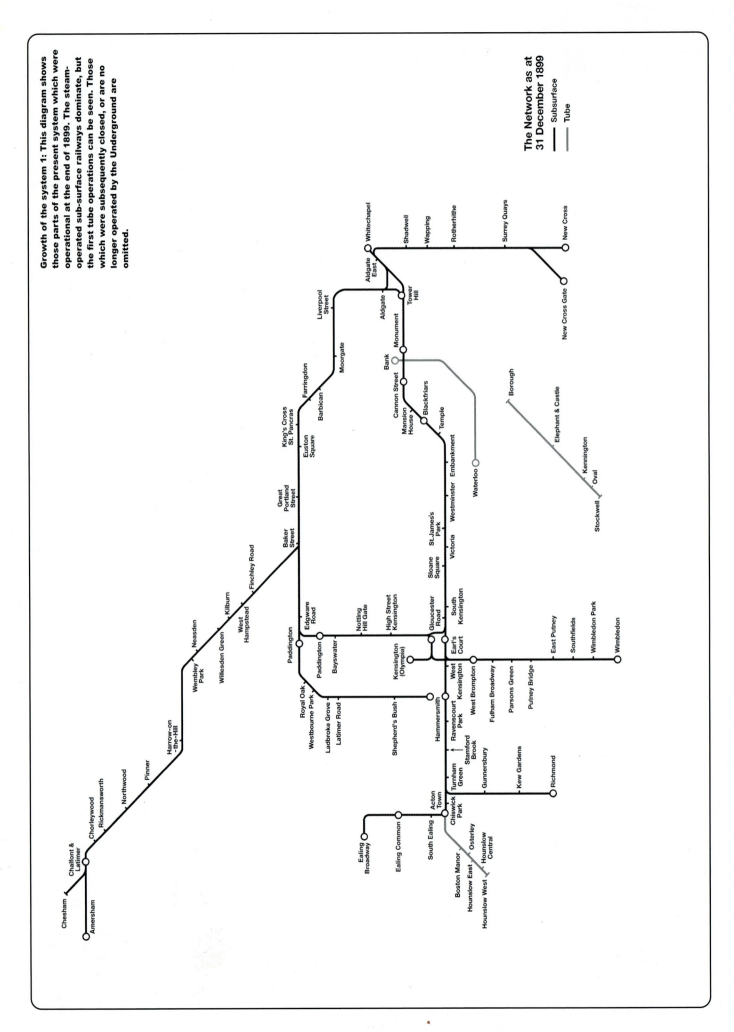

Growth of the system 1: This diagram shows those parts of the present system which were operational at the end of 1899. The steam-operated sub-surface railways dominate, but the first tube operations can be seen. Those which were subsequently closed, or are no longer operated by the Underground are omitted.

The Network as at 31 December 1899

Subsurface
Tube

CHAPTER TWO

The First Tube Railways

> 'The delicious name "Bakerloo" invented by "Quex" of the *Evening News* was an object of particular horror (to G. A. Sekon, editor of *The Railway Magazine*).'
>
> *C. Hamilton Ellis, 1959*

The basic process of driving a large tunnel without disturbing the surface directly above is old. The first significant example for the London Underground was completed in 1843, although there was then no intention of putting it to railway use.

On 25 March of that year, the first tunnel beneath the Thames was opened, connecting Rotherhithe on the south bank with Wapping on the north, without impeding river traffic. Its length was 365m. In fact, it was the first tunnel for public traffic ever to be driven beneath a river, anywhere in the world. The engineer responsible was Sir Marc Isambard Brunel, with the considerable assistance of his even more illustrious son.

THE BRUNEL TUNNEL

Brunel's method of tunnel construction was inspired by a study of the shipworm, *teredo navalis*. A shell, scored with parallel rows of small teeth that resemble the cutting edges of a file, forms the head of the shipworm. As the shipworm burrows its way inward, the wood dust is passed through its body and a secretion containing carbonate of lime is deposited. This lines the tunnel created with a whitish, shell-like substance. Brunel patented a process for tunnelling based on the mollusc's own principle.

The result was a shield forced into the earth and excavated from within. Although primitive by modern standards, it worked, and the idea has yet to be bettered. For the Thames Tunnel, Brunel employed a rectangular shield made of iron, shaped like a huge box with open ends, and furnished with projecting teeth. It was placed at the working face of the tunnel, and as the face was gradually excavated the shield was moved forward, protecting the men within against the great pressure of the ground above them. The shield was honeycombed with compartments wherein worked miners and bricklayers, and as it moved forward beneath the river bed, the miners excavated the soil and strengthened the cavity they made. The bricklayers followed and lined it with bricks.

This tunnel was intended to expedite the work of the London Docks and to save horse-drawn traffic from making the long detour via London Bridge. Long sloping approaches would have been necessary for this purpose, but when the tunnel was completed after a series of misfortunes, the promoting company had no funds left. The only access was by stairways down the circular shafts which had been used for construction purposes, and usage was thus confined to pedestrians. It was an extremely costly project which took 18 years to complete, including a seven-year period during which it was abandoned through lack of funds. This followed an accident in which the Thames had burst through the roof, flooding the workings and drowning seven men; the project also claimed the health of Marc Brunel.

As early as 1832 it was stated that 'it is confidently hoped that the public approbation and admiration which have hitherto encouraged the labours of those who have designed and undertaken this magnificent work, will not be withheld'. The 1843 opening saw a band of the Coldstream Guards at the head of a procession in which Brunel took part, but the tunnel was quickly dubbed a white elephant by a sceptical public. It languished until it was acquired, as already related, by the East London Railway. Nevertheless, Brunel had shown a way which many others would follow.

TOWER SUBWAY

In 1869 Peter Barlow was engaged to drive a second Thames tunnel, this time between the Tower and Bermondsey. He improved on Brunel's method, using a circular shield and dispensing with the brickwork, lining the tunnel instead with cast-iron segments. These were bolted flange to flange. The Tower Subway, as it was named, had a minimum depth of 6.7m in comparison with the shallower Brunel tunnel, but it was only 2.13m in diameter when completed. This severely limited its usefulness. Barlow's shield was driven forward through the earth by levers and jacks, cutting into the clay and progressing an average of 1.52m a day.

Both the method of tunnelling and the tunnel itself are notable in railway history, for Barlow's iron-lined tube was the first of its kind in the world. It was opened formally on 2 August 1870. Since it also contained a small railway, it was also the very first tube railway. Passengers descended a shaft in a lift, and at the bottom took their seats in a car which was drawn through the tube by cable, worked by a small stationary engine. The rail track gauge was 2ft 6in (762mm) and the car held 12 passengers. After a life of only three months, the company went bankrupt and the railway closed on 24 December the same year. The lifts and the cable car were removed.

It lingered on as a pedestrian walkway until March 1896, shortly after the opening of Tower Bridge in 1894. Since then, it has been used to carry hydraulic power and a water main (later abandoned) under the river.

Below: **A new Brush-built driving motor (No 48) for the Bakerloo in 1914, which was one of a batch of 10 from that builder plus two from Leeds Forge. The centre doors were controlled manually and swung inwards. They were locked electrically by the gatemen. Later, they were replaced by single doors.**
Author's collection

THE GREATHEAD SHIELD

From these two beginnings evolved the famous Greathead shield, which cut most of London's subsequent tube tunnels. James Henry Greathead drove the tunnels for the King William Street-Stockwell tube railway in 1886, using a shield of his own design. The Greathead shield consisted of an iron cylinder divided into two by a bulkhead, with a rectangular hole for access to the workface.

It differed from Barlow's in so far as it was driven forward into the earth by hydraulic rams working at pressure. The rams pressed against the tunnel segments already fixed in place and forced the 3.65m diameter shield into the earth, enclosing a great core. Clay was removed from the face by hand, to a depth of about 600mm, with the spoil thrown back into the tunnel proper and removed by a small temporary railway. The excavated section of tunnel was then sprayed with liquid cement and a lining of cast-iron rings bolted together within the trailing end of the shield. As the shield moved forward, more cement was forced through the holes in the plates to fill the gap left between the lining and the clay, a process known as grouting.

The driving of tunnels required a great deal of precision if they were to meet accurately, since an error of only 2.5mm in sighting would throw the actual driving seriously out of alignment. Sufficient was now known to enable the whole of the tube network to be cut accurately.

Along the line of route, a series of vertical shafts was sunk, from which headings were driven at right angles. To find the exact centre line along which to bore the running tunnel, a theodolite (an instrument for measuring angles by optical means) was set on the surface over the end of a heading and precisely over the subterranean line of route, but way above it. Two plumb lines were next hung down the working shaft and exactly aligned with a sight on the instrument. The theodolite, thus set, was taken to the bottom of the shaft, and its position adjusted

until this time it agreed with the plumb lines already adjusted from above. In other words, a sight line taken above ground was about to be transferred below, and it was then only necessary to determine a true right angle off the vertical plummets and to fix a true depth. When the correct distance along the heading had been measured, and the true right angle determined, the point and direction of the running tunnel's centre line was known, and work could begin.

The shield was erected in position in a chamber formed by several rings of iron lining, and a short excavation was made in the working face of the running tunnel. Provided the earth was soft enough for the purpose, piles were inserted between it and the edge of the shield, and a forward thrust of the shield drove the piles into the face and broke up the earth for easy removal. With the Greathead type of shield it was necessary thereafter to cut a small chamber in the face in advance of the shield, so that the earth enclosed by the ring of the shield after each forward thrust might collapse into the space made.

BUILDING THE RAILWAY

On certain sections of the London tubes, the tunnels may be seen to dip on leaving the stations and to rise on approach to them; by looking through the end windows of a car where a sight along the interior of several successive cars can be had, the bend of the train on meeting each change in direction is perceptible. It has become the practice that running tunnels should be so graded for the double purpose of accelerating the departure of a train and retarding its speed on approach. The falling gradient of about 3.3% (1 in 30) results in a saving in current consumption, and

Below: **The conditions in the tube tunnels during construction must have been fairly unpleasant, at least in the early days. This reconstruction may be found in London's Transport Museum.** *Author*

conversely the rising gradient, which is made rather less acute, results in an economy on brake wear. With modern trains possessing reserves of tractive power and powerful brakes these switchbacks are less important, although they still augment appreciably the overall speed when stations are closely spaced. The double reverse curve encountered on the Piccadilly Line at South Kensington though, and the fearsome bend on the Central Line at Bank, stem from a different reason, in that the builders preferred to follow the street patterns above rather than tussle with property owners over possible compensation problems.

Engineers may have to contend with more than clay or workable earth. They have encountered waterlogged sand or have had to tunnel below rivers and streams where normal methods would have quickly resulted in flooded workings. The general procedure is to construct airtight working chambers and compress the air within them, so that there is sufficient pressure to keep out the water or, sometimes, to help support the periphery of the tunnel face. If a waterlogged stratum is met when sinking a shaft, a vertical chamber is constructed; and if a tunnel has to be driven through a bed of soaked sand, for instance, then a horizontal chamber is made. In both cases a smaller compartment is constructed at the entrance to the pressure chamber to form an airlock, so that men and material do not enter or leave the pressure chamber direct from the outer air. The move from atmospheric pressure is thus via a chamber in which pressure can be increased until it equals that at the work face. On tube construction work, air pressures can reach a multiple of three times atmospheric pressure.

The greater proportion of tunnelling for London's tubes has been driven through what is known as London clay, varying in colour from grey-green to yellow, and which lies on top of the chalk and sand that once formed a seabed. The tunnels burrow beneath shallow beds of gravel and river drift which the Thames and its tributaries have deposited over the clay during the ages. Roughly north of a line represented by Euston Road, the London clay comes to the surface, and stretches out as far as the chalk of the Chiltern hills. In central and southern districts of London, pockets of sand and gravel, often waterlogged, are found lying beneath layers of 'made ground' formed by the foundations of older London. The depth of the made ground is as much as 7.5m at Farringdon. Under a few parts of London the predominant clay is shallow in depth, and chalk is encountered, but generally London rests on a very thick layer of clay which is anything up to 140m deep.

Little of this was known to the tube pioneers, but even in Victorian London it was clear that the 'cut and cover' method of railway construction was unacceptably disruptive to normal day-to-day living. At the same time, the need to improve transport facilities within the central area, that is within the area of London

THE FIRST ELECTRIC TUBE RAILWAY, 1890.

Above: **The caption says it all!** *Author's collection*

Right: **The body of 1907-built C&SLR coach No 163 rests on oil drums after its rescue from East Molesey, Surrey, on 16 September 1974.** *R. J. Greenaway*

Bottom right: **The small size of the trains is noticeable in this view of the City & South London Railway at Stockwell station on the original section of line. Island platforms of this sort, below ground, can still be seen today at Clapham Common and Clapham South stations.** *South London Press*

encompassed by the Circle Line, became ever more pressing. An effective tunnelling method was therefore a prerequisite for the expansion which was to follow.

Another necessary technical development was the means of traction. Cable haulage had been used since the earliest days of railways, until it was supplanted by the steam locomotive. Could cables be used satisfactorily for underground railways?

CITY & SOUTH LONDON

The City & South London Railway was built on the premise that they could. The original route length was 2.5km, but this was quickly extended to nearly 5km after work started, since it was realised that the full potential of the line was unlikely to be developed otherwise. The C&SLR was to be powered by a stationary engine at Elephant & Castle. Two cables were to be provided, one at 16km/h on the sharply curving section north to King William Street, the other at 19km/h on the straighter and easier Stockwell section. Contracts were signed, but the work was never carried out as in the meantime the decision was made to adopt electricity as the motive power. This promised to offer a higher average speed and, ultimately, to be a cheaper medium than cable.

On 4 November 1890 Prince Edward (the future King Edward VII) visited Stockwell to perform a formal opening ceremony; public services began on 18 December. The trains were of three bogie trailer cars hauled by 11.8-tonne electric locomotives at an average speed of 18.5km/h.

Only by their freedom from steam and smoke could these early trains have commended themselves to travellers. Unlike the creature comforts of the traditional steam-hauled rolling stock found on the Metropolitan and District railways, the City & South London offered little amenity. It was a railway designed for a purpose, without the constraints of the compatibility needed for an installation which was part of a system. Its function as the 'Sardine-box Railway', a name bestowed on it by *Punch*, was to take passengers from one station to another, avoiding the delays from road traffic.

This it did with remarkable success, and within three years of its opening was carrying 15,000 passengers each day. The coaches, appropriately nicknamed 'padded cells', were a mere 2.08m wide, designed for a tunnel purposely made as small as possible to reduce construction costs. Passengers sat on longitudinal benches, above which were tiny windows that were little more than ventilators, so that in the absence of advertisements passengers could do little more than sit and stare at one another. Electric lighting was provided, which was a luxury compared with the gas lights in the Metropolitan and District stock, so perhaps the

fortunates who sat below one of the low-powered bulbs were able to read their newspapers. A curious notice on the inside of all cars read: 'No passenger shall be permitted to ride on the roof on penalty of 40s [£2.00] fine'.

If the general description sounds less than enticing, the tram alternative was worse, with oil lamps and seats with negligible upholstery. The two guards on each train were responsible for control of the gates at the ends of the cars and also for informing passengers of the names of the stations. It seems that ridicule as much as anything else persuaded the company to build their future stock with larger windows, the fleet reaching 170 cars by 1908. Describing a journey on the C&SLR between Monument and Bank, *Punch* said: 'The train rocked alarmingly. It was so packed with people that getting in and out was a regular scrimmage. We entirely endorse the railway company's advertisement in that it is the "warmest line in London".'

LOCOMOTIVES

There were basically two types of locomotives, represented by Nos 1-14 with flat sides, distinguished from later builds with rounded sides which gave more space for housing the air brake reservoirs. This was a matter of some moment, since the locomotives at first carried no compressors, and for their braking had to rely

on a fresh supply of compressed air taken in at the terminus. The train pipe of the braking system was routed over the roof of the locomotive and its cars. The first 14 locomotives were built by Mather & Platt of Manchester, Nos 15 and 16 by Siemens, and most of the others by Crompton. The maximum fleet of 52 was in service in 1901. All were driven by a pair of modest 37kW (50hp) motors; No 22 was subsequently remotored in 1912 with two 90kW interpole units and was thus the most powerful on the line. The four-wheeled locomotives were minute, being only 4.27m long, 1.98m wide and 2.59m high. Even so, the driving cabs extended from front to rear of the locomotive, with the driver facing sideways. Passengers waiting on platforms were thus presented with the odd sight of the driver facing them as the train rumbled in. Perhaps it was as well that he was provided with an assistant.

These midgets of locomotives were designed for an uncomplicated run under known conditions, and were therefore both simple in design and sturdy in build, with a minimum of fittings which could give trouble. There was no

Below: **One of the original and very short locomotives for the C&SLR, No 5. Although it carries an 1889 builder's plate, close inspection shows that it was reconstructed at Stockwell Works in 1906.** *IAL*

Above: **Kennington station on the City & South London Railway was built with the distinctive domed roof shared with other C&SLR stations, but is the only one to retain it today. By the time this photograph was taken, the roundel had appeared.** *Author's collection*

reduction gear in the drive, and the motor armature was mounted directly on the axle. Wiring was equally simple; the traction current merely passed from the collector shoes to a fuse cut-out and main switch, thence to a rheostat (or variable control), and through the motors back to earth via the axlebox, wheel and rail. In short, the locomotives were the absolute embodiment of electric motors on wheels. This highly practical engineering approach was rewarded by many years of hard work, hauling 40-tonne trains at speeds of up to 40km/h.

The whole of the running line was below ground, as much as 32m down at the Thames crossing and never less than 13.5m. The workshops and depot were on the surface, reached by an amazingly steep 29% (1-in 3^1/$_2$) inclined ramp at Stockwell. Later, and after an unfortunate mishap when the tow-rope broke and a car took a headlong flight back to the main line, a hoist similar to the one which graced the Waterloo & City was installed. The up and down running lines were in their own separate tunnels of 3.1m diameter north of the Elephant and 3.2m to the south. This reflected the greater speed planned with cable haulage on the southern section and which would thus increase the sway of the trains! Today's engineers refer grandly to the 'kinematic envelope'; this was an early practical response to the problem.

At the termini, the running tunnels merged into one larger elliptical tunnel. Locomotives had

to be placed on the other end of the trains, and this was carried out by 'stepping back' the locomotive of each incoming train so that it returned with the subsequent train. Coupling and uncoupling were jobs for the driver's assistant. The stations and passages were entirely lined with white tiles, except where space was monopolised by advertisements, and the effect was recorded as being 'to provide a bright and cheerful gleam under the artificial light'.

Adequate passenger access to the deep-level tube platforms was the remaining technical necessity. All the original stations were furnished with Armstrong hydraulic lifts, with two cars in each shaft and driven by high-pressure water. They lasted between 10 and 15 years; later stations were equipped with electric ones.

Power for the system was taken from the company's own power house at Stockwell, where three dynamos were belt-driven by steam engines with massive 4.27m-diameter flywheels. The current was taken along the tunnels by feeder cable to signal cabins at each station, where other cables led to the conductor rails.

SYSTEM EXPANSION

The City & South London Railway proved so popular during peak hours that capacity became a real problem. It was decided to raise the 2d (0.8p) flat fare during the morning peak, but modification of the signalling system allowed more trains to be run and this early example of a

peak hour surcharge was not introduced. However, passenger traffic continued to grow, so that the small single-road terminus at King William Street, which had been designed for use with cable haulage, became overcrowded. The company's solution here was to abandon the terminus with its steeply inclined approaches, and to build a replacement at Bank. The extension diverged from the old line at London Bridge and was opened in 1900. In the next two years the tube was extended south to Clapham Common and north to Moorgate, after which it continued beneath the line of City Road to the Angel at Islington. It subsequently reached King's Cross and then Euston by following the slope of Pentonville Road. This final section opened in 1907.

Traffic continued to increase in the years preceding World War 1, until it became obvious that the C&SLR would have to be completely modernised. This was the penalty for the pioneer, upon whose work others had subsequently improved. It meant the installation of a new signalling system, the enlargement of the stations to take longer trains, and the reconstruction of the tunnels to what became the increased standard diameter of 3.56m. Such work was well beyond the financial capabilities of the company to carry out unaided, and an agreement was sought with the Underground Electric Railways Company of London, which by then controlled most of the other underground lines in the capital. Consequently, control of the C&SLR passed to the UERL in 1913, although the war delayed a start on the expansion work for a further nine years.

Since tube railway schemes were now coming before Parliament in some numbers, an attempt was made to set out some ground rules. With the example of the C&SLR no doubt in mind, a Parliamentary Committee of 1892 suggested that future tubes should be of a minimum 3.5m in diameter. They also proposed that the principle which required companies to purchase properties they passed beneath should be abandoned, and replaced by a wayleave system. The ability to obtain such permission might avoid some of the tortuous curves which resulted in following the streets above, although it would still leave the companies open to claims of extortionate compensation payments. Wayleaves would be granted free of charge when running under public streets. These sensible reforms were to be of benefit to London, although they did not solve the problems of funding highly capital-intensive railway construction.

WATERLOO & CITY

The completion of the Circle Line in 1882 had resulted in the linking of all the main-line railway termini that were not within walking distance of the City; all, that is, except Waterloo. In the days when the West End was of less importance, this was a serious shortcoming as far as the London & South Western Railway was concerned, and to remedy it they promoted a direct tube link using the newly developed technology and backed with that company's substantial resources.

The second tube railway in the capital was opened in 1898 after a construction period of less than four years. Completely self-contained and with the two stations at Waterloo and Bank only, this modest 2.03km line crosses beneath the Thames near Blackfriars Bridge. An inclined tunnel, which meant a long wearisome walk, formed the exit from the system at Bank, and remained thus for the next 62 years. The line's power station and sidings were at Waterloo, where a hoist brought cars to the surface.

This was the first tube line to use rolling stock with motor cars instead of locomotives. The bodywork of the 22 cars was built in America by Jackson & Sharpe, with electrical equipment by Siemens and bogies from the LSWR workshops at Eastleigh where the vehicles were assembled. The open saloons were of distinctively transatlantic appearance, and the seats were formed of perforated plywood without any upholstery. To reduce the cost of operation during the day when traffic was light, five additional single-unit motor cars were supplied by Dick, Kerr & Co of Preston the following year.

Current collection was from a centre conductor rail, and the trains were formed of a pair of motor cars with two intermediate trailers. Eight power cables ran along the roofs of the trailers to connect the power cars, a feature which was not allowed on any other tube railway. Commendably, all electrical gear was arranged so that it did not reduce the length of the vehicles which was available for passenger use, although the truly massive motor bogies with their 838mm diameter wheels had a raised floor level above them.

A Siemens shunting locomotive was provided to work in the sidings at Waterloo.

The original system proved to be sound both in design and construction, and few changes were made until the next generation of rolling stock was acquired in 1940.

Historically, the line never had any formal connection with the Underground railways or London Transport. The Waterloo & City remained with the LSWR and its successors until it passed to London Underground in 1994.

CENTRAL LONDON RAILWAY

The C&SLR and the W&C came; the public saw; the Central London Railway conquered. At 9.14km in length, what became the core of today's Central Line ran through the heart of London in an area which until then had not seen a railway of any kind.

Its route was from Bank and westwards in a straight line to Shepherd's Bush. There were 11 intermediate stations. It was decided not to use the island platform arrangement favoured by the C&SLR (and still to be seen today at Clapham North and Clapham Common), and instead to separate the twin tubes widely enough to allow a platform for each direction, joined to its neighbour by cross passages. Where the streets were narrow as at St Paul's (formerly Post Office), Chancery Lane and Notting Hill Gate, one tube was placed directly above the other to take advantage of the free wayleaves thus obtained. In the anxiety not to incur compensation costs as a result of undermining buildings, some ferocious curves were introduced between St Paul's and Bank. These were sufficiently tight that the tunnel diameter had to be increased by up to 229mm to accommodate the 'throwover' of the cars as they negotiated the line. This has proved to be a lasting nuisance, particularly at Bank station where the train-to-platform gap can be excessive.

The stations were finished with white tiling and had large nameboards in white enamel picked out in blue, but in addition, the train guards were instructed to call out the name of the next station on leaving the previous one, and repeat it on arrival. (A voice synthesised version is incorporated in the current rolling stock; such is scientific progress!) Electric arc lamps illuminated the platforms, which were reached by electric lifts, offering an altogether more attractive environment than the C&SLR. This superiority was continued in the 170 cars, which were built by Ashbury and Brush to take

full advantage of the increased tunnel size. These were long, low vehicles with a platform at each end enclosed by a lattice gate structure, and with slightly bowed sides and a clerestory roof. Although the intention had been to use the recommended 3.50m diameter tunnels, a later decision not to line the cast-iron segments of the tubes resulted in an effective diameter of 3.56m, which became the standard.

The platforms were 99m long, and it was envisaged that a locomotive would be provided at each end of the seven-car trains. This was vetoed by the Board of Trade's Railway Department, who this time refused to allow power cables to run between the two. They were doubtless influenced by recent incidents at Dingle on the Liverpool Overhead Railway, and Cournonnes on the Paris Metro, where electrical faults had set fire to wooden-bodied rolling stock. So the Company had to confine itself to one locomotive per train, which then required time-wasting shunting movements at each terminus. This restricted the minimum service interval to 3$\frac{1}{2}$ minutes, or 17 trains per hour.

The Central London Railway was opened on 27 June 1900, again by Prince Edward, who rode on it from Bank to Shepherd's Bush, although it was 30 July before the start of public services. It deserved to be, and was, an instant success, and managed to avoid falling into the trap of catering for business traffic only. By tapping the theatre, shopping and hotel areas of the West End as well, it attracted over 40 million passengers in its first full year of operation in 1901. This was eight times the numbers generated by the City & South London after a similar period.

It was a tremendous improvement on the Metropolitan, still wedded to steam. Hamilton Ellis recalled that the ever-present *Punch* published 'a happy cartoon of sweet little Fairy Electra riding on a sort of sparkling Catherine wheel, waving a minatory wand at a hideous demon with a smoking chimney hat, and remarking that now people had seen her, she fancied his days were numbered'. However, the Central London too had its share of problems.

For a start, the locomotives required the use of valuable platform space but, more seriously, they gave rise to complaints of vibration. Fortunately, a technical solution was at hand thanks to the work of Frank J. Sprague in Chicago. Sprague is credited with the invention of multiple-unit working, whereby a single master controller uses a low-voltage circuit to achieve simultaneous control of all the traction motors in a train. This overcomes concerns about the wisdom of allowing high current traction power to be transferred by cable along its length. Experimentally, four trailers were converted to driving motors cars with two motors in each, and sandwiching four trailers in between. Success led to an order for 64 new motor cars, and these were delivered in 1903 from the Metropolitan Railway Carriage & Wagon Co and the Birmingham Railway Carriage & Wagon Co. However, much valuable space was still taken up by the control equipment and switchgear, which were housed above the car frame. Another hugely worthwhile outcome was the ability to run trains at two-minute intervals (30tph) if required, thanks to the quick turnrounds which could be achieved.

The electric locomotives were scrapped, apart from two which were fitted with trolley poles and sent to join the company's pair of steam locomotives, which had been built by Hunslet to tube gauge. These condensing 0-6-0Ts were used for shunting duties at the Wood Lane depot beyond the Shepherd's Bush terminus, and for maintenance work in the tunnels when the power was off. The power station was also located here.

CLR EXPANSION

The first extension to the Central London Railway was opened in 1908 to serve the Franco-British Exhibition at White City. In view of the existing depot connections, the terminal loop provided was negotiated in an anticlockwise direction, with a single platform at Wood Lane situated on the loop. This introduced some operating and technical problems, since cars were 'handed' depending on the direction they faced and they could now be turned in the course of their journeys. The importance of 'handing' lies in the electrical and air pipe connections made between cars, since unless these are arranged symmetrically about the centre (and are thus expensively duplicated), a car to be coupled to another cannot reverse. The penalty for not providing full reversibility is the constraint in limiting what may be coupled to what.

At the eastern end, the line to Liverpool Street was completed in 1912. Motor bus competition ate into receipts from 1905 onwards, and the Central London Railway was drawn inexorably into closer co-operation with the Underground Group, under whose control it fell in 1913. Commercially, it was known by the nickname 'Twopenny Tube' long after graduated fares were adopted. From 1911 the company decided to carry parcels in compartments set aside on the trains. A porter sorted these during the journey, and they were then delivered by messenger boys on tricycles. Parcels could be up to 56lb (25.4kg) in weight, not exceeding 1,216mm x 760mm x 304mm in size, and with a collection and delivery radius of 800 metres from any station. Passengers were also wooed with season tickets, and with reduced rates for those under 18. The company also indicated how a model passenger should behave 'in order to aid in rendering the service expeditious, clean and comfortable for all':

- To enter and pass along the lifts quickly and not congregate around the entrances
- To be ready to leave the train immediately on arrival at destination
- To be careful to extinguish matches, cigar and cigarette ends before throwing them away
- To refrain from spitting
- To refrain from smoking in the lifts

GREAT NORTHERN & CITY

By far the most massive of all tube construction in London resulted in the building of the big 4.88m diameter bores of the Great Northern & City Railway, between Finsbury Park and Moorgate. The original intention was to allow Great Northern trains to reach the City direct via a connection at Drayton Park. This would have rendered the continuation to the underground station below the GNR premises at Finsbury Park unnecessary, but this ambition was frustrated for over 70 years.

This 5.6km line was built by using an extra powerful Greathead shield, but as the shield progressed the lower cast-iron segments were removed and replaced by a blue brick invert as an economy. It was the only economy which was practised, since the stations were built to a full 128m long (and 137m at the termini), in the fond hope that one day they would be needed by Great Northern trains. They appeared immense and deserted, as indeed they mostly were, with trains occupying only a small portion of the platform length during the slack hours. 'Slack hours' was a period term for what is now known as the off-peak.

The line opened in 1904 and was electrified from the outset using multiple-units on the Sprague principle. The conductor rails followed closely the arrangement used in the earlier Metropolitan and District trials to be described in the next chapter, with both positive and negative rails placed 254mm outside the running rails and 51mm above their level. This ensured that no traction currents were present in the running rails. For the first time, these were being used to carry track circuits in the modern sense and provide automatic signalling using treadles. The unique conductor rail arrangement remained in use until the original cars were replaced in 1939. It was then converted to Underground standard.

Thirty-two motor and 44 trailer cars were built for the service by Brush and Dick, Kerr.

Below: **Great Northern, Piccadilly & Brompton Railway tube-stock motor car No 51 of 1906, known as Gate Stock. Built in France, the United States or Hungary, there was a total of 108 cars of the same design for each of the three Yerkes tube companies. They were finished at Lillie Bridge. The open nature of the car end is apparent.** *Author*

Trains of six cars operated in the peak, and two cars at other times. The cars had open end platforms where the guard stood and worked the lattice gates by levers. There were also sliding doors in the centre of each car, but these were opened only from the outside, and then only at the termini, by porters specially detailed for the job. The line had its own power station near Essex Road, which allowed for direct cables to be run to four connections along the line, thus making substations unnecessary.

Somewhat enigmatically, in 1913 the line was acquired by the Metropolitan Railway, with which it never had any physical connections. The new owners promptly abandoned the GN&CR power station and provided their own supplies from Neasden.

Success for entrepreneurs in the promotion of underground railways was thus far from a foregone conclusion, and many lesser schemes fell by the wayside. Nevertheless, all the interest now being shown resulted in some which were deserving of being built, but found themselves struggling. The common denominator was a lack of sufficient financial backing, but the industry was to find this in the person of an American banker and stockbroker.

THE YERKES TUBES

Charles Tyson Yerkes was born in 1837, and spent many years in making fortunes for himself out of tram companies. Despite resorting to bribes, he was nevertheless hounded out of Chicago in 1899. He came to London, backed by a new and unwary group of US investors.

Underground railway expansion in London was faltering. There were a number of tube railway schemes beyond those already discussed which had secured their Acts, but construction work was advancing slowly at best. For the Metropolitan and the Metropolitan District, the question of electrification or not, and then on what system, was looming.

Yerkes was quickly involved in the District, confirmed by his taking a controlling stake in that company in 1901. His interests quickly expanded. The Metropolitan District Electric Traction Co (MDET) was created for the purpose of electrifying that railway and the building of a power station at Lots Road, Chelsea, to supply it. Within a year the company had bought out the Charing Cross, Euston & Hampstead Railway interests (a constituent of the Northern Line), the Brompton & Piccadilly Circus and the Great Northern & Strand (which were combined and enhanced to become the Great Northern, Piccadilly & Brompton) and the partially-constructed Baker Street & Waterloo. In 1902 the MDET was revamped as the Underground Electric Railway Company of London Ltd (UERL). Yerkes was its chairman, and although some variations to schemes already authorised were approved, no more underground railway proposals outside the UERL empire survived to be built.

Yerkes's backer was Edgar Speyer, the American-born son of a German-Jewish banker.

Through his international banking concern and the Old Colony Trust of Boston, Massachusetts, it proved possible for Yerkes and the UERL to raise the capital to build the lines. To what extent financial chicanery was resorted to remains unclear, but the result was that central London gained a network of underground lines about 24m below ground level, which was to remain in its 1907 form for a further 60 years. Yerkes died in 1905 before any of his tubes were opened; he was succeeded by Speyer, while George Gibb of the North Eastern Railway was brought into manage the undertaking.

The Baker Street & Waterloo Railway, or Bakerloo, was opened to traffic in March 1906 between Baker Street and what is now Lambeth North. By the end of 1907 the Piccadilly and Hampstead tubes had also come into being. Using current station names, the Yerkes tube lines therefore were:
- Edgware Road and Elephant & Castle
- Finsbury Park and Hammersmith, with a branch from Holborn to Aldwych
- Golders Green and Charing Cross, with a branch from Camden Town to Archway

BUILDINGS AND EQUIPMENT

Common ownership had brought a number of common features, one of the most distinctive being the stations. Designed by Leslie Green, many of the 'ox-blood' coloured tiles cladding steel-framed buildings, sometimes with further offices above, were designed to catch the attention of passers-by. Like them or not, they were certainly distinctive. At platform level (there were no islands), a common approach saw tiles on the walls spelling out the station name in large letters, while the tiled surrounds were colour coded to aid station recognition.

On the track itself, the rails were carried on sleepers of Jarrah and Karri wood, which is practically non-combustible, and the spaces between sleepers were filled with concrete so that passengers might have no difficulty in walking to the nearest station in the event of trains being held up in the tunnels. All platforms were constructed of concrete slabs.

The Yerkes tube lines were all fitted with automatic signalling which relied on track circuits, with the additional refinement of the automatic train stop. In this the practice of the District was followed.

With a requirement for nearly 500 tube stock cars in the space of a couple of years, many manufacturers were involved, although there was little enough British input. The major orders were fulfilled by the American Car & Foundry Co of Pennsylvania, Les Ateliers de Construction du Nord de la France, and the Hungarian Carriage & Wagon Works. Considerable attention was paid to fire-proofing the system in general and the cars in particular, which had steel body shells.

The spring-loaded 'dead man's handle' was fitted. This device interlocks the driver's control of the train to the braking system; if hand pressure on the handle slackens or is removed, the brakes are applied automatically. This

enabled the trains to be worked in safety by a motorman only, without an assistant. The passenger 'gate stock' as it was called required staffing by a man between each pair of cars to open the twin saloon doors and the gates onto the platforms. A single-stroke bell was provided on each car platform, operated from the platform at the other end of the car. When the train was ready to start, the guard at the rear passed a signal to the motorman via each of the gatemen *en route*.

The cars were all compatible with each other, although this was of limited importance as there was then no physical connection between any of the lines. Each car was 15.2m long, but a 2.43m or 3.65m section of the body of the motor cars was taken up with a control compartment. Doors were provided at the ends of the cars only, leading to the platforms, but the interiors were already adopting transverse seats in the centre with longitudinal seats over the bogies in the ends, which would be familiar to succeeding generations.

Depots were provided at London Road for the Bakerloo, the only part of that line which was above ground in the beginning, at Lillie Bridge for the Piccadilly, which needed to run over District tracks to gain access, and at Golders Green for the Hampstead tube. This rural crossroads, later described in group advertising as 'a place of delightful prospects' made an ideal site, and thus the story that Yerkes made a spot decision to extend his line beyond Hampstead on the basis of a chance trip with his coachman is perhaps an exaggeration. Whatever the reason, the judgement was not flawed, and 10 million passengers a year (from 5,000 new homes) were using the associated station by the outbreak of World War 1.

COMPETITION AND REORGANISATION

The onset of competition from the electric tramways and motor buses in the latter part of the decade depressed the fortunes of all the underground railways. Further American involvement came with the recruitment of Albert Henry Stanley, a young and fast-rising tramway manager. He was born in Derby in 1874 but emigrated with his family at an early age. He came to London to support Gibb, and ultimately to succeed him. Later created Lord Ashfield, he was destined to become the future driving force of London Transport. Here, as chairman, he was to combine the disciplines of commercial management with public accountability, and an awareness of the social benefits that a co-ordinated public transport system could bring.

Right: **This undated view of Strand station, Northern Line, shows a familiar scene, although the platform walls of what is now Charing Cross were later adorned with David Gentleman's drawings depicting the bringing of the Eleanor Cross to the station forecourt above. The track appears to be ballasted, and the 'suicide pits' were later additions.**
Author's collection

Financially, the situation was slowly restored, helped on its way by the establishment of the London Traffic Conference (or operator cartel). Fares were gradually forced up to avoid the ruinous competition which was taking place, and the companies agreed to a joint marketing policy with the use of the word 'Underground'. Thus Frank Pick entered the scene; from that time on, the contribution of good design was to be exploited wherever possible.

In 1910 the Yerkes tubes were formally merged. Now under the guidance of Stanley, the UERL began to swallow up bus and tramway companies. The UERL became known as the 'Combine', and co-ordination with the development of through fares became the order of the day. Of the underground railways, by 1912 only the Metropolitan with its Great Northern & City appendage stood apart, as did that child of the LSWR, the Waterloo & City.

At this time there was one more oddity in London's railed transport below ground, and this was the Kingsway tram subway. Broadly parallel to the Piccadilly's Aldwych spur from Holborn, which opened on 30 November 1907, were the London County Council trams.

Remarkably, the LCC had got there first, opening the 890m-long tunnel less than two years earlier, on 24 February 1906. Its purpose was to provide a fast and unobstructed tram link between Bloomsbury and the Embankment. The subway ran from the junction of Theobalds Road and Southampton Row to the Embankment, passing below Holborn and Aldwych, with 'stations' at both of the latter. These had island platforms and were in many ways of a similar style to contemporary Underground practice.

Gradients were stiff at up to 10% (1 in 10) for the open-air incline at the northern end (which though long disused still exists), and again on the approaches to Holborn tram station. On straight track, the tram subway was 6.1m wide and built for single deckers, but was later reconstructed for double-deck use. Closure took place on 5 April 1952, towards the end of traditional London trams.

CONSOLIDATION

An early result of the combine was the promotion of a terminal loop for the Hampstead tube. Projection of the (present names) Northern Line southwards beyond Charing Cross in a terminal loop running under the Thames and calling at what is now the northbound platform at Embankment offered interchange with both the District and Bakerloo. It was opened in 1914 as part of a rebuilding scheme for the station.

It followed a projection of the Bakerloo to Paddington in 1913, after the Great Western with some agonising had brought itself to make a contribution towards the cost. The London & North Western Railway followed suit and provided the capital needed for a further extension of the Bakerloo to Queen's Park. This was to enable an integrated service to be offered with its own electric trains using the 'New Line', built to tap the suburban potential of local services out as far as Watford.

Bakerloo trains were extended as electrification permitted, reaching Watford Junction in 1917. This was the first time that a tube line had come into direct physical contact with a main-line railway, and this raised some floor height compatibility problems at station platforms. Due to the war, cars from the unfinished Central London extension were used initially, together with gate stock. The guards' and conductors' positions on these cars were provided with a sort of footstep, which enabled them to help passengers mount the large difference in platform heights. The Joint Stock compromised and the floor level of the new trains, which were finished in LNWR livery, was 143mm higher.

Incidentally, when the same problem arose later because of joint running between the District and Piccadilly lines, the track was raised so that the difference was spread between the two floor heights.

A number of other schemes were started before the onset of World War 1 hostilities, but completion had to wait for a while. War brought with it traffic growth and staff loss to the forces; female labour was employed for the first time, but strictly for the duration only. Damage to the system was negligible. The use of the tube stations as shelters during Zeppelin airship raids caused minor chaos, but this was nothing to what was to be experienced in the next conflict.

The physical scale of what was being achieved was quite breathtaking. In 1863, the Metropolitan Railway had started operation with a mere seven stations. By 1902, the number of stations on what was to become London Underground had expanded to 97, and by 1911 there were as many as 155. Over the same period, the route km rose from 5.88km (1863) to 109km (1902) and 174km (1911).

Although not all of it was below ground level, this equated to the building of well over 3km of railway and three stations *in each and every year for almost half a century.*

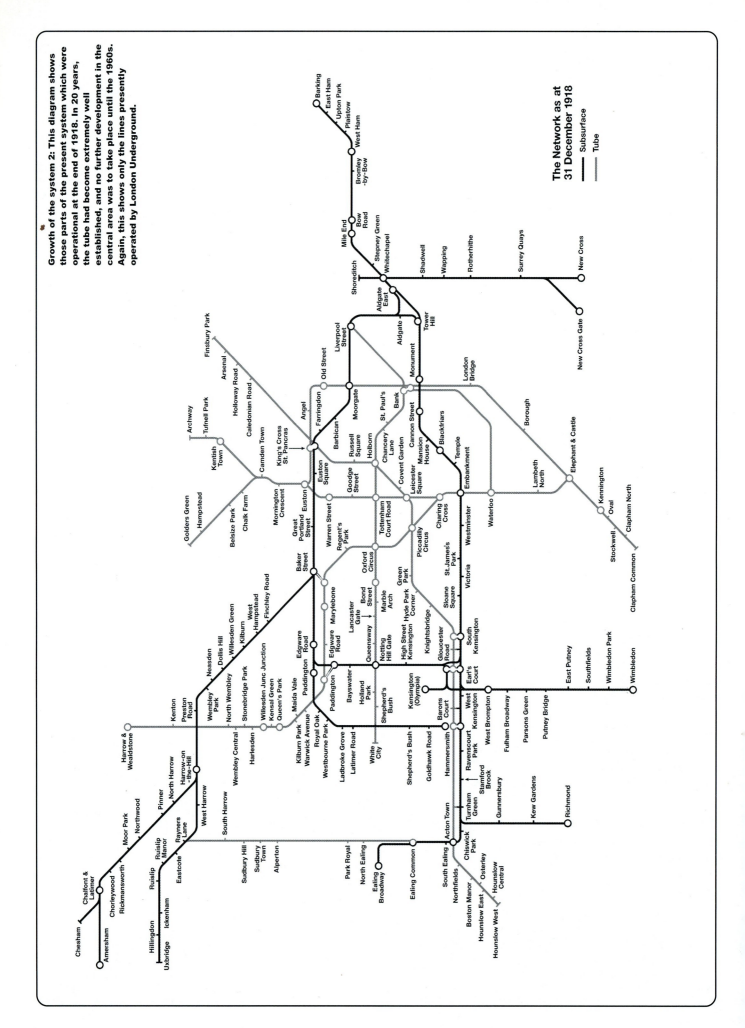

Growth of the system 2: This diagram shows those parts of the present system which were operational at the end of 1918. In 20 years, the tube had become extremely well established, and no further development in the central area was to take place until the 1960s. Again, this shows only the lines presently operated by London Underground.

The Network as at 31 December 1918

▬ Subsurface
— Tube

CHAPTER THREE

Consolidation and Development

> '**I tell you, young man, that the day will come when electricity will be the great motive power of the world.**'
>
> *George Stephenson, to a young engineer, 1847*

So far, this book has examined the origins of the steam railways and the electric tube lines which supplemented them in the central area. The latter put the offerings of the surface railways to shame, and it was at the turn of the century that serious talk began of converting the Metropolitan and its District counterpart to the joys of electric traction. It was almost a case of electrify or die, for with steam power their position was deteriorating rapidly in the face of competition from the tubes and rapidly evolving road transport. But what system of electrification should they choose? Logic dictated compatibility, and it was agreed to conduct an experiment.

CONDUCTING THE TRIALS

The two lines decided to electrify both tracks between Earl's Court and High Street Kensington. This joint decision was taken in 1898, and conductor rails were laid each side of the running rails and electrified at 600V dc. It was decided to purchase a new, six-coach train rather than convert existing stock, and this consisted of two motor coaches and four intermediate trailers. Through control lines were not installed, and thus only the leading motor coach provided power. The experimental service commenced at the close of 1899, and a premium fare of one shilling (5p) was charged as against 2d to 4d (0.8p to 1.7p) by steam train. It was thought that people would pay extra for the privilege of riding in an electric train, but in fact the novelty had already worn off since the City & South London had by now been running for a decade.

The train was retired a year later, with (inevitably!) three cars reverting to each

company. It had fulfilled its purpose by proving the case for low-voltage dc traction – or so it seemed. Yet when the tenders came in, the one which most impressed the adjudicators of the committee of the two companies was that submitted by Ganz of Budapest. This system used three-phase alternating current at 3,000V, supplied by a pair of overhead copper wires insulated from each other and with separate collection devices for each, with the third phase provided by the running rails. It was however untried in any conditions remotely like those of London, and when the Board of Trade demanded a demonstration, the companies were unwilling to finance it.

The Metropolitan remained firmly behind the Ganz option on the grounds of economy, since it would require only simple substations and no heavy conductor rail. It did, however, require a pair of overhead wires instead. Another claimed advantage was that the static transformers would not need attendants and could be left to look after themselves. The District, on the other hand, favoured the British Thomson-Houston Company's dc system. There was, however, an element of unreality in the argument for, truth to tell, the District was all but bankrupt. The Metropolitan offered terms for acquisition, but was rebuffed.

THE DISTRICT GETS ITS WAY

In the end, a growing American influence was consolidated by the arrival of Yerkes and his acquisition of the ailing District. With electrification as a top priority, Yerkes rejected the 'expert' advice he was offered, and sent his engineers to find out for themselves. By then Ganz's experimental section of line had been dismantled, but they were able to inspect the 108km Valtellina line in Italy from Lecco to Sondrio, then all but complete. However, Yerkes remained unconvinced of the merits of untried ac systems, having seen what dc traction could achieve in his native USA. The Metropolitan fought a rearguard action on the merits of the Ganz system, pursuing it even to arbitration. The Board of Trade gave judgement for the dc system, albeit with some hard words to say on how the District had conducted itself in the process. The tremendous jobs of building the power stations at Lots Road and Neasden, many substations, and laying miles of cable, were at last put in hand.

Some 42 route km of the Metropolitan were electrified in three years, a very creditable performance considering the line was clear for work to take place in only about six hours out of every 24. The length of the District to be electrified was even greater. At first, an experimental electrified line between Acton Town and South Harrow was laid down and used both for testing the installation and training crews to operate the new electric trains. Two seven-car trains of the open saloon type, seating an average of 46 passengers a car, were run on the 9km length of District track to South Harrow. Larger and heavier than any tube stock, and with three 130kW motor cars in each train, a top speed of 97km/h was claimed for them. They were fitted with hand-operated sliding doors in the middle and gates at each end platform. Both electrical and braking equipment came from different sources to compare the results. These District cars, with their angular appearance and open platforms, bore

Left: **A District Railway B-stock car, No 200, which used a very early example of air-operated sliding doors.** *Author's collection*

Above: **This view is from the south end of Aldgate station looking towards what was then Mark Lane, but later Tower Hill station, on 11 September 1922. The tracks on the left of the picture lead to and from Aldgate East. Noticeable is the use of bull-head rail, which was long an Underground favourite, and the ramps to guide pick-up shoes across the running rails they will meet. At the point on the left can be seen a split centre conductor rail, to accommodate shoes approaching from both directions.** *IAL*

Services, Ealing Broadway to Mansion House

Year	Traction	Trains per day, each way	Fare	Journey time
1891	Steam	n/a	10d	49min
1901	Steam	40	7d	48min
1913	Electric	187	5d	35min

unmistakable signs of their American origins. This influence remained in future building, and henceforth carriages became cars, and bogies became trucks.

Once these cars had proved themselves, mass production was undertaken, although two thirds of the 420 cars ordered were constructed in France. Sliding doors were provided throughout, and pneumatic cylinders were installed to allow their operation by the gateman. However, this turned out to be over-ambitious for the technology of the era, and the apparatus was removed.

INFRASTRUCTURE WORK

While this was going on, the work of electrification was proceeding steadily, and eventually, on 22 September 1905, the last steam train puffed around the Inner Circle. Not many months after its exit, the major programme of electrification of both railways was completed.

Henceforth there were long, well-lit saloon coaches for the delectation of passengers, and the stuffy compartment coaches were withdrawn. It was as if the authorities wished to wipe the memories of steam trains from the minds of their passengers, for stations and tunnels were thoroughly cleaned of accumulated layers of soot and grime, and there was much repainting and a general brightening up. Such, some would observe, is the value of competition.

The District committed itself to total electrification, and purchased 10 electric locomotives which normally worked in pairs. In appearance, these were among the nearest to boxes on wheels ever to run in Britain. Built to haul LNWR trains on the Outer Circle service between Mansion House and Earl's Court where engines were changed, the locomotives found new employment in 1910 in conjunction with the Tilbury line. The basic services out to Barking were provided by jointly owned trains of a similar type to those already owned by the District. For the new services, the London, Tilbury & Southend company constructed two rather splendid trains of gangwayed stock with sliding doors and, be it noted, retention toilets; these were put into service between Ealing Broadway and Southend. The District locomotives hauled

these trains as far as Barking, then the limit of electrification. The new coaches entered service in 1912, and the operation continued until 1939.

There is little doubt that electrification did much for the railways and their passengers. A comparison of what was offered as the years advanced and technology developed is revealing. Today, there is less than half the 1913 number of trains, while journey times have been eased slightly.

FLEET REQUIREMENTS

The Metropolitan had other preoccupations. Its various lines differed greatly in type and requirements, and the blanket solution applied by the District was felt to be inappropriate. Steam traction would continue, albeit on a much curtailed basis. Although the 'A' class 4-4-0Ts had provided the majority of the steam services, there were other small classes of locomotives which saw most use on the main line. Of these, the five 0-4-4Ts of the 'E' class built from 1896 were notably successful, as were the four similar 'F' class 0-6-2T locomotives which followed them, for freight working. The third of the 'E' class, No 1, was built at Neasden and has survived into preservation in working order.

Above: **Steam locomotive development did not cease with the onset of electrification. Metropolitan Railway 0-6-4T No 96 is one of the four 'G' class locomotives. They were built by the Yorkshire Engine Co in 1915 and formed part of the fleet which went to the London & North Eastern Railway in 1937. The name,** *Charles Jones,* **referred to the Metropolitan's locomotive superintendent at Neasden from 1906 to 1923.** *Author's collection*

Right: **A train of early District electric stock arrives at Ealing Broadway c1912. The non-stop cachet was applied to workings from Mansion House, but only a few stations were omitted. In reality, the trains tended to stop in tunnels outside the stations, anyway, but it was not until 1964 that such workings were abolished entirely.**
Bucknall collection/IAL

Further steam-locomotive building saw four massive 'G' class 0-6-4Ts in 1915 for freight, which the Metropolitan took the unusual step of naming. Eight graceful 'H' class 4-4-4Ts for express passenger work were built in 1920/1, and finally six 'K' class 2-6-4Ts were constructed from the parts manufactured at Woolwich Arsenal to a South Eastern & Chatham design after World War 1. Bearing a strong resemblance to a tank engine version of Maunsell's 'N' class (which in effect they were), their main purpose was freight work. These 18 locomotives all went to the London & North Eastern Railway in 1937, when that company assumed responsibility for non-electric passenger haulage on what was by then London Transport. Few survived the war years to come.

The Metropolitan's main interest now was in electric traction. Deliveries of multiple-units were in batches from a variety of British manufacturers. However, they differed fundamentally from the District stock in that the latter opted for a single-motor bogie and associated equipment, whereas the Metropolitan's motor cars had two motor bogies and thus no trailing bogie. Like the District,

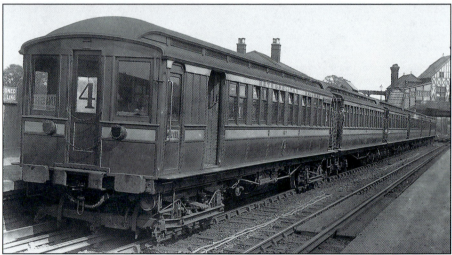

Above: **The Metropolitan had some large and impressive tank locomotives; this is No 111 of the 'K' class 2-6-4T type, with side tanks. The six locomotives were assembled by Armstrong Whitworth & Co in 1925 from surplus SECR locomotive parts from Woolwich Arsenal which had been ordered by the Government. They were intended primarily for freight work; all went to the LNER in 1937.** *IAL*

Right: **Initially, both the Metropolitan and the District provided rolling stock for the operation of the Inner Circle service. The Metropolitan later became the predominant operator. This is one of the original 1904-stock trains, seen here on the Metropolitan main line.** *IAL*

though, the Metropolitan quickly found BTH equipment to be much more reliable than that offered by the Westinghouse company. Unfortunately, by the time this became apparent, the Metropolitan was lumbered with a substantial number of orders for Westinghouse traction controls which they were unable to cancel. These cars were later converted to trailers to operate with new motor cars.

The Metropolitan provided all the outer rail trains on the Circle and some of the inner rail ones as well, since it owned the greater part of the mileage. From 1907, it took over the whole service provision, and this hastened the conversion of some of the steam stock, built only a few years previously, to electric operation. These later vehicles had been constructed with bogies, as opposed to the rigid eight-wheeler designs previously used.

A further 20 trains, later increased to 24, were built for the joint Metropolitan and GWR

Hammersmith & City electrification, completed in 1906; this included the branch to Addison Road. For this, the GWR built its own power station at Park Royal and became the owner of some of the trains, although all were maintained by the Metropolitan.

METROPOLITAN ELECTRIC LOCOMOTIVES

The first electric locomotives for the Metropolitan were of Bo-Bo centre-cab type and were built between 1904 and 1906. They were intended for hauling through Great Western main-line trains from origins such as Windsor on the Bishop's Road and Aldgate section. A second type, for domestic Metropolitan use, resembled those supplied to the District. Neither design lasted long, all 20 being replaced by new

machines built by Metropolitan Vickers at Barrow in 1922 to handle the increasingly heavy trains on the main line out to Harrow and, from 1925 when electrification was extended, to Rickmansworth.

These celebrated locomotives were equipped with 224kW motors, one geared to each of the four axles, with electro-magnetic control to provide special slow speed control for shunting purposes. Besides the 12 current collector shoes on the locomotives, other shoes were fitted to the guards' vehicles at the extreme ends of the rakes and connected by power cable, to ensure that the whole was not brought to an unseemly halt by the locomotive becoming 'gapped' at a break in the conductor rail at junctions. In such subtle ways was the excellent steam 'Dreadnought' compartment stock modified for

Above: **The Metropolitan's first electric locomotives were of the camel-backed variety. This is No 1 from the first, Westinghouse batch, delivered in 1906.** *Author's collection*

electric traction! The other change was the fitting of electric heating.

The overall length of the locomotives was 12.04m, and their weight 61.5 tonnes. Double-ended, they were fitted with dual Westinghouse compressed air and vacuum brakes, also trip cocks for train control (a separate one for each brake type). In 25 seconds 32km/h was attainable, with 183 tonnes in tow, and a maximum speed of 105km/h on the level. No 15 was exhibited, with some rolling stock, at the Wembley Empire Exhibition in 1924/5 (an event of considerable commercial significance for the Metropolitan), and carried a commemorative nameplate. The whole class received names, associated in some way or other with the area served.

The bronze nameplates were removed from 1943, and the lake livery with gold lining was dropped for utility grey. The names were restored from 1953, together with the lake and gold; this time No 2 became *Thomas Lord*, No 9 never received a new nameplate as it was then in the service stock, and No 10's name was shortened to *W. E. Gladstone*. By this time, Nos 15, 17, 19 and 20 had been withdrawn from service.

Long term, two have survived. Locomotive No 12 *Sarah Siddons* remained in the service stock fleet for many years, while No 5 *John Hampden* is in London's Transport Museum at Covent Garden.

Metropolitan electric locomotives of 1922/3, as named in 1927

No	Name
1	*John Lyon*
2	*Oliver Cromwell*
3	*Sir Ralph Verney*
4	*Lord Byron*
5	*John Hampden*
6	*William Penn*
7	*Edmund Burke*
8	*Sherlock Holmes*
9	*John Milton*
10	*William Ewart Gladstone*
11	*George Romney*
12	*Sarah Siddons*
13	*Dick Whittington*
14	*Benjamin Disraeli*
15	*Wembley 1924*
16	*Oliver Goldsmith*
17	*Florence Nightingale*
18	*Michael Faraday*
19	*John Wycliffe*
20	*Sir Christopher Wren*

Above: **Metropolitan electric locomotive No 10** *William Ewart Gladstone* **is seen at an unidentified location.** *Author's collection*

activity did achieve was to establish the need for additional trains, and both the surface railways had new stock delivered in this period.

Although the small bore tube railways had never contemplated more than one class of travel, the Metropolitan and District continued to provide selectively for First-class passengers until October 1941. The Metropolitan, indeed, was prepared to go to considerable lengths for its important passengers. The Rothschild saloon was a 1905 reconstruction of two luxury six-wheeled vehicles built 10 years earlier for the use of Ferdinand de Rothschild, who lived at Wendover. It became the company's directors' saloon, its last official duty being to form an inspection special over the Brill branch before services were withdrawn in 1935.

Of greater fame were the legendary Pullman Cars constructed by the Birmingham RCW Co for Pullman, but fitted out to Metropolitan specifications. Built to Circle Line gauge, they entered service in 1910 and were retained until 1939. *Mayflower* and *Galatea* were the Metropolitan's response to Great Central competition, and although initially they ran in ordinary trains throughout the day, including a late-night theatre train arriving back at Aylesbury at 00.55, lack of patronage soon restricted their use to the principal business services. Their value was in the publicity they gave the company, seen as a matter of increasing importance, rather than the revenue they generated.

The addition of the Uxbridge branch to the Metropolitan at Harrow had proved successful in generating traffic, to the extent that quadrupling of the double track north of Finchley Road was undertaken as far as Wembley Park by 1915. Similar capacity constraints had affected the District, and west of Hammersmith the sharing of the LSWR's tracks was producing unacceptable delays. Consequently, the District quadrupled this section in 1911, only to find the LSWR withdrawing its service five years later. As matters turned out, this was to much simplify the subsequent westward extension of the Piccadilly, so the work was not wasted. What this

THE TUBE GOES FURTHER

By the 1920s the Underground map was beginning to look familiar to modern eyes, although as yet the extensive incursions into what became vast swathes of suburbs had hardly begun. The experience of Golders Green in the Edwardian era had however shown the potential for suburban development, and this decade witnessed further extensions. The first to get under way were projects, which had been deferred by the war.

The Central London had been determined to press on westwards, and agreement was secured with the Great Western that it would construct the Ealing & Shepherd's Bush Railway. Reconstruction of the terminal loop was called for, especially in view of the opening of White City Stadium. The platform on the outside of the sharp curve was causing delays to trains, as there was a very substantial gap between the doors newly installed in the centre of the cars (replacing those at the ends), and the platform edge. The platform on the inside of the curve could take only six cars, due to the positioning of the depot entrance and exit roads, and was not used in consequence. The solution adopted was to construct a movable 10.8m extension to the short platform, which was capable of being swivelled through a 1.07m arc away from the tracks when use of the depot roads was required. Movement was electro-pneumatic, controlled from the signalbox and interlocked in the normal way. This ingenious contraption lasted from 1920, when the Ealing extension was brought into use, until 1947.

The two tracks which continued west from Wood Lane were arranged for right-hand running, so a flyover was constructed to restore the normal rule of the road before the next station at East Acton was reached. Electric power came from the GWR's plant at Park Royal.

Legal powers to project the Hampstead tube northwards had been obtained as early as 1902, but it was late in 1923 that the extension to Hendon Central was opened, and August 1924 by the time the tube reached Edgware. The tardiness had cost the Combine dear, as land values had risen (due, one imagines, almost entirely to its own efforts), and some demolition was needed before the railway could proceed on brick arches and viaduct, north from Golders Green. These gave way to cutting as the line reached Brent (now Brent Cross), and the formation widened. Later, passing loops to be used for express working would be provided each side of the tracks serving the island platform. Crossing the North Circular Road on viaduct again, the line reached Hendon Central. As with others on the extension, this station was finished in a Georgian style to complement the suburban housing developments.

The twin tunnels at The Burroughs, Hendon, took the new railway under the Midland main line and today's M1. Above the northern end of the tunnel was sited a semaphore signal, but not for train control purposes. It offered a range of positions, most of which were unknown in the railway rule book. Viewed from Colindale station 914m distant, this was an eyesight test for train drivers. Not being allowed to wear spectacles, failing an eyesight medical was a serious matter for the individual, who was entitled to demand this practical test if he did not pass.

Continuing to Edgware, the line passed through the embankment of the Great Northern Railway, to make its own island platform

terminus with an overall roof which covered also a pair of adjoining sidings. Additional sidings and a car shed were also provided. A frequent snappy Underground service was to galvanise Edgware's growth in a way that the modest offerings by the longer GNR route could never have done; in 1919, ordinary bookings from Edgware GNR were as low as 20 per day.

INTEGRATING THE C&SLR

Bolstered by the allocation of cheap money from the Government, the much-needed rehabilitation of the City & South London and its integration into the Hampstead tube began at last in 1922. Two distinct elements were involved: the enlargement of the old tunnels to standard bore, and the construction of the complex series of underground junctions at Camden Town. While work was in progress, further powers were obtained to extend south from Clapham to Morden, and to construct a new link from Embankment under the river to Waterloo and to junctions at Kennington. With the Edgware extension underway as well, the 'Edgware, Highgate and Morden Line', one of the names by which the combination was uneasily known, largely assumed its present Northern Line form.

The C&SLR's tunnels were built to a mixture of dimensions, successively 3.20m (Euston to Moorgate), 3.50m (Moorgate to Borough Junction), 3.09m (Borough Junction to Elephant), and 3.20m Elephant to Clapham Common. To enable the enlargement work to be carried out, the line north of Moorgate was closed

completely, while trains continued to run on the southern section. This latter policy came to grief in November 1923 when a minor roof fall stopped a northbound train near Elephant & Castle. Fortunately the driver was able to remove the obstruction and reach Borough station before large quantities of earth cascaded into the tunnel and blocked it completely. After this episode, it was decided to close the line until work was finished. The substitute bus service was increased to a one-minute headway as a result.

Where the tunnel diameter was 3.50m, hand enlargement and use of larger key pieces in the tunnel linings was sufficient, but elsewhere the existing lining rings were removed and shields used to bore out the tunnels to the standard 3.56m diameter. The ring-like shields were designed to allow the diminutive trains to continue to run; perhaps the odd C&SLR rule forbidding passengers to ride on the roof of trains had some relevance after all! Four new segment pieces replacing the originals were

Right: **A potted history of the reconstruction of the City & South London Railway at the time of its reopening on 1 December 1924, and carried in** *Modern Transport.*
F. H. Stingemore/Author's collection

Below: **London Electric Railway rolling stock developed over the years, and as these drawings show, the car lengths remained broadly constant. Clearly, it was the doors which were giving most problems – how many, of what design, and where to put them?**
Author's collection

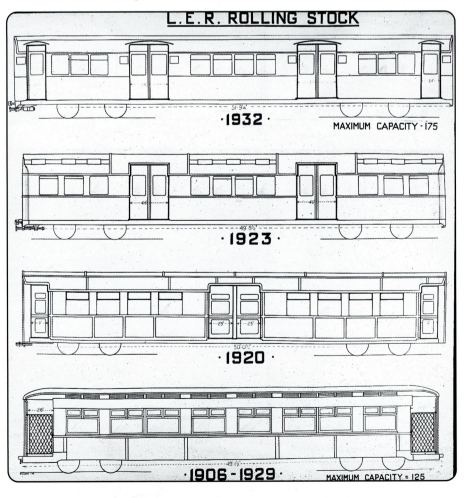

L.E.R. ROLLING STOCK

·1932·   MAXIMUM CAPACITY ·175

·1923·

·1920·

·1906-1929·   MAXIMUM CAPACITY = 125

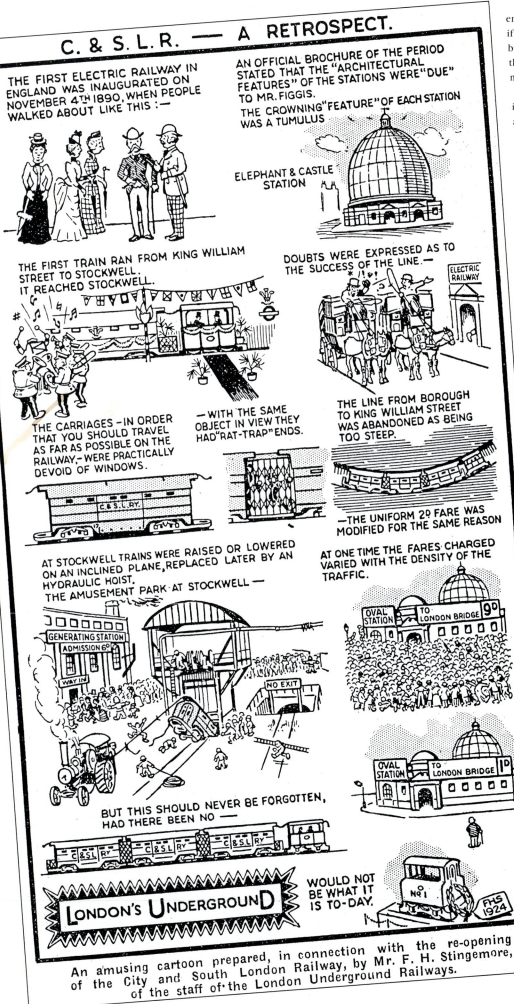

An amusing cartoon prepared, in connection with the re-opening of the City and South London Railway, by Mr. F. H. Stingemore, of the staff of the London Underground Railways.

enough for the 3.20m tunnels, even if the result was hardly circular, but the smallest tunnels had new linings throughout. There were some realignments to eliminate speed restrictions.

Modernisation also covered the installation of standard Underground automatic signalling and the conversion of the power supply to fourth rail. Station platform tunnels were lengthened to 107m (a standard C&SLR three-car train was only 33.5m long). The stations themselves were suitably updated, many being provided with escalators. Alone, City Road station between Euston and Angel did not reopen. The reconstruction effected a major improvement, and with new rolling stock as well, the running time between Euston and Clapham Common was reduced by one quarter from 31½ to 23½ minutes.

CAMDEN TOWN

At Camden Town the requirement was to insert junctions between the Hampstead tube's two diverging northern branches and the C&SLR's Euston terminus. Since the latter was aligned east-west and well below the newer tube, and there was only about 1.5km in which to effect a junction, steep gradients at a maximum of 2.5% (1 in 40) uphill and 3.3% (1 in 30) down were needed. The 'stomach diagram' of this complex of underground lines which enables parallel and non-conflicting movements to be made through-out was proudly publicised. Interestingly, this junction has since been claimed to be the major limitation to expanding train frequencies. It does have the benefit that trains from Bank to Edgware do not conflict at all with Charing Cross to High Barnet services. The reconstruction work was completed in April 1924, and a through service between Moorgate and Golders Green was instituted.

For rather different reasons, such an arrangement has been enforced following the derailment of a High Barnet-bound train on 19 October 2003.

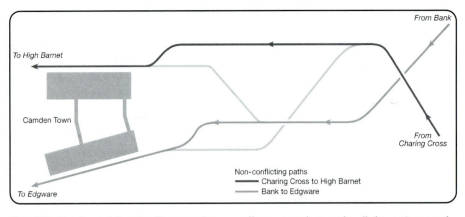

Above: **The junctions at Camden Town can be used to run two separate services which each become part of a separate railway. The equivalent track layout applies in both directions. Likewise, all trains via Charing Cross can use the Kennington loop.**

In the diagram:
- To High Barnet
- From Bank
- Camden Town
- To Edgware
- From Charing Cross
- Non-conflicting paths
  - Charing Cross to High Barnet
  - Bank to Edgware

TO MORDEN, BUT NO FURTHER

The Morden extension was the result of horse trading with the Southern Railway interests, which drew a physical as well as a metaphorical line across the tube's path with the building of the Wimbledon & Sutton Railway. As so often in south London, tube construction was problematic due to waterlogged ground; nowhere was this more apparent than at Tooting Broadway. In the past, the village of Tooting had been noted for its plentiful water supply, and the tube station lay over what amounted to an underground lake. The station and its approaches had to be built under compressed air conditions, work being first conducted from beneath air locks in vertical working shafts, and then from behind horizontal air locks in the sections of tunnel completed. From a final 'cut and cover' section due to wet ground, the tube emerged to an open-air cutting at Morden, where a three-track/five-platform face layout was built. The tracks continued beyond to extensive stabling facilities on the surface. A conscious effort was made to make all the stations on the extension conspicuous, and the angular surface buildings made much use of Portland stone in their construction.

Calls from time to time to extend the Underground fell on deaf ears; in consequence Morden station forecourt has remained a busy and important bus-rail interchange point. In any event, it is doubtful whether the Northern Line has the capacity to carry much additional traffic over this section.

Work on the last piece in the jigsaw began immediately after the Camden Town junctions were opened. Immediately south of Charing Cross (then Strand), the new southbound line forged straight ahead to Embankment (then Charing Cross), through the return part of the loop at a point below the river, and on to Waterloo and Kennington. Here, the new connection divided and rose each side of the City Line platforms, giving level and quick interchange for passengers. Connections enabled trains to continue south, and a conventional turnback siding was provided between the running tunnels. However, a terminal loop was and is the principal means of reversing direction, and the author admits to having watched a train disappear into the tunnel at the end of Platform 2 and then nipping across to Platform 1 to see if the same train really would reappear! Terminal loops are not all they might be from the operator's point of view, and are discussed later.

The opening of the Kennington extension coincided with the completion to Morden, and on 13 September 1926 work was finished for the time being. (Balham station opening was delayed to December). These extensions created what was then the world's longest rail tunnel, from Golders Green to Morden via Bank, a distance of 26.75km. Subsequently, this was exceeded by the High Barnet branch of the Northern line, whose East Finchley to Morden via Bank distance is 27.84km or 17 miles 528yd.

The following year, a single-track link was made at King's Cross between the eastbound Piccadilly and the northbound City Line, both in a trailing direction. This was purely for rolling stock and engineering train movements, and gave the Northern access to Acton Works.

WATFORD BY THE MET

Jointly with the Great Central Railway, the Metropolitan built a 3km branch from Moor Park to Croxley Green and Watford. Or rather, the line was built to the edge of Cassiobury Park, through which the railway was not allowed to pass. This unsatisfactory terminal arrangement severely limited the practical usefulness of the line, which has always remained something of a backwater. Services commenced in 1925.

Below: **The London & North Western Railway's New Line to Watford opened in 1916 with borrowed stock, as the rolling stock ordered was not ready. As can be seen, the six-car production trains looked smart in their 'plum and spilt milk' LNWR livery. They were jointly owned with the LER. This was the first time that motor cars had been provided in Underground trains other than at the ends; the cars (from right to left) were M-CT-M-T-T-M.** *IAL*

Right: **'Metro-land for Health'. An advertisement which appeared in** *Modern Transport***, 30 May 1931.** *Author's collection*

TYPICAL RESIDENCE ON CEDARS ESTATE, RICKMANSWORTH.

METRO-LAND FOR HEALTH

HAVE you ever realised the joy of living in the country; the pleasure of rural surroundings and bracing air? Have you ever thought of the definite advantages to be gained; the economies to be effected; the new viewpoint that a change of scene, occupation and interest will undoubtedly bring?

In Metro-land—London's nearest countryside—you will find all that you can reasonably ask. It has character and charm; variety and interest.

It is the most accessible and least spoiled residential district around London and its train service is the envy of all. There are through trains to and from the City both morning and evening; there are "non-stop" trains, "cheap" trains; "theatre" trains—everything in fact that you can possibly desire.

But this is not all. Metro-land lays definite claim to be the most healthy district around London. The climate is mild and equable; the air is clean and invigorating, and the subsoil, for the most part, is gravel. There are unlimited facilities for outdoor recreation; there are fifteen golf courses from which to choose; educational and shopping facilities are exceptionally liberal, whilst the Season Ticket Rates will be found within the reach of all.

In Metro-land there are neat little villas standing in their own trim gardens; stately mansions surrounded by park-like grounds and there is also a multitude of out-of-the-way nooks and corners where the life of the countryside goes on serene, unspoilt by the changes that have overwhelmed it elsewhere.

The residential districts nearest at hand are Neasden, Wembley Park, Northwick Park and Harrow. Then comes Rayners Lane, immediately serving the delightful Harrow Garden Village, then Eastcote, Ruislip, Uxbridge and Pinner. Further afield, yet still within easy reach, are Rickmansworth and Chorley Wood. Beyond these are Chesham, Amersham and Great Missenden, and then, as a fitting climax, comes Wendover, a gem of rural scenery.

It will pay you to consider carefully the many advantages of living in Metro-land and to review the active housing development that is taking place in all directions. To help you in this connection, a profusely illustrated Handbook has been prepared containing a varied selection of exclusive designs and plans of charming houses, and also a "Broadsheet" that sets out in detail the various housing propositions obtaining in Metro-land.

The coupon below will bring you a free copy, of each, by return.

The Commercial Manager,
Metropolitan Railway,
Baker St. Station, N.W.1.

Please send, post free, copy of "Where to Live" Handbook and also House-Seekers' Broadsheet.

NAME.........

ADDRE........

A triangular junction was built to provide direct access to Rickmansworth, but full passenger operation over the north curve lasted only until 1933, since when it has seen occasional use only. Future possibilities in this area are discussed later.

The housing boom of the inter-war years transformed great expanses of open country around London into street upon street of detached and semi-detached houses. This growth was not confined to any particular area, but went on at a rapid pace wherever there was easy access to London. Perhaps the most sustained attempt to stimulate suburban living was the building of Metro-Land. This is an extract from a 'Live in Metro-Land' press advertisement of 1931:

'The delightful residential area served by the Metropolitan Railway claims the serious attention of every Home Seeker...The train service provided is unequalled for frequency and rapidity; the educational and shopping facilities are unlimited; the season ticket rates are low and the local housing developments especially attractive. Residents in this district also have the added advantage of being able to travel to and from the City without change of carriage...'

During the inter-war period, 4,000 homes were built in Middlesex and Buckinghamshire on the back of the Metropolitan Railway Co, with the concurrent expansion of the railway facilities. That this was possible was in large measure due to the Metropolitan's ability to exploit its excessive land holdings in the area to the benefit of the railway's finances. This was achieved through the associated Metropolitan Railway Country Estates Ltd. British railway companies were generally discouraged or forbidden from ownership of land which they did not require for carrying on their main business.

Continued congestion on the Metropolitan main line resulted in the four tracking reaching out to Harrow by 1932, the same year in which the 7.24km Stanmore branch was completed. The latter was designed to tap the housing spreading out from Edgware, Canons Park station being less than a 2km bus ride from Edgware tube. However, the Metropolitan's relatively high fares policy compared with the Underground group acted as a disincentive to traffic growth, and single-car units transferred from the Rickmansworth-Watford service sufficed for the limited off-peak traffic between Wembley Park and Stanmore. In view of the two track bottleneck between Finchley Road and Baker Street, growth was the last thing the Metropolitan really needed. Both schemes were financed by cheap government money, provided for the relief of unemployment.

In the east, the District extended its interests another 12.5km from Barking to Upminster in 1932; this extension of electrification to Upminster was to serve the vast new London County Council Becontree housing estate. Two additional lines were laid in for the new service to the north of the Tilbury tracks by the London Midland & Scottish Railway as successors to the LT&S company, with additional stations provided at Upney and Dagenham Heathway (1932); also at Upminster Bridge (1934) and Elm Park (1935).

THE PICCADILLY GOES NORTH

The Great Northern, Piccadilly & Brompton Railway, to give the line its earlier title, had provided a direct connection from its northern terminus at Finsbury Park with the West End from 1906. Finsbury Park was one massive, not to say notorious, interchange, with passengers in those days arriving by Great Northern suburban services from Edgware, High Barnet and Dunstable, as well as today's Hatfield and Hertford lines. To this was added the traffic from the extensive tram and motor bus systems. The tube terminus was built on Great Northern property, and one of the consequences had been an undertaking given in 1902 that the Piccadilly would not be extended northwards without GNR consent.

By 1925, with 30,000 passengers changing between different forms of transport daily, the public pressure to relieve the congestion was intense. 'There is enormous overcrowding on the trams and on the other vehicles during the peak hours of the day, and there is no possibility of augmenting accommodation save by providing increased railway accommodation either by tube or electrification of existing lines or by introducing electric signalling,' Sir Henry Maybury told the Royal Commission.

Part of the problem was finance. The Underground Chairman, Lord Ashfield, noting the disparity of traffic between the peak and the 'valley hours' was blunt: 'It may be a great surprise to you to know that the Underground railways in London have never been, in their whole career, a financial success. In other words, they have failed to earn anything approaching a reasonable return on capital invested in them ...' One result was the Act of 1927 under which the Underground Group was able to borrow capital at 3% to finance the Piccadilly improvements, which were started in 1930, following the waiving (under protest) of the LNER veto five years earlier.

PHYSICAL FEATURES

As might be expected of a line which runs partly in tube, and partly across undulating country, the Cockfosters extension has several interesting features. For the 6.5km from Finsbury Park until it emerges from the long tunnel which starts at Barons Court, the line runs in twin tunnels driven beneath Seven Sisters Road to Manor House. Here they swing north through a 300m radius curve (the sharpest on this line of otherwise easy curvature), and continue beneath Green Lanes to Bounds Green. The gradient falls all the way to Turnpike Lane, and then rises at an average of 1.7% (1 in 60) to the summit at Enfield West.

Where the tube emerges at Tewkesbury Road, the tunnel is enlarged to 4.88m, and bell-mouthed to reduce the air pressure on trains entering at speed. Just after the line leaves the twin tunnel, it is carried obliquely across the North Circular Road on a 53m girder bridge, followed by a long viaduct to reach Arnos Grove station. It then enters an 850m tunnel, towards the far end of which is Southgate station. Cutting followed by viaduct and embankment takes the line to Oakwood and Cockfosters terminus, between which points the highest and coldest car sheds on the Underground system, 84m above sea level, are passed on the west side of the line.

The tunnelling was through the yielding London clay, using a variety of shields and pneumatically operated shovels. One particularly delicate operation involved strengthening the brick tunnel through which the New River flowed at Bounds Green. Here it was necessary to insert an iron lining for a distance of 27m, as the railway was to pass 7.5m below the river bed.

The naming of the stations produced a flurry of local excitement. Perhaps unwisely, the Underground Group invited the public to respond to ideas put forward by the Group for the names of most of the stations. The new line extended well beyond the built-up area, partly to reach a suitable depot site. The route was carefully chosen to split the distance between the two existing Great Northern Railway suburban branches, and as a result the stations initially served nowhere in particular. The most controversial choice proved to be the present Oakwood, for which the suggested alternatives were Merryhills (a nearby public house) and East Barnet (then the name of the road alongside the station). However, the Group then determined to call the station Enfield West, which upset the sensibilities of the Southgate Urban District Council on the grounds that the station was nearly a quarter of a mile outside the Enfield UDC area and the name would confuse passengers. Alternatives of Southgate North and Oakwood Park were rejected by the Group, who stuck to their intentions and opened the station as Enfield West in 1933. But offence of this

Above: **Heston-Hounslow station, later Hounslow West, after conversion to an island platform in 1912. The semaphore signal on the left is protecting the entrance to the single-line section.** IAL

nature, once given, is rarely forgotten, and a year later the station became Enfield West (Oakwood). It took the UDC until 1946 to secure the final adoption of plain Oakwood.

WEST FROM HAMMERSMITH

As the country filled up in the northern districts of Southgate and beyond, so it did in places like Hounslow, Ealing and Harrow, and it was considered advisable to balance the working of the Piccadilly Line by extending it at the other end also.

Services were projected concurrently to the west and north west, not so much by breaking fresh ground but by the adaptation of existing lines. The Piccadilly was extended from Hammersmith to South Harrow in 1932, then to Northfields in 1933, and later the same year to Hounslow West. Finally, in October 1933, the Piccadilly was extended from South Harrow to Uxbridge, where it replaced the District shuttle service from Acton Town, itself inaugurated in 1910.

The District tracks already extended through Hammersmith to Hounslow, and from Northfields onwards it was simply a matter of Piccadilly trains using the District Line. But the District tracks as far as Turnham Green, on the way to Northfields, were far too busy to accommodate additional Piccadilly trains, plus a lesser number of Richmond trains, and some major work was called for. The problem was solved by constructing a new tunnel by 'cut and cover' methods under Hammersmith Broadway for two new tracks, completely rebuilding the station as well for good measure. That was coupled with the adaptation of the disused Southern Railway viaduct which had once given LSWR trains from Richmond access to Kensington, and included a connection to the Metropolitan's Hammersmith & City line.

Above: **This undated photograph is of South Kensington station, with a train of Metropolitan Railway stock. Like so many others, the station boasted an overall roof in the early years. The leading vehicle would appear to be one of the 1905 batch of stock, with enclosed – as opposed to open (and gated) – ends.** *IAL*

The rebuilding was designed to offer complete physical separation between the Piccadilly trains which were to use the two centre tracks, and those of the District line which flanked them. The latter had junctions to accommodate both the Ealing Broadway and Richmond services, and the diagram below shows how the changes in the layout were made. This also illustrates how it came to be that Stamford Brook station, which was opened in 1912 and never had platforms on the LSWR line, has no platform today on the eastbound Piccadilly Line.

West of Turnham Green junction, the tracks were quadrupled through Acton Town to Northfields by widening works; between Northfields and Boston Manor, a new car depot was built, with access from the running lines via a flyover junction. Services to Uxbridge from Acton Town used a grade separated junction, and followed the District and then the Metropolitan

tracks to reach their objective. Thus the western extensions used existing lines almost throughout.

The layout between Hammersmith and Acton Town required a different stopping pattern for the two lines, the Piccadilly providing the non-stop service and gaining a modest couple of minutes in the process. The four tracks west of Acton Town have proved less useful, particularly since the withdrawal of District line services on this section in 1964. The former District eastbound track between South Ealing and Acton Town was devoted to testing purposes.

Hammersmith station was completely rebuilt during the 1990s.

PICCADILLY CIRCUS AND HOLBORN

The extensions brought renewed pressure on the central-London section of the Piccadilly, and extensive rebuilding of Leicester Square, Green Park (formerly Dover Street), Hyde Park Corner

and Knightsbridge followed. The classic rebuilding was that of Piccadilly Circus, completed in 1928. The old station which dealt with 1½ million passengers in 1907 could now look forward to a traffic of anything up to 50 million journeys annually, and total reconstruction was called for. The solution was to create a 1,394sq m ticket-hall area 4.5m below the surface of the Circus itself, surrounded by a circular walkway which was accessed from five subways leading to the street and directly into the basement of Swan & Edgar's prestigious department store. (It has become a branch of Tower Records, but the facility remains). 'Passimeter' ticket offices with the clerks in the middle like goldfish in a bowl were installed, as were no fewer than 26 self-service ticket machines. Five escalators in two shafts led down to a common landing 17m below ground level, from which two sets of triple escalators led to the Piccadilly and Bakerloo lines respectively. The booking hall was intended to recall Nash's Circus, obliterated by Edwardian rebuilding. Shops and showcases lined the perimeter, which was lit by lanterns on the red scagliola columns. Fitments were in bronze, and travertine marble was used for surrounds. A 'world clock' built at Lillie Bridge workshops was installed, as were the 'see how they run' indicators from which service regularity could be observed by the public. It was a masterpiece of its time, described by S. E. Rasmussen in 1937 as 'an excellent example of what the Underground has done for modern civilisation'.

Also on the agenda was the closing of three of the lesser-used stations, thus speeding up the services. Brompton Road, Down Street and York Road all ceased to trade between 1932 and 1934.

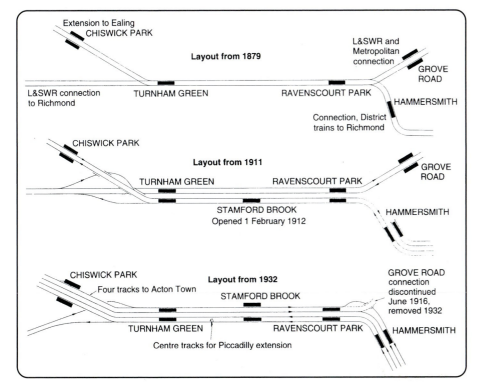

Rebuilding at Holborn, completed in 1933, was to make it an interchange station between the Central Line, which had previously served British Museum station, and the Piccadilly. The new platform tunnels were built around the running tunnels, so that until the old tunnels were dismantled trains were running in a tube within a tube. At the same time, escalator tunnels had to be built to connect the lines with each other and to the surface ticket hall.

A NEW APPROACH

The general thrust of legislation in the 19th century had been to preserve as many small and competing industries as possible, with the ever-present fears of monopoly power and consequent exploitation of the public being uppermost. However, views changed in the 20th century. The London Electric Railways Facilities Act was passed in 1915, allowing the C&SLR, CLR, LER, MDR and also the LGOC to create a pooled revenue agreement into which all moneys collected would be paid, and each would draw upon in agreed proportions. The first steps by government to co-ordinate London's transport

Below: **Passengers need to hold tickets, and self-service ticket machines offered some clear advantages if they could be made reliable and reasonably foolproof. This is an early example, but its location is not known.**
Author's collection

were taken by the setting up of the Ministry of Transport in 1919, and the benefits of mass production and the planned approach became part of the general ethos. By 1931, it was possible for Herbert Morrison to say when introducing the second reading of the London Passenger Transport Bill into the House, that 'Competition must go; it stultifies progress,

The Underground in 1932			
Company	*Number of locomotives*	*Passenger vehicles*	*Passengers (millions)*
Metropolitan	57	719	119.7
District	7	564	126.5
London Electric	-	1,295	149.8
City & South London	-	114	61.2
Central London	-	259	41.2
Total	64	2,951	498.4

Note: The Metropolitan totals include the GN&C; of the company's 57 locomotives, 36 were steam. The vehicle stock also included 18 parcels and 544 goods vehicles.

endangers the standard of life of the workpeople in the industry, and is too expensive'. It is of interest that the Bill, first promoted by a Labour administration, was subsequently enacted by the new 'National' Government.

That Ashfield, as chairman of the Underground Group, was in favour of the formation of what became the LPTB, there can be little doubt. In his concern at the possible effect of the change in government, he was reported in *Modern Transport* in 1932 as saying that there could be 'no true or permanent solution of the problems of London passenger

transport without a unification of ownership, administration and finance, in capable and independent business hands, extending to all the local passenger transport undertakings within a widely defined London traffic area'.

Before turning to the London Passenger Transport Board, the achievements of the Underground and the Metropolitan should perhaps be recorded. In 1932, the last full year of their separate existence, the trains of what was to become London Transport in popular parlance carried 498 million passengers using 2,951 passenger vehicles. The table shows how passenger journeys were spread almost equally between the surface and the tube lines.

THE BECK DIAGRAM

By now, the London Passenger Transport Board era was fast approaching. Like all new organisations, it was gong to need an early success. This came from an unlikely quarter, and to be fair to the Combine, it was actually introduced under their stewardship. It was to become an important symbol of the unity of an undertaking which had been newly created by statute.

January 1933 saw the first printing of Harry Beck's diagrammatic representation of London Underground, at first as a pocket folder and later as a poster. With this stylised representation, all attempts at geographical accuracy as used in the maps up to that time ceased. The only other physical feature is a stylised representation of the River Thames, a helpful locational device for visitors to the capital and residents alike.

Beck's original, the inspiration for which came from the circuit diagrams which he used in his work as an engineering draughtsman, depicted an Underground rather smaller than it is today. Thus, the Central Line was still stuck at its 1920 size of Ealing Broadway (only) to Liverpool Street. On the other hand, the Bakerloo, which in the first poster version shared the colour red with the Central, was then operating to Watford Junction courtesy of the LMS. The eastern ambitions of the District were acknowledged by a box on the edge of the diagram listing the stations beyond Mile End to Upminster '& Southend'. The Circle Line was not distinguished separately.

It was immediately successful, and has remained so ever since. Although it has always been updated at intervals, a complete redrawing of Beck's work was undertaken by Harold Hutchison in 1960, and again by Paul Garbutt in 1964. Garbutt toned down the angularity of the preceding version, and his work remains the basis of the computerised version seen today.

Above all, though, the diagram was of immense use to the travelling public. There can be few households in Britain which do not have a copy, somewhere, if only in a diary. Such has been its impact that it has been voted as one of the top icons of the 20th century. Sadly, though, it is now called the 'Tube map' by London Underground. As readers of this book will be aware, it covers much more than just the tubes, and a map it is not.

TAKE TICKETS FROM THESE MACHINES

BOOK HERE

CHAPTER FOUR

The London Passenger Transport Board

The new Board, which quickly became known as London Transport, was dominated by Lord Ashfield as Chairman and Frank Pick as Vice Chairman and Chief Executive. With these two men in charge of what was now a public authority, given also the expectation of some capital funding, rapid advance was only to be expected.

> 'The New Works Programme 1935/40 was by far the biggest single programme of local transport development ever undertaken in the London area.'
>
> *LPTB Annual Report, 1947*

PRINCIPAL DUTIES

The London Passenger Transport Act, 1933 established a public authority, the London Passenger Transport Board (LPTB), with a general duty to secure the provision of an adequate and properly co-ordinated system of passenger transport for the London Passenger Transport Area. This Area extended about 32km to the west and east of central London, rising to 48km to the north and south. It thus included all the Board's own railways, save only the extremities of the Metropolitan. The Board were entreated to take steps for extending and improving transport facilities, and were given wide powers. They also had a duty to break even, and to fix their fares and charges accordingly.

The chairman and the six Board members were to be appointed by a panel of Trustees, who themselves represented local authority, professional and commercial interests.

The Act provided for the LPTB to acquire all the undertakings owned by the Underground Group (which included tramways and bus companies) and the Metropolitan Railway. Other acquisitions were the local authority-owned tramways, bus companies owned by the Thomas Tilling group, and independent bus operators in the London area. The Board was also given borrowing powers for capital purposes. The vesting date was 1 July 1933.

REVENUE POOLING

The only omissions from the 1933 Act were the 'Big Four' main-line railway companies.

To cover this situation and to meet the co-ordinating objectives for London, the Act required the establishment of a Standing Joint Committee to ensure that suburban rail services were properly co-ordinated with those of the LPTB. A specific statutory requirement was the establishment of 'the pooling scheme'. This provided for the pooling of:

● the whole of the LPTB's receipts, net of the mileage-related operating costs and with allowance for capital expenditure
● the commensurate amounts for the suburban services operated by the main-line railways within the Board's area

Above: **A train of pre-1938 Standard stock on a Piccadilly Line Arnos Grove service.** *IAL*

The pool included the LPTB's bus, tram and trolleybus operations. It was then to be distributed between the parties in Standard Proportions; these reflected their receipts in an earlier year, which turned out to be 1932.

The LPTB's Annual Report and Accounts are decidedly opaque about the financial details, but some results for the first year of its existence are shown on the right.

It will be noted that the total number of passenger journeys on the LPTB's railways were fewer than those on the Big Four companies, but that the latter's share of the pool varied enormously. The predominance of what by then was the mainly electrified Southern in the area concerned may be seen,' and at first glance it is perhaps

surprising that the LNER did not make a better showing. However, the London, Tilbury & Southend line was part of the LMSR, as were the electrified North London and Watford dc lines. In all of this, the Great Western involvement was marginal.

ABSORBING THE METROPOLITAN

The Metropolitan never ceased to believe that it was a 'real' railway, and in terms of its geographical extent the company had a point. But the Metropolitan was not absorbed into the LNER along with the Great Central Railway at the time of the Grouping, and to have left it

Statutory Revenue Pooling Scheme, 1933/4		
	Passenger journeys (millions)	% of pool to which entitled
LPTB		
Railways	415.9	
Buses	1,950.5	
Trams	1,002.4	
Trolleybuses	27.2	
Total LPTB	3,396.0	62.00
Big Four		
GWR		1.34
Southern		25.55
LMSR		5.09
LNER		6.02
Total Big Four	525.9	38.00
Grand total	3,921.9	100.00

Above: **A train of Metropolitan MW (later T) stock, seen at Neasden. Motor coach No 237 was built by Birmingham Railway Carriage & Wagon Co. These capacious compartment trains lasted until the Amersham electrification 30 years later.** *Author's collection*

independent in 1933 would have been even more awkward. It did in fact have a claim to both camps, but it fought the formation of the LPTB.

One of the problems may have been perceptions. As a new BR Eastern Region employee in the 1960s, the author was told that there were only tram lines south of the river, while the Underground was hardly mentioned. Views in the other direction were on the lines 'we carry passengers, they only run trains'. This is not a book about management, but the above are relevant considerations when a unified organisation is sought.

It was to the remote corners of the Metropolitan that the Board initially turned its attention. There was the small matter of the Brill branch in deepest Buckinghamshire. By now the branch train was sometimes quite empty, in which case the crew would often stop and go rabbiting in the woods. Another practice was the swapping of milk and eggs from nearby farms for lumps of coal from the engine. It was not unusual for the locomotive to derail on the deteriorating track, in which case the occasional passenger had no choice but to walk.

So, with fewer than 50 passengers and 20 tons of freight a day, closure was inevitable and took place on 30 November 1935. Locomotive power in later years had been Metropolitan Railway Sharp, Stewart 2-4-0T locomotives, and then the familiar Beyer Peacock 4-4-0Ts were substituted until closure. However, the Aveling & Porter locomotive No 807 was rescued from dereliction by the Industrial Locomotive Society in 1950 and subsequently restored at Neasden. It passed to the National Collection in 1957 and is currently displayed at the Covent Garden museum.

The Aylesbury–Verney Junction service followed the Brill branch into oblivion the following summer.

KING'S CROSS

On a more positive note, it was common knowledge that King's Cross Metropolitan station fell well below the standards which were being achieved elsewhere. To reach it from the main-line station or from the tube station meant a long walk; work spanning several years surrounded its closure and replacement by the present station in 1941. As a result, the station entrance became adjacent to (but not integrated with) the deep-level tube lines; both had their own ticket hall.

At this point, Euston Road runs roughly east and west past the frontages of King's Cross and St Pancras main-line stations; 11m below lies the Metropolitan Line, following the course of the roadway. A tunnel curves out from St Pancras, carrying the tracks of the Widened Lines which meet those of the Metropolitan and run alongside it to Moorgate. The tunnels connecting with the LNER then formed a similar junction. West of the point where the tunnels converge, and running parallel to the Metropolitan, was a short length of abandoned tunnel, built in 1868 towards Euston Square, but never completed.

To provide for the new Metropolitan station, the eastbound Metropolitan track was diverted into the abandoned tunnel, and a new tunnel was constructed on the south side of the main tunnel. This was to allow the newly redundant portion of the main tunnel to be used partly as an entrance and ticket hall, and partly as a reversing bay, although it was never electrified. Additional space was thus secured for passenger circulation because the main tunnel was generously proportioned to accommodate a double track of the old Great Western broad gauge. In the early 1960s the reversing bay was filled in and converted for use as an additional 75m-long concourse area. This allowed the resiting of the

ticket office, and the separation of flows of passengers entering and leaving the station.

Construction exposed both the Underground and St Pancras tunnel lines below, which had to be bridged with girders while keeping the Euston Road traffic moving. Then the 70-year-old abandoned tunnel, wet and layered with accumulated debris, had to be cleaned and waterproofed to make it fit for its new use. The 21st century rebuilding is discussed in Chapter 12.

BAKERLOO TO STANMORE

A major shortcoming of the Metropolitan main line was the capacity limitation represented by the two-track section between Baker Street and Finchley Road. What was to prove an abortive scheme had, in 1926, resulted in the Metropolitan's enlarging Edgware Road station to two island platforms with a view to constructing a relief line broadly parallel to its existing one. How this would have been operated is a matter for conjecture, but no more work was ever done.

With the addition of passengers from the Stanmore branch, completed in 1932, the strain was becoming intolerable. The LPTB now determined to construct a new tube line from Baker Street to Finchley Road to enable the Bakerloo Line trains to run to Wembley Park and then over the Metropolitan's branch to Stanmore. For such projects, the direct ownership of all the assets and operations involved was likely to make progress much simpler.

The new scheme involved the building of entirely new double tubes branching off the Bakerloo system at Baker Street and proceeding along and beneath the line of the Metropolitan for 4km to a point approaching Finchley Road. Here they had to rise between the Metropolitan tracks. The layout thence to Wembley Park was rearranged to give the Bakerloo trains exclusive use of the two lines in the middle of the four-track formation. New island platforms were provided where necessary to allow the (unusual) fast-slow-slow-fast layout of tracks.

As part of the plan, the Metropolitan services were to be speeded up by allowing them a clear run for the 7.24km between Finchley Road and Wembley Park. The same would happen between Baker Street and Finchley Road, where new tube stations at Swiss Cottage and St John's Wood were to replace Lord's, Marlborough Road and Swiss Cottage (Met). Today, an all-stations train on what is now the Jubilee Line takes 19 minutes between Baker Street and Wembley Park; with one stop only, the Met takes 12 minutes.

At Neasden, new depot facilities were built for both lines, as the workshops element of the Metropolitan's premises was relocated to Acton. This allowed the Bakerloo's tightly constricted London Road depot site to be reduced in status to stabling sidings. A new diveunder connected Neasden depot to the running lines. The Wembley Park junction for the Stanmore branch had been constructed on the flat, and a burrowing junction north of the station removed the conflict with southbound Metropolitan trains. Further work rearranged the layout at Harrow-on-the-Hill.

At Baker Street the work required a new tube junction and a new southbound tube platform so that Bakerloo trains from both branches could enter the station together. Station rebuilding included the provision of escalators. Step-plate junctions, in which successive lining rings in the running tunnels are progressively increased in diameter, were built at the divergences, but Finchley Road provided the major tests of engineering ingenuity. To accommodate the Bakerloo, the northbound Metropolitan Line had to be diverted further west and below the North Star hotel, which itself required underpinning. Only 50mm of concrete separated the hotel's cellars from the crown of the new tunnel when it was finished. The northbound Bakerloo tube then broke surface via the abandoned Metropolitan tunnel. Also at Finchley Road, a 15m girder supporting the buildings above the trains was found to be partly in the way of the new ticket hall. It had to have a top section cut away and a strengthening flange welded on while the station was in continuous use.

Predictably, the Metropolitan crews referred disparagingly to the tube-sized newcomers, which were not seen at Stanmore until 1939, as 'toy trains'. What the Underground crews might have called the Brill branch, had they ever seen it, is another matter!

As part of the same development programme, the rest of the Bakerloo station platforms were lengthened to 115m to take seven cars instead of six, and at Elephant & Castle terminus a new length of double tube siding was constructed beyond the station to provide two tunnel sidings. They were pointed in the direction of Camberwell, but remain today as completed in 1939. Resignalling enabled extra trains to be run.

DISTRICT CAPITAL WORKS

The District Line had been extended to Upminster in 1932, but the traffic thus generated served only to increase the passenger volumes to be carried. The major constraint was the series of junctions which form a triangle in the Aldgate area. Before reconstruction, delays occurred through trains already in Aldgate East station fouling the spur line on which Aldgate station stands, and the points controlling it. The other two sides of the triangle were only long enough to accommodate six-car trains. It was to lengthen these sides to take eight-car trains (by

Below: **The new Uxbridge station, opened in 1938, was at a lower level and further west and south than the one it replaced. This is the view of the work under way in the station approach taken from York Road, just beyond the station platforms. A battery locomotive is in the foreground, with 'F' class 0-6-2T No L52 beyond.** *IAL*

utilising the space occupied by the old platforms), as well as to provide better passenger facilities and a larger station, that the work of resiting the station some 450m further to the east was undertaken.

To get the required headroom for two new ticket halls beneath Whitechapel Road, one at each end of the new station, the tracks had to be lowered by up to 2.2m. The work of enlarging the tunnel, which included installing girders up to 21m in length to support the roadway above, had to allow the continued passage of trains and road traffic, and required extreme care as many of the surface buildings were old and more liable to collapse.

The fishbelly girders spanning the line and part of the platforms were brought in by road and lowered into the space where the tunnel crown had been demolished. The longer and heavier girders for the work further west, where they were to span the new four-track layout on the old station site, were brought in at night by

rail in two halves from opposite ends of the site. They were halted below their final positions, and swung round on ball races through 90° to straddle both platform and track. Bolted together, the ensemble was then lifted to its resting place.

At the same time, work had been going on below, building the new platforms, although the tracks were left more or less at their original level for the time being, supported increasingly on wooden trestles as construction progressed. From the trains, it was possible to peer down to the station taking shape below. Lowering was accomplished by suspending the track from the new roof, dismantling the trestles, and letting down the 425m of double track using blocks and tackle by a maximum of 2.2m. This work

Below: **Test running and staff training with 1938 stock for the Northern Line extensions was taking place between East Finchley and High Barnet on 4 April 1940. There are at least three people in the cab.** *Author's collection*

commenced at 01.00 Sunday, and by 05.00 Monday the first train ran through on the new alignment. Nine hundred men were employed on the changeover, which also required the demolition of the old platforms, completion of the new ticket hall which had been left unfinished as it would have obstructed the old tracks, and the new signalling installation completed and tested. The new station was opened on 31 October 1938.

Another development on the Metropolitan was the rebuilding of Uxbridge station on a new site closer to the town centre, completed in 1938. It contains the only stained glass window on the Underground, featuring the coats of arms of the local authorities.

Before work started on these improvements though, the London Passenger Transport Board launched one of its major acts of policy in its five-year plan — the New Works Programme, 1935-40. Originally estimated to involve an expenditure of £40 million, and planned for completion by about 1940, this was by far the biggest single programme of transport development ever undertaken in the London area.

CO-ORDINATION AT WORK

The need for railway development in London, particularly in the eastern and north eastern sectors where there had been long-standing complaints, had been recognised for many years. But it was only with the creation of the Board in 1933 that it became practicable to consider the needs of London as a whole.

A duty falling on the Standing Joint Committee with the four main-line railways was the review of projects to electrify suburban lines of the main line Groups. The aims were to improve facilities and to open tubes and surface railways, while holding down costs of construction. This was one of the advantages, it was hoped, that would be gained from the revenue-pooling arrangements. Even more specifically, it was unlikely to be achieved without them.

The parties wasted no time, and the 1935-40 Programme had as a major feature the projection of tube lines up to the surface and extended over newly electrified main-line tracks. In this way, the outer suburbs were to be connected direct to both the West End and the City by tube. Lord Ashfield, who was Chairman of the Standing Joint Committee as well as the LPTB, prevailed successfully on the Government to finance such electrification schemes, and two of the main-line railways were involved in what emerged at the New Works Programme.

Only a fragment of the works were completed before World War 2, but two fundamental principles were established. These were:
- Suburban lines carrying a dense traffic within the London Transport area should be electrified as soon as circumstances permitted
- as far as practicable, the Underground should work short-distance suburban services, and link them with their own tubes or surface lines

Right: **Inside a 1938 tube-stock driving motor, looking towards the guard's panel. The horizontal bar was used to keep the passengers at bay, although it was not always used.** *Author*

NEW WORKS PROGRAMME

The main proposals as they directly affected the Underground were as follows:

- Central Line. Extension east from Liverpool Street to Stratford and over LNER tracks to Leytonstone, Woodford and Loughton (and also thence to Ongar[1]). New tube constructed from Leytonstone to Newbury Park, then by LNER route via Hainault and Woodford. Extension west from North Acton Junction to West Ruislip (later to Denham[1]) over additional tracks laid alongside GWR Birmingham main line. Withdrawal of LNER/GWR services.

- Northern Line. Highly complex extensions from Moorgate-Finsbury Park line over the LNER to both the Alexandra Palace branch (diverging at Highgate) and to East Finchley, meeting at the latter with a new projection of the Archway line. Trains would continue over the LNER to Finchley Central, junction for the High Barnet branch. Trains would also continue over the LNER's branch to Edgware via Mill Hill East. (There would be a new extension from an enlarged Edgware Underground station to Bushey Heath[1]). Withdrawal of LNER services.

- Metropolitan Line. Quadrupling of the section Harrow-on-the-Hill-Rickmansworth and extension of electrification from Rickmansworth to Amersham, including the Chesham branch.

While work was put in hand quickly, no extensions of the Central Line were ready for traffic before the war. However, improvement to the original central core, onto which the new tracks were to converge from east and west, was finished by 1938. To enable the standard tube stock to run, the track was renewed and laid on transverse sleepers, and the original third rail electrification converted to the fourth rail London Transport standard. In order to give the required clearances, it was necessary to install the positive conductor rail slightly higher than the standard position, necessitating a modification to the current collection shoes of the rolling stock. Finally, the old station platforms were lengthened to 130m to take eight-car trains.

On a level line, these alterations could have been achieved by encircling the running tunnel with the larger sections of station tunnel. But as the tracks were originally constructed to enter and leave each station on rising and falling gradients respectively, some rebuilding of the tunnel approaches to the stations was needed. The nearer portions of each gradient had to be brought more nearly level, which

[1] Not part of the New Works Programme

meant steepening the remainder of each slope by up to 0.9m to gain the extended platforms. All was achieved during night-time engineering occupations.

The results of this work remain plainly visible, but Health and Safety at Work requirements would make such enlargements far more complex, more time consuming and thus more costly to carry out today. This should not be seen as an argument against safety-related rules and regulations, but merely to record that they do exact a price.

With all the work in central London finished, the original Central London Railway was adapted to carry the traffic from the extensions, which was expected to total some 300 trains daily.

THE NORTHERN IN STEAM DAYS

Before considering the Northern line scheme itself, it is instructive to examine what travel to the Northern Heights was like during the inter-war period. This account comes from Jack Gaywood, a regular passenger then in his early twenties, living at Woodside Park and working in the City.

'The (mostly) LNER suburban service was very grubby, both inside and out. It did have its compensations, for one, it had a good punctuality record. In the mid-1930s I could leave home at 8.14am and run to catch the 8.16am Moorgate train (via Farringdon). This was helped by the complete lack of kerbs or steps as one approached Woodside Park and rushed onto the platform. This train called at Finchley Church End and was then non-stop to Finsbury Park. Arriving there at 8.30, it was down the spiral stairs and on to a fast Underground train on the Great Northern & City Line (alternate ones non-stopped Drayton Park and Essex Road), arriving at Old Street at about 8.40 or 8.45. The gate stock trains ran every three to four minutes. Then I would either catch a tram or walk down Great Eastern Street to my Shoreditch office, arriving just after 8.50.'

By comparison, the present-day running time from Woodside Park to Old Street is 27½min, as opposed to the 24-29min taken via Finsbury Park.

'Maybe the Underground didn't really take any longer,' said Jack, 'but it seemed to and it was crowded. The steam service was much more fun.

'Neither were the peak services infrequent. From Woodside Park, trains left at:

- 8.10 King's Cross, missing some stations.
- 8.16 Moorgate, calling at Finchley Church End, then Finsbury Park.
- 8.25 LMS to Broad Street, calling at all stations except Highgate and, I think, Stroud Green.
- 8.32 Moorgate, but that one was too late for me.

On the homeward journey, there was the remarkable arrangement on the down side at Finsbury Park where three suburban trains drew up alongside each other, at line with platforms on both sides. They would have come from Broad Street or Moorgate, with some Finsbury Park starters. From west to east there might be a High Barnet or Alexandra Palace (Platform 10), a Gordon Hill (between Nos 8 and 9), and a New Barnet train (between Nos 6 and 7). These were the normal destinations. Passengers sitting in the Gordon Hill train had a very good chance of having their toes trampled!

'I usually managed to avoid the Finsbury Park scrum. In the evening I would walk to Shoreditch station on the North London Line. My train home was the 4.55pm LMS service from Broad Street to High Barnet, which then called at Haggerston, Dalston Junction, Mildmay Park, Canonbury, Finsbury Park, Stroud Green, Crouch End, Highgate, East Finchley, Finchley Church End and West Finchley, before dropping me at Woodside Park. The drivers used to forget about West Finchley (opened 1933) and only remembered about it as they came round the bend on the downhill. They would then slam the brakes on, but often didn't stop in time. When this happened they might set the train back; otherwise they carried on.

'Outside the rush hours, to get home from the West End; we used the tube to Golders Green and then a tram or a bus to North Finchley Tally Ho! For some reason, we never travelled via (the present) Archway. The tram routes later became trolleybuses.'

Thus there were some reservations about the benefits of the Underground.

As part of their education, HRH Princess Elizabeth and HRH Princess Margaret rode from St James's Park to Tottenham Court Road and back on 15 May 1939, accompanied by a lady-in-waiting and a governess.

THE NORTHERN EXTENSIONS

To begin with, all went well. Archway (formerly Highgate) is a deep-level tube station, from which trains were required to rise to a distinctly higher level at East Finchley. Archway had been constructed as a terminus, and two dead-end siding tunnels projected north for a short distance. One was extended to form a reversing siding with crossover connections, and the other was continued as the new northbound line. This, with its twin tunnel, rose at 2% (1 in 50) to Highgate, where it was still 24m below the old LNER station. Lengthy escalators were therefore needed to connect the new platforms (which themselves were 146m long to suit the proposed operation of nine-car trains) with the ticket hall situated immediately below the LNER platforms.

But the LNER station was itself built in a cutting between two tunnels, and Archway Road (which was the principal access) was another 18m above that. A further escalator was (later) built up the side of the embankment in the open air, to complete the access to the platforms a full 42m below.

Beyond Highgate the tubes continue to rise, breaking surface one each side of the LNER tracks at East Finchley, with all four tracks crossing the Great North Road together by bridge. At this point there was some difficulty with the levelling-off of the tube, as the tunnel exit had to be high enough for the line to cross the main road, yet as far from Highgate as possible to flatten out the gradient. This brought the tunnel mouths very close to East Finchley station, and as a result the southbound track plunges rather abruptly at 2.5% (1 in 40) into a tunnel mouth which is slightly lower than its counterpart. This drop was necessary as the southbound tunnel had to pass below the LNER lines to Finsbury Park.

There was insufficient width of land at this point to enlarge the tunnel entry into the usual bell-mouth, and other means had to be found to minimise the rush of air as trains entered the tunnel. It took the form of a number of pressure

Below: **The extension of tube services out to former LNER lines meant that platforms were too high. This then required the construction of a double ramp to reach the steps which were of course already there. This was not always done, but at Finchley Central it was. Similar problems arise with building access.** *Author*

relief openings in the top of the tunnel and these were strung out for some distance, gradually spacing out as they went. The intention was to avoid unpleasant 'popping' of the ears by minimising the piston effect as a train dropped into the tunnel at about 56km/h; the air ahead of the train is allowed to escape rapidly through the vents, and then less rapidly as the train passes deeper into the tunnel. The pressure thus builds up more gradually, but even so it can be an uncomfortable experience sitting in the front car of a train.

North of East Finchley, the lines converge on two tracks for the long straight run to Finchley Central; had the intended schemes been completed this section might have proved to be a major operational problem with two busy routes diverging at both ends. This station was to have been an imposing complex with a pair of island platforms serving four tracks, but no work other than platform lowering was ever carried out, and it remains today a pleasant typically Great Northern station. The (historically) later High Barnet line curves to the right through a cutting to the 'odds and ends' built station of 1933 at West Finchley and further GNR stations to the terminus. At all the intermediate branch stations, platform heights were left untouched when the Underground took over, and passengers thus stepped down into trains and up out of them.

From Finchley Central the Edgware tracks carried straight on, over the imposing Dollis Brook Viaduct which carries the Underground

Above: **This view of a pre-1938 stock was seen on a train bound for Uxbridge, just after it had left Ickenham. The wire mesh still visible on the windows suggests that the picture was taken in wartime or soon after.** *J. Jefferson*

18m above ground level(!) to Mill Hill East. Electrification was extended this far on a single line only on 14 March 1941 to serve the barracks — and there matters stuck fast. As with the proposed Metropolitan electrification, only minor preparatory work was undertaken.

Although much work was done on LNER premises in the Finsbury Park area and thence to both Alexandra Palace and East Finchley, this was not completed.

WAR BEGINS

The outbreak of the war brought great changes, not least in the control of the undertaking passing to the Minister of Transport on 1 September 1939 under the Defence Regulations. Control of the LPTB, as of the main-line railway companies, was exercised through the Railway Executive Committee. This body acted as an agent for the Minister, and gave directions on his behalf. Again, Ashfield represented the Board. In 1939 the Board employed 17,812 staff on its railways, but this represented only 3% of those employed on railways nationwide.

Arising from this, all the company net revenues were to be pooled, and the Government effectively guaranteed their net revenues at amounts equivalent to those they were receiving in the immediate prewar period. For the Board, this was the year ended 30 June 1939. Any surplus revenue (subject to a maximum) was to be distributed to the companies in proportion to a fixed scale; that accruing to the LPTB was 11%. In 1941, a fixed annual sum was substituted, out of which the Board did slightly better.

The Board's traffic, swollen at times by troop movements, was substantially reduced by the evacuation, by the blackout, and later by the bombing of London. The population in the area served fell by 2,700,000 so that by late 1944, only 7,147,000 remained. The financial implications were not welcome.

A major early test was the evacuation. Not only children but also expectant mothers, mothers with children under five, the blind and the elderly were to be moved out. The plan was to evacuate 1,250,000 persons in the space of four days. In the event, 600,000 were ferried out of inner London by the LPTB and the main-line railways. Lack of bombing resulted in many returning, only to be sent on their way again in 1940 and subsequently. This required a team effort between public organisations; the police, local authorities and the government departments concerned all had major contributions to make.

As the war progressed, development work gradually ceased. Uncompleted parts of the New Works Programme were suspended, in some cases to be completed up to 20 years after the intention, in others to face eventual abandonment. The replacement of rolling stock came to an end, and a reduction in maintenance programmes, brought about by an acute shortage of labour and materials, had to be accepted. At the same time, with many staff away on active service in the Forces, there was a need to make a contribution to the national effort in aircraft manufacture and war supplies generally. Rolling stock and equipment for such a mundane purpose as providing transport facilities in London were thus maintained in service with great difficulty, while older stock needed a special rehabilitation overhaul after the end of hostilities.

WARTIME PRECAUTIONS

The war formed a test of altogether unprecedented severity for the Underground and its parent organisation. The first concern was to take adequate air raid precautions. The most obvious threat to the Underground in central London was that of flooding. It was well known that if any of the tunnels carrying the tube railways under the Thames were breached, the whole of the tube system would be at risk. Similar consequences might result from a breach of the Embankment's wall paralleling the centre section of the District Line. Certain stations had also to be protected against the

Above: **Wood Green, on the Piccadilly Line extension north of Finsbury Park, dates from 1932 and was a Charles Holden production. Situated on a busy crossroads, it is not the sort of building one is going to miss.** *Author*

possibility of burst water mains, while a breach of Marc Brunel's Thames Tunnel, now carrying the East London Line, might lead to flooding over a wide area.

For traffic reasons, any permanent sealing of the underwater tunnels could not be entertained. At the time of the Munich Crisis in 1938 both the Bakerloo and Northern Line tunnels were plugged with concrete, but this was an emergency expedient only. Plans were prepared early in 1939 to install a complete system of electrically operated floodgates on those lines each side of the Thames so that the underwater sections could be isolated from the remainder of the system. Time did not allow the completion of this work by the outbreak of war, and closure of the portions of line affected followed; the last section to be reopened between London Bridge and Moorgate did not do so until May 1940. These construction works represented the most major disruption of the system during the entire war period.

Use of the gates needed care to ensure both the continuation of train services and the safety of passengers. Two independent sources of electricity supply were arranged, and hand operation could be resorted to. Manned continuously, all 18 gates could be closed following the receipt of air raid warnings by Leicester Square traffic control office. Track circuit diagrams indicated locally the positions of all trains, and the signalling was interlocked with the gate mechanisms; the gates themselves could be closed in less than a minute. Arrangements were put in hand to work the

severed sections separately. As a second line of defence, steel diaphragms were placed nearby in case they were wanted.

The similar works on the District Line were not needed at low tide, and an automatic tide indicator was installed. Acoustic bombs were another hazard, and detection devices were placed on the river bed to record any which posed a threat to the Underground tunnels.

Other less extensive preparatory work included:

- the duplication and paralleling of electricity supply cables,
- modifying ventilation arrangements to minimise the effects of a poison gas attack,
- strengthening the structures of essential buildings ranging from generating stations to traffic control offices
- the use of disused tube stations as secure accommodation for government and other purposes

The Aldwych branch was closed for the duration and used to store items from the British Museum, including the Elgin Marbles.

The blackout regulations produced major difficulties. As well as all the stations, depots and workshops, every vehicle had to be fitted with special lighting which was the minimum possible to enable the job to be done. Miles of cream netting (which not-so-gradually turned black) covered all but the centre of the windows on underground cars; it adhered so firmly that traces remained on many cars until their final scrapping. Passengers were much tempted to peel it off, and an obnoxious individual called Billy Brown was invented, who by means of car advertisements told the reader:

'I trust you'll pardon my correction
that stuff is there for your protection.'

This invited a reply, such as the addition of:

'We thank you for your information
but want to see the bloody station!'

Signals had to be hooded and dimmed, while all kinds of maintenance work became that much more awkward. The strain on passengers and staff alike was great, and many experiments were carried out to see what improvements could be made to illumination levels without incurring unnecessary risks. These met with a fair degree of success.

A CLASSLESS SOCIETY

The tube lines of what became London Underground have always offered one-class travel, but the same was not true of the sub-surface lines. Both the Metropolitan and the Metropolitan District had First, Second and Third class in their steam-operated days, but their Second class was abolished in stages between 1904 and 1906.

Thus, the London Passenger Transport Board inherited a system in which there was no Second-class accommodation. It survived on the main lines, but was abolished by the LNER on its Great Northern and Great Eastern London suburban services on 1 January 1938. This was a prelude to sizeable chunks of both being ceded to London Transport upon electrification as part of the tube extensions then under way.

First class remained, but it was the LPTB which took the first step towards abolition. Traffic growth at peak periods was intensified as a result of World War 2, but while most passengers travelled Third class, the retention of First class on the Metropolitan and District lines reduced accommodation for passengers as a whole, and led to uneven loading of trains. Consequently, one-class accommodation became universal on 1 February 1940, with the exception only of those trains serving the Aylesbury and Watford joint lines.

Matters did not, however, rest there. In general, the uneven loading of trains continued, and from 18 April 1941 the Minister of Transport allowed passengers with Third-class tickets to occupy First-class seats when Third-class ones were fully occupied. Less than six months later, on 11 September 1941, the Minister of War Transport announced that from 6 October, all trains which both began and ended their journeys within the London Passenger Transport area would be Third-class-only.

This did not affect services between, for instance, Fenchurch Street and Southend, which could still pick up and set down First-class passengers at stations such as Barking and Upminster. It was, though, the end of First class for all journeys by Underground.

BOMBING

Bombing from August 1940 onwards inevitably brought disruption to services, although never to the extent of causing the shutdown of the system as a whole. Most incidents resulted in partial line closures for periods of 10 days or less. Those that took longer to repair included the sad destruction at Balham on 14 October 1940 when a bomb pierced the station tunnel roof causing flooding from burst mains and an inrush of gravel and rubbish which half filled both tunnels. Four staff and 68 shelterers died, and the line was closed for three months. Again, at Bank on 11 January 1941, the roadway was penetrated and collapsed, leaving a crater 46m across. The escalators were wrecked and blast damage was inflicted on trains in the platforms 19m below street level. Four staff and 53 shelterers lost their lives and two months elapsed before the station reopened.

One of the longest breaks in service was the five-month suspension between King's Cross and Euston Square after the massive air raid of 10 May 1941. Perhaps the worst incident took place at Bethnal Green on 3 March 1943, when a woman carrying a baby tripped and fell down a short staircase only 19 steps long. The press of others behind her seeking shelter during an air raid at the yet-unopened station resulted in those behind also falling. Within minutes, 173 died of suffocation in a space the size of a living room. Over 2,000 incidents relating to damage to railway buildings were recorded, and 1,050 cases of damage to rolling stock. Nineteen railway cars were totally destroyed.

TUBE-STATION SHELTERS

The tube stations made natural shelters from the bombing, and although at first resisted, there proved to be no practicable means of denying people refuge. Indeed, men used crowbars to force the locks on the station entrances, and the authorities quietly capitulated. The first use was on 7 September 1940. Sanitary arrangements were hastily installed, with a drainage system at 81 stations eventually allowing sewage to be pumped to the surface. A refreshment service provided by train or otherwise was feeding

Above: **Gants Hill was well known for its debt to the Moscow subway system in its general construction; it opened in 1947 with the commissioning of the Central Line as it was extended. It has recently been refurbished, as shown in this picture from May 2001. The platforms are in sight of the passengers, through the gaps in the walls, on either side.** *Author*

120,000 nightly in late 1940. Most slept on the platforms, although bunks for 22,800 were built. Later, bunk allocations were provided by ticket, and medical posts, washing facilities, storage for bedding and even small libraries eventually made an appearance.

The peak night was 27 September 1940, when 177,000 spent the night as guests of the London Underground. Thereafter the numbers declined gradually. An oddity was Highgate, still unopened in 1940 because the escalator installation had not been finished, but otherwise complete. The Inner London stations became so crowded as shelters that special trains for shelterers were run to Highgate and unloaded there. The rest of the train service ran non-stop through a brightly lit station full of sleeping people! Some of the

uncompleted sections of the Central Line east of Liverpool Street were also used for this purpose, but under the aegis of the local authorities.

REFRESHMENT TRAINS

At the request of the Ministry of Food the LPTB added a public catering department to their range of activities, to supply food to shelterers every night. Catering stores were set up at Wood Lane in the former CLR workshops, and supplies included items such as electric boilers, as well as the food which was distributed in containers.

A special train left Wood Lane at 09.30 to collect the empties, returning at 11.00. Bins containing unsold food and the fresh orders for the following night were brought into the depot, and girls worked from 11.00 to 13.45 to refill the bins with the orders. The bins were transferred to a hand trolley, which had an

Below: **A Tube Refreshments Special leaves Wood Lane as a three-car unit on this occasion, its windows covered with notices of 'Stand clear please' and 'No entry'. The interior must have been very full, but not to the extent that it was going to overtax the traction motors.** *Charles Klapper/Author's collection*

adjustable platform that slid out to match the train doorway level.

Seats had been removed from the train, and were substituted by boards labelled with the names of the stations at which the containers were to be set down. At each station, it was the driver's job to stop the three or four-car set so that the right car door was opposite the refreshment point. The containers were pushed out; no more than 20-25 seconds was allowed for this, and the train continued. The train left Wood Lane at 14.00, immediately behind a service train. Conspicuous window labels were designed to warn passengers against entry.

The service began on 6 November 1940. As an example of nightly sales, at the 70 canteens then open, daily orders were running at 28,000 buns, 20,000 slabs of cake, as well as more than 180,000 litres of tea and cocoa. Equipment for the supply of refreshments, the brewing of tea and coffee or the making of soup at stations was provided from the Lord Mayor's Air Raid Distress Fund. It was intended that six other depots would soon follow, supplying over 120 canteens at 72 shelter stations.

DEEP-LEVEL SHELTERS

Once the principle of using the Underground as shelter accommodation had been accepted, it was natural to consider what else could be done. This resulted in the limited construction of deep-level station platforms below some existing Northern (and Central) Line platforms, in the fond hope that under peacetime conditions they could be utilised as part of an express tube network. Eight shelters were built (out of 10

proposed) at an average depth of 24m below ground level underneath existing stations. The shelters had a shaft head at each end with a lift for five persons, as well as a double-spiral staircase. The pairs of 'station' tunnels were to be 427m long. Their 5.03m diameter was divided into two levels with a floor installed at the midway point, with around 8,000 bunk beds installed. There were first aid facilities, kitchens and sanitation, and also connections to the LT station. Although completed from 1942 onwards, the shelters were not used by the public until mid-1944. These were located at Belsize Park, Camden Town, Goodge Street, Stockwell, Clapham North, Clapham Common and Clapham South – and Chancery Lane. Three (Goodge Street, Clapham Common and Chancery Lane) were retained for government use.

After the war, Jamaican immigrants had the misfortune to be housed in Clapham South, which also accommodated detachments from the Royal Navy and Royal Marines for the funeral of King George VI, and it was used again during the 1953 Coronation. The last example of any of these tunnels being employed as living quarters was at Goodge Street where an Army Transit Camp had been established, but following a fire there in 1956, such use was abandoned.

WARTIME PRODUCTION

The section of tunnel between Leytonstone and Gants Hill was turned into an aircraft component factory. The Plessey Company installed the factory in 1942, converting the 4km stretch into a wartime production line employing more than 2,000 workers.

In 1940 Lord Beaverbrook, as Minister of Aircraft Production, had approached the LPTB about the possibility of using the Underground for the protection of vital production machinery. Construction of the Central Line extension was

Right: **Working in a tube tunnel, albeit one that has yet to be commissioned, is more restrictive in space than might be imagined. This is the scene somewhere on the then uncompleted route between Leytonstone and Newbury Park during the war years, when it was used as a factory.** *Plessey/Author's collection*

nearly complete when it was agreed to turn the 28,000sq m of floor space into a factory, which was used to make items such as fuel pumps and aero engine starter motors. Interviewed by *The Times* in 1985, Mr Dennis Barron, who, at the age of 16, had been paid a mere £1 per week, described working there:

'It was strange, really, like working in a mine, only you could hear the bombing overhead – a terrific bang, and all the lights would shake. Men and women worked side by side; we all liked it because there was such a good group of people working together. We took our work seriously, arrived at 7.30 in the morning and worked until past dinner time and on Saturdays, with no overtime pay.'

The tunnels were equipped to handle raw materials inwards and finished parts outwards on a narrow gauge railway, which was also used for taking visiting VIPs on tours of inspection. Other adaptations to the tunnels were the provision of entrances so that no worker had to walk more than 400m, extra ventilation shafts, cloakrooms and sanitations. A canteen for 600 was erected at Redbridge.

Less well known is the use made of the Exhibition Subway at Earl's Court station, where a factory manned by voluntary part-time workers for making aircraft components was established.

COMMERCIAL POLICY

The structure of fares that had grown up over the years was not inviolate. A thoughtful paper to the Institute of Transport by the LPTB's Commercial Officer Alec Valentine in 1943 suggested major changes that could be in the offing after the war.

Valentine's basic proposition was that the piecemeal structure of fares which had evolved satisfied nobody, and that the early postwar years would present an opportunity for reform. He further suggested that economic and commercial considerations for the passenger transport industry as a whole should be uppermost in deciding the path to be followed, and it was far preferable for the industry to make its own case rather than have the solution handed to it by others.

A key question he asked was whether the season ticket was justified at all. Compared with ordinary fares, the Underground saved in booking clerks and their accommodation, and received moneys in advance. There was, perhaps, greater efficiency in fares collection, and that was about all. Together, these benefits were worth at most a 10% discount. Added to this was greater convenience to the passenger.

Below: **Oakwood station has the square box appearance, following the approach used earlier at Sudbury Hill. It is seen here in May 2001.** *Author*

Perhaps surprisingly, he did not mention the high cost of providing peak services.

Valentine also questioned the unlimited validity of such tickets, citing the American example of commutation tickets which could be used for one return journey, per day. (As a point of interest, 2003 weekly Travelcard pricing was based on slightly less than 10 times the Underground single fare, but the validity was of course much wider than any conventional season ticket.)

Also criticised were reduced fares for various groups, with suggestions that workmen's fares had become an anachronism, and that the economic case for half fares for children (then defined as being aged 3 and under 14) needed re-examination. Low charges for 'poor and unfortunate persons' should not be costs to be borne by the transport industry. In this last category, he included wounded soldiers, shipwrecked mariners, nurses, scholars over 14 and juveniles on low incomes. 'Free school milk,' he said, 'is not a charge upon the dairies.' Interestingly, in view of later developments, cheap fares for the elderly did not figure in his list. Workmen's fares were subsequently abandoned as were scholars' fares for the over 14s, but child fares later became available to

those aged 5 and under 16, with some reductions for those under 18.

Valentine did however state that he was in favour of cheap fares if they stimulated travel, to the extent that a net increase in revenue was the result. 'As far as possible,' he said, 'they should avoid being made available to those who would otherwise pay full fares.' The 1938/9 Annual Report showed that Underground-originating revenue then derived 67% from Third-class ordinary fares, 17% from workmen's fares and 15% from Third-class season tickets. The small residue came from First-class ticket-holders. This did not however include those whose journeys originated on the national rail network. Today, Travelcards account for roundly two thirds of Underground revenues, and ordinary tickets for most of the remainder.

Right: **A public tribute to the staff – particularly the women – of London Transport, in 1942.** *Author's collection*

THEY KEEP THE WHEELS RUNNING *smoothly*

Speeding millions to and from their war jobs is the wartime task of London Transport workers—24 hours a day. It's a big job and with 18,000 of the staff in H.M. Forces, it's not an easy one. London Transport is proud of the fine work of its staff—including the 11,000 women now doing such a fine job in filling the ranks. Aided by many little acts of consideration on the part of passengers, the staff manage, even in these testing times, to keep the wheels running smoothly.

LONDON TRANSPORT

Do you use Kings Cross?

If you do, you will find this map very useful

Map of the London Underground by H. C. Beck, with routes to:
TO HARROW UXBRIDGE WATFORD CHESHAM AYLESBURY, TO WEMBLEY WATFORD, TO HAMMERSMITH, TO EALING BROADWAY, TO EDGWARE ROAD, TO HAMMERSMITH RICHMOND HOUNSLOW EALING BROADWAY SOUTH HARROW UXBRIDGE, TO WIMBLEDON, TO STANMORE, TO EDGWARE, TO HIGH BARNET, TO COCKFOSTERS, TO LOUGHTON ONGAR HAINAULT, TO BARKING UPMINSTER SOUTHEND, TO MORDEN.

INTERCHANGE STATIONS
ESCALATOR CONNECTION
UNDER CONSTRUCTION

LONDON UNDERGROUND TRANSPORT

H.C.BECK

Paddington: Metropolitan Line to Paddington, 13 minutes.

Marylebone: Metropolitan Line to Baker Street, 9 minutes—thence short walk.

Euston: Northern Line to Euston, 6 minutes. Or Bus 14, 18, 30, 71 or 73; 4 minutes.

Liverpool Street: Metropolitan Line to Liverpool Street, 12 minutes.

Fenchurch Street: Metropolitan Line to Aldgate, 14 minutes—thence short walk.

London Bridge: Northern Line to London Bridge, 14 minutes.

Cannon Street: Metropolitan Line to Cannon Street, 19 minutes. Or Bus 18 to Queen Street, 16 minutes —thence short walk.

Blackfriars: Metropolitan Line to Blackfriars, 21 mins.; or Northern Line, change at Bank, 21 mins. Or Bus 63; 16 minutes.

Charing Cross: Piccadilly Line and change at Leicester Square for Strand, 16 minutes.

Waterloo: Piccadilly Line, change at Leicester Square, 18 minutes. Or Bus 77 or 77a to Kingsway, change to 68 or 169; 18 minutes.

Victoria: Metropolitan Line to Victoria, 26 minutes; or Piccadilly Line, change at Leicester Square and Charing cross, 27 minutes.

There are Travel Information Booths at Kings Cross and at many other of the chief traffic points. If the normal routes shown above are interrupted, officials at the booths will tell you your best alternative routes.

UNDERGROUND TRAFFIC

The volume of traffic carried reflected the course of the war and is outlined in the table on the right.

Evacuation and the subsequent bombing depressed traffic levels in 1940 and 1941, after which they slowly recovered with the intensification of the war effort and greater movement of HM Forces. Services were also restricted due to coal shortages limiting electricity generation. Although initially the number of passengers carried fell faster than the drop in car km operated, leading on the whole to easier travelling conditions, the later expansion of demand was met by further restrictions on the service provided. In 1945, 543 million passenger journeys were catered for by 261 million car km — a ratio 23% worse than that for 1938/9 and over 60% worse than in 1941. The figures mask any differences in average journey lengths which may have taken place, and do not take account of the way that distribution of traffic over the working day may have changed. But here was the genesis of a problem which was to dog the Underground for the next 20 years, when system capacity consistently failed to meet the demands placed upon it.

	Passenger journeys (millions)	Underground car km (millions)	Passenger journeys per car km
Underground Originating Traffic During the War Years			
1938/9	473	280	1.7
1940	352	267	1.3
1941	334	257	1.3
1942	419	269	1.6
1943	473	262	1.8
1944	492	257	1.9
1945	543	261	2.1

THE POSTWAR WORLD

What sort of a world did the Underground emerge into in 1945 with the cessation of hostilities? Short term, the ending of the strain of wartime operation could not be matched by easier travelling conditions. In the words of the 1945 Annual Report, 'Shortages of staff and fuel remained and no immediate increases in services were possible. Rather did victory bring some embarrassment to the Board, for the general reaction after six years of war manifested itself in a desire for enjoyment and celebration, and heavier loadings were the result.' The focus of all the effort had gone, the staff were exhausted, and the system was run-down and lacking in new equipment.

The longer-term scene was influenced by the planners. In 1943 Patrick Abercrombie finished his huge survey of the planning needs of

Top left: **The pre-1938 stock kept going on services like the Aldwych shuttle from Holborn. The train crew are happy to pose for their photograph here, at Aldwych. Thoughtfully, the cab and destination panel lights have been left on to illuminate the front end.** *O. J. Morris*

Left: **This advertisement appeared in *Modern Transport* at the end of 1940, suggesting alternative routes which might be available between the main line terminals. The rectangles adjacent to many main line stations are presumed to refer to the Travel Information Booths, although this is not explained.** *Author's collection*

London; it was full of visions of an orderly, beautiful city with fresh air and lively tranquillity to take over after the war. There were to be substantial implications for the railway system. One result was a plan to build new underground railways all over the central area, co-ordinating the efforts of the main-line railways and the Underground. Another was to confirm the creation of a 'Green Belt' to surround the capital and limit urban sprawl, which was now seen to be growing at an alarming rate and something to be discouraged. The catch was the complete lack of public money to make any advance towards the goals; not to put too fine a point on it, there wasn't any left.

These are matters considered further in the next chapter, as are the pressures which determined the fate of the uncompleted parts of the New Works Programme. In fact, the resumption of the Central Line work brought Greenford, Newbury Park and Woodford into the tube network by the end of 1947, and thus within the pre-nationalisation LPTB era. Curiously, in one sense, this made the Underground system older. The section from the junction with the LNER east of Stratford through to Loughton had been built by the Eastern Counties Railway and opened on 22 August

Above: **The exit escalator at St John's Wood is very much as it has always been; the station opened under LPTB auspices in 1939.** *Author*

1856, or over six years before the opening of the Metropolitan. A service of eight trains per day in each direction was offered initially. It became part of the Great Eastern Railway in 1862, and in 1865 Loughton station was reconstructed to offer through services to Epping and to Ongar.

The development of the trains and the huge influx of new rolling stock during the Board's existence is described in Chapter 6.

Writing their own epitaph in the 1947 Annual Report, the Board recorded that they had 'sought to provide a passenger transport service, by rail and road, worthy of London as a great metropolitan city; at the same time, they had pursued a long-term policy of financial soundness, supported by an appropriate fares structure which could also be justified both by the adequacy of the services and the efficiency of their operation'. Looking forward they added, perhaps a little plaintively, that they 'had done all in their power to press on with new railway works and to obtain new supplies of rolling stock'. The emerging postwar situation was not encouraging for capital schemes.

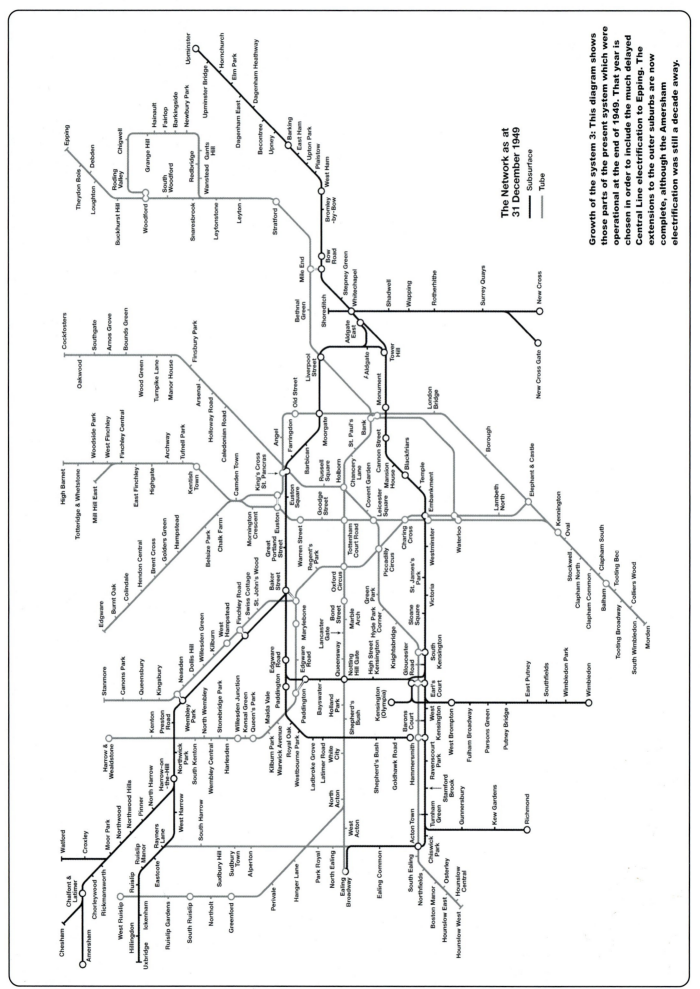

The Network as at
31 December 1949

Subsurface
Tube

Growth of the system 3: This diagram shows those parts of the present system which were operational at the end of 1949. That year is chosen in order to include the much delayed Central Line electrification to Epping. The extensions to the outer suburbs are now complete, although the Amersham electrification was still a decade away.

CHAPTER FIVE

Postwar Gloom

'The poor prospects for attracting traffic to the projected (Northern Line) extensions make the completion of the electrification unjustifiable.'

London Transport in 1953, BTC

The Transport Act 1947 saw London Transport nationalised for, as it turned out, the first time. Or, in the jargon of the day, it was 'socialised'. The new body which emerged was to be known as the London Transport Executive. As such, it was one of five which were under the direction and control of the newly created British Transport Commission (BTC); the others were the Railway, Docks & Inland Waterways, the Road Haulage and the Hotels Executives. The political nature became apparent, the appointment of the chairman and members of the Executive being a matter for the Transport Minister.

THE NEW ORGANISATION
Responsibility for the day-to-day management of the undertaking was devolved by the BTC to the London Transport Executive (LTE) before vesting, which took place on 1 January 1948. The Executive thus assumed the obligation, in conjunction with the Railway Executive, of providing an efficient, adequate, economical and properly integrated system of passenger transport, by rail and by road, in the London Transport area.

Fares became the province of the newly created Transport Tribunal, to which the BTC had to make application for variations.

In practice, it turned out that the BTC had enough to do in agonising over the affairs of the infant British Railways, and the LTE was left mainly to its own devices. A minor rash of boundary changes in the Metropolitan line's area put LT in charge of the section from Harrow-on-the-Hill to south of Aylesbury, the Chesham and the Watford branches. Likewise, British Railways Western Region lost most of the western end of the Central Line, including the uncompleted works on the West Ruislip branch, while the Eastern Region lost the chunks of Great Northern and Great Eastern suburban lines which were in the course of conversion to Underground operation as part of the 1935-40 programme. Other LT acquisitions were the East London Line and the District Line east of Whitechapel and really only reflected reality, in that the providers of the services should be responsible also for the infrastructure. (Such an approach is not reflected in current thinking!)

However, these were hardly matters which were fundamental to the running of the Underground; indeed, change was noticeable by its absence. But public expectations were rising, and it was perhaps in these years that London Transport, as the 1948 nationalisation renamed the undertaking, lost the respect of the public which had been so ably harnessed and demonstrated a long decade ago.

CENTRAL LINE GOES WEST
It had been bad luck for the would-be commuters on the Central Line. The New Works Programme had promised them great things both east and west of the capital, and a large proportion of the work had been carried out before the war stopped activity. Instead, the hapless passengers along the Eastern Avenue had watched the running tunnels being turned over to war work, and then fitted out with an 8km long concrete floor – which took a correspondingly long time to remove afterwards. The extension works turned a short inner suburban railway line between Ealing Broadway and Liverpool Street into a veritable railway system of its own, extending way into the country.

There were two main reasons for the western projection. First, there was a need to balance the workings in the west with those into the Essex borders, and second to provide direct West End and City access for the developing areas of Greenford and Ruislip. They also offered a modest measure of relief for the Piccadilly Line.

The first obstacle to be tackled was the total rebuilding of the inconvenient and makeshift arrangements at Wood Lane, where the original platform on the sharply curved terminating loop had been supplemented by the through platforms of the Ealing & Shepherd's Bush Railway in 1920. The present westbound Central Line takes a wide sweep around the old site on

Right: **The Victoria Line was the first new line to be constructed post-war. This is the black horse motif outside Black Horse Road station.**
Author

its way to the replacement station of White City, opened in 1947, above ground and just to the west. Built in brick and concrete and in unprepossessing style, it nevertheless gained a Festival of Britain architectural award. The twin island platforms retained the right-hand running inherited from the old layout, giving a curious back-to-front feeling to the station. The central track, normally used for terminating trains, was flanked by platforms on both sides; access to the depot was retained. Eastbound trains still pass one of the old platform sites in tunnel.

Between Wood Lane and North Acton there were, until 1938, only two Great Western-owned tracks, used by Ealing-bound tube trains and steam-hauled services; quadrupling was undertaken to separate the GW and LT trains. At North Acton, a new burrowing junction was built so that West Ruislip-bound trains could diverge from the Ealing line without crossing its metals.

THE WEST RUISLIP ROUTE

There was a considerable amount of construction work needed for the new tube to parallel the (now) former Birmingham main line, although none was in tunnel. Much of it was carried on a long succession of bridges and viaducts over roads, other railways and waterways. Thus there is a brick viaduct over the River Brent between Hanger Lane and Perivale, followed by three long viaducts in concrete and several bridges or girder spans to carry the line over the east and west forks of the Network Rail line from West Ealing. Beyond Greenford, distinguished by its central bay which accommodates all that remains of National Rail local services in the area, the tracks multiply at Northolt Junction where the line from Marylebone joins that from Paddington. The result is a great area of land dedicated for railway

Below: **The West Ruislip extension of the Central Line from Greenford to the terminus was opened on 21 November 1948. This detailed diagram shows its track layout and its relationship with the other lines in the areas.**
Railway Gazette, 26 November 1948/Author's collection

purposes, but with little traffic other than the tube trains running every 10-15 minutes and a five-times-an-hour Chiltern Railways diesel unit.

At Ruislip Gardens the line passes over West End Lane on a plate-girder bridge set very much on the skew, to the extent that the girders have a maximum span of 30m. On the south side of the line is the Underground's extensive Ruislip depot. This has 16 tracks, each with its own inspection pit 134m long, and, together with the carriage sidings, there are 23 parallel lines of track here besides the running lines. West Ruislip is the terminus, the proposed further extension to Denham never having been pursued. From here, Epping is nearly 55km and 90min of running time away – the longest continuous journey which can be undertaken on the Underground. All the extension works in west London, including the modernistic stations, were built by the GWR, with London Transport being granted running powers. After nationalisation, management and ownership were transferred in stages to London Transport – a process completed in 1963.

Opening of the western extensions by stages in 1947/8 saw the replacement of a modest steam-worked suburban operation, many of the stations served being no more than halts. The traffic growth engendered by the new tube railway, although substantial, has never perhaps quite matched expectations.

CONTINUING EAST

It was a very different matter in the east, where the LNER was under severe pressure. Southwest Essex, without a tube railway before, had a splendidly long one when work was completed.

The grand scheme for the area included electrification (at 1,500V dc) of the LNER suburban service between Liverpool Street and Shenfield, and the extension of the Central Line from Liverpool Street to Loughton to connect with the Grange Hill loop. At Loughton, tube trains would connect with the LNER Loughton–Epping–Ongar service. London Transport was always keen to extend

electrification to Epping, but the Government was hostile. This was only authorised postwar, on the strength of works already carried out, and with some housing development. All would be electrified and resignalled.

The extended tube ran from the Central Line platforms at Liverpool Street to a deep-level station at Bethnal Green, afterwards rising to the sub-surface level of the District Line at Mile End through water-bearing ground. The compressed air method of boring could not be employed here because the depth of covering earth was insufficient and the ground too porous to prevent air leakage. The problem was met by chemically treating the earth, both to consolidate it and to hold back the water so that tunnelling could proceed. Some complicated engineering was also needed at the station, for the tube emerges on either side of the District Line tracks, and the old station had to be transformed into a new one with a double island platform layout. Mile End is unusual as a tube line station in that it is partly open to daylight on the westbound platform, and access is by stairs only.

For the 2.77km between Mile End and Stratford the line had to run beneath several streams that form part of the River Lea system. It was imperative to use compressed air under the east London marshes, and, to provide sufficient ground cover, the twin tubes were located beneath the LNER embankments. At river crossings, however, those embankments ceased, and the tubes were deprived of cover. Beneath the City Mill River only a few feet of waterlogged ballast lay between the tunnel shield and the bed of the river. A 'blow' here would have resulted in disaster, so the ground again had to be artificially consolidated, the injection pipes for forcing the chemical into the ground being driven from pontoons anchored in the river.

Beneath the Carpenter's Road LNER bridge, west of Stratford station, it was impossible to use compressed air, because at this point the tubes were rising to the level of the main line, lying

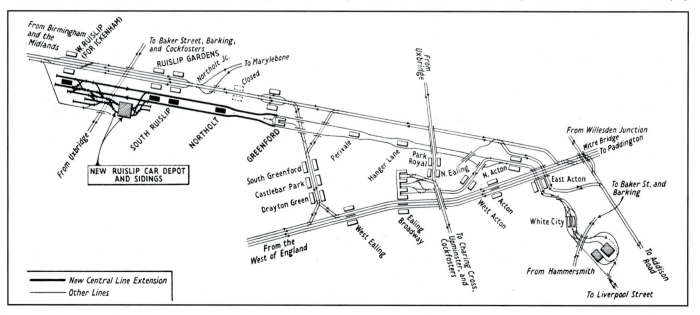

Above: **Watford High Street station may be reasonably central to Watford, but the station itself is decidedly depressing on a rainy day like this. A southbound 1938-stock train arrives on 20 April 1977. The last such services were withdrawn five years later, but services could one day be restored with Underground trains approaching from the Croxley branch.** *Author*

only a little way below the road surface. Here, it was necessary to sink two coffer dams (a kind of watertight enclosure) and partly build the tubes within them. A portion of the tunnel under the roadway had to be made only 2.13m in diameter to start with, owing to the presence of a large sewer; but after the diversion of this the tunnel was enlarged to 3.66m.

STRATFORD CROSS-PLATFORM

At Stratford itself the tube shared the LNER station, making cross-platform connections in both directions with the Shenfield electric suburban services provided from 1949, and then dived back into the tube tunnel until it was clear of this extensive railway complex. It rose to the surface in an open cutting to a junction (originally) with the LNER west of Leyton

station. The eastbound tunnel was positioned directly below the Loughton branch signalbox with minimal clearance beneath the ballast; the consolidating chemical treatment was administered from inside the cabin amongst all the levers and locking mechanisms, without interrupting traffic.

Tube operations did not cover early morning running, and staff trains were retained to and from Stratford BR. They outlived the BR operation of goods services on the branch, and the diesel units used latterly did not run north of Loughton. Such a service is no longer possible, as all physical connections have been severed. For many years, it was possible to buy a fully printed BR Edmondson card ticket with Central Line destinations, at the Liverpool Street east-side ticket office, long since demolished. This ticket was valid on Underground trains.

At Leytonstone the route forked, some trains continuing on former LNER metals via Woodford, while others entered the new tube (previously used as a factory) to come to the surface again at Newbury Park. Redbridge station on the extension was built by the 'cut and cover' method, being only 4.5m below ground level, but Gants Hill was given a unique

treatment. Situated below a roundabout and thus with an underground ticket hall, escalators led down to a concourse between the platforms 45m long and 6m high. The domed roof was supported by rows of columns. Some kindly folk compared it with the monumental stations on the Moscow underground, but while the approach was the same, the execution was mundane.

At Newbury Park the tube joined the LNER tracks from Ilford (later abandoned). Alterations at this station and others on former LNER lines were carried out by that company. Here a huge copper-covered concrete arch shaped like an aircraft hangar, and just as draughty, was erected alongside to serve as a bus station. For the next 40 years, Hainault station was a terminus for trains from the south, and extensive depot facilities with car washing plant and housing for up to 344 cars were built beyond the station.

On the former main line, the LPTB managed to close level crossings as part of the electrification package. Mostly, alternative facilities were provided, but the severing of Snakes Lane at Woodford station, which required traffic to make a diversion of about 1.5km, provoked much indignation among local motorists. Loughton station underwent rebuilding, but elsewhere structures were largely preserved. The lines were opened in sections from 1946 and it was unfortunate that the LNER's domestic electrification to Shenfield was delayed, since the tube service immediately attracted more traffic than it could cope with, resulting in questions in the House as early as 1948.

EPPING–ONGAR

The completion of electrification to Epping on 25 September 1949 would no doubt have been the end of the matter had there not been two further sections of line to be considered. The loop from Hainault to Woodford passed through the countryside and was incorporated in the electrification programme from the outset. Justified or not, the work was completed in 1948 and the line worked as a shuttle. A contemporary description of the scene north of Grange Hill referred to 'a tunnel mouth surmounted by a haystack, and a trial train disappearing with much sparking from the newly electrified track, that pleasantly contrasted with cattle munching in the fields'. Little has since changed.

The other section was the wholly rural single-track route for 9.85km from Epping on to Ongar. The Great Eastern Railway may or may not have had Chelmsford in their sights when pressing out to Ongar, but the line was so patently of a different nature from the rest of the Underground system. The completion of electrification to Epping and the transfer of responsibility for the line to London Transport meant that the latter specified the services to be run. They were still dependent upon British Railways Eastern Region for the service, and this

was provided by a push-pull set and an ex-Great Eastern 'F5' class 2-4-2T or similar. The service was generous: Mondays to Fridays in 1952 there were 36 departures from Ongar, the first leaving at 05.09. The last train back arrived Ongar at 00.45, but 00.50 on Saturday nights and a disgracefully early 00.18 on Sundays!

Several years elapsed before London Transport could bring themselves to allocate the capital, but in 1957 electrification was completed and a shuttle service using two electric trains was introduced. These would cross each other in the passing loop at North Weald, and it was said that if each started simultaneously from Epping and Ongar after dark, the lights on the intermediate stations would dim to a dull glow! Thus was the Central Line work completed, more or less as planned, if a little late. It was on the Northern Line that the hard luck stories really began.

NORTHERN HEIGHTS STYMIED

There was no good news for the inhabitants of Mill Hill, Alexandra Palace and Brockley Hill. Substantial progress had been made, yet slowly it all slipped away. Preparations for the extensions beyond Edgware which included the commencement of the boring of Elstree tunnel, the building of substations and of Aldenham depot were all to no avail. Aldenham later became the bus overhaul workshops of London Transport, but the rest of the work went to waste.

The cessation of work on the Northern Heights electrification and its subsequent postwar abandonment created much antagonism, traces of which can still be found today. However, it is difficult to see what has really been lost.

By 1952 the Mill Hill East–Edgware rail service had long been replaced by the 240A bus, which started from the forecourt of Mill Hill East station and for which through rail tickets were issued for many years. It was operated by single-deckers of the TD type.

ALEXANDRA PALACE

Further south, the half-completed bridge across Seven Sisters Road at Finsbury Park was abandoned. At Drayton Park, where the Great Northern & City between Moorgate and Finsbury Park was in the open but at a depth of about 12m, new running lines were constructed, leaving the old line just north of the station in a 'cut and cover' tunnel. They then emerged through trough-shaped cuttings to the surface, and the intention was that they should continue to rise to a new high-level island platform at Finsbury Park. Thence the former flyover curve crossing the LNER main-line tracks was to have been adapted to carry the tube trains on their way via Highgate to the dizzy heights of Alexandra Palace station, and to East Finchley for onward projection. Work got as far as erecting the London Transport roundels on Highgate high-level platforms, but again, no further work was carried out once it had stopped in 1941. The only part of the new work retained was the access to the depot at Highgate from East Finchley's centre platforms.

The LNER (and, later, BR Eastern Region) trains kept an Alexandra Palace service going after a fashion, although low usage and coal shortages meant all passenger operations were suspended between 29 October 1951 and 7 January 1952.

This was not, be it said, the fastest of services due at least in part to the circuitous nature of the route. Journey time from Alexandra Palace to King's Cross by through train was 23min for a distance of 11km, in comparison with the 16min for the 8km from the nearby Wood Green (itself now renamed Alexandra Palace) on the Great Northern main line. Both timings were with steam traction.

In the 1952/3 winter timetable, nine services departed from Alexandra Palace in the Monday–Friday morning peak and six in the evening; there were no services at all between 09.42 and 17.05. The timetable was better balanced on Saturdays, which saw the same morning peak pattern and an alternating 20/40min frequency service from 12.25 until close with the 17.25 departure from Alexandra Palace. For some reason, there was no 15.45 departure to fit into this otherwise regular pattern.

The steam passenger services were withdrawn formally on 5 July 1954, with the last vestiges of goods traffic ceasing on 18 May 1957.

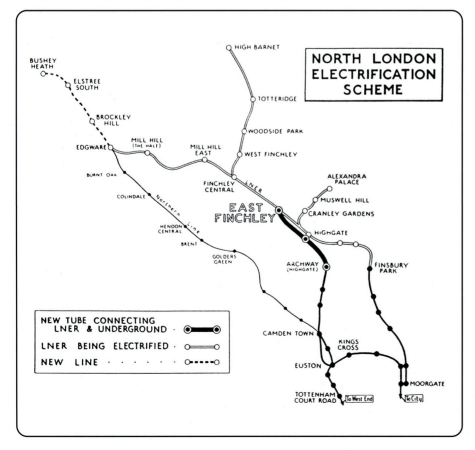

Left: **The North London Electrification Scheme following the New Works Programme, 1935-40.**

BUSHEY HEATH

As the plan emerged eventually and was authorised, the proposal was for the construction of a new railway from the existing Edgware LPTB station to Brockley Hill, 1.25km from Edgware and on viaduct. From there it would continue a further 1.88km to Elstree South, the last section being in 1.44km twin-bore tunnels. Elstree station would have been in a cutting, and from there the final 1.46km of the line to the Bushey Heath terminus would have had the new Aldenham Northern Line depot alongside. The total length of the branch would have been 4.61km.

However, the habitation in the area was minimal, one reason why the Watford & Edgware Railway's Act of 1903 had never resulted in any construction work over the 10km separating these towns. Apart from offering a site for a new depot, the justification was going to be the new housing which it would serve. As Chambers (see later) concluded in 1955:

'The plan to extend the tube (to Elstree) was abandoned after the war because a large part of the area which the proposed extension was intended to serve was subsequently scheduled as Green Belt, and the traffic would thus not have warranted the completion of the project.'

One can hardly blame the postwar planners for their refusal to contemplate further continuous urban development. The Underground companies had quite unashamedly capitalised on the drawing power of their services and the consequent suburbanisation of London. Indeed, the Group was proud of its achievements. The Underground's Operating Manager J. P. Thomas, writing in 1928, had this to say of the extension to Morden, completed two years earlier:

'The surrounding countryside is probably the most undulating and pleasant of any on the outskirts of London, and it is likely that the growth which has taken place at Golders Green, Hendon, and Edgware will be repeated here... The railway, which enables the dweller in this

Above: **Pre-1938-stock driving motor No 3327 of 1927. As can be seen, the inspection hatches have been removed to show what lies behind; it was this equipment which was relocated beneath the cars in the 1938-stock design. It was on show at the Science Museum in London as seen here, but later went to London's Transport Museum.** *Author*

district to reach the City or West End within half an hour, will convert the countryside into a modern suburb and will provide one more incentive to the Londoner to forsake the congested areas for the healthier localities on the outer fringe.'

Expectations were fulfilled, and more. Suburbia was extended by the buses which brought in the passengers from further afield, and who were to be encouraged by the issue of combined bus and Underground tickets. The identical result was achieved elsewhere, whether at Barking, Ealing, Harrow, Putney or Wembley.

Yet it was all far from plain sailing for the railway companies, and Lord Ashfield's admission that the Underground had never been a profitable enterprise has already been noted. In the 1930s, Frank Pick, as managing director of the Underground, acknowledged gloomily that his problem had no solution; to make the Underground pay he had to stimulate suburban traffic which, when poured into the centre, overloaded the buses and congested the roads.

LACK OF PROFITABILITY

Part of the problem lay in the nature of passenger transport itself, where the costs and benefits which resulted were distributed on a much wider canvas than the company and its customers. The issues raised by the suburbanisation of Morden *et al* could not be dismissed as a merely private matter between two parties to a commercial transaction, especially in an age which believed in the efficacy of the planned approach.

From the earliest days, entrepreneurs realised that while transport facilities might be provided profitably to meet a demand which was already there, the provision of such facilities in themselves could stimulate traffic and increase the values of the surrounding properties. The problem has always been that while the railway interests would benefit from the generated traffic revenues, this was not enough to finance

Left: **In 1969 a Northern Line train of 1938 stock took a nosedive onto the road at the bottom of Barnet Hill, causing extensive damage to the bridge. Reinstatement is underway there on 25 September 1969, as a train heads (left to right) towards High Barnet.** *Author*

extensions and regeneration of the systems. The gains represented by rises in property values went into the hands of private individual property owners.

One might compare this with the extensions of the Underground under the New Works Programme 1935-40, which became possible only because of the availability of cheap government loan capital.

Cheap finance, or grants, tended to set the scene; if it was investment in urban railways that was wanted, funding of capital costs would have to be mainly a matter for either central or local government. But what was wanted in the postwar era?

RAILWAYS LONDON PLAN COMMITTEE

The County of London Plan had spawned various subsidiary work. Even after the more exotic ideas of the Railway (London Plan) Committee of 1944 had been watered down, the British Transport Commission's 1949 Working Party proposals were vast in conception. They suggested a quite remarkable network of new routes lettered from A through to M, crossing London in tunnel. Everything would be electrified.

The Working Party were careful to distinguish between urban tube railways with intensive services and frequent but short stops, and outer suburban railways running in 5.18m diameter tunnels taking main-line rolling stock but with lower service frequencies, fewer stops and higher average speeds. These do not mix, particularly in the design of rolling stock provided. For a satisfactory outer suburban

service, there must be a high seating capacity. In the in-town area, there must be a high overload capacity requiring ample standing space. This can only be obtained at the expense of seats, while the door arrangements need to permit rapid loading and unloading at stations to minimise stop times.

The proposed works may be summarised as follows. It should be noted that the Working Party accepted the need to demolish Blackfriars Bridge, but not Charing Cross or Cannon Street bridges, on planning grounds. (Environment was not a word then in general use.) Routes A and B were to have been new underground lines, passenger and freight respectively, linking the main-line services north and south of the river which were then using Blackfriars Bridge. Route C was to be a new tube from the Tottenham and Edmonton area via Finsbury Park, King's Cross, Euston, Oxford Circus, Green Park, Victoria, Vauxhall, Stockwell, Brixton and Streatham to East Croydon. Branch lines on the alignment of the Cambridge Road and from Seven Sisters to Walthamstow were 'possibly desirable'.

Route D was the Chingford/Enfield electrification, then via new tube from Hackney Downs to Liverpool Street, Bank, Ludgate Circus, Aldwych and Trafalgar Square to Victoria. A westward extension of this line had lower priority. A low priority Route E would have duplicated the Northern Line south of Kennington with extensions on to the Southern. Route F was the electrification of Marylebone services; again tube projection southwards was of lesser importance. Yet again, Route G, the electrification of Fenchurch Street services,

could have resulted eventually in a new westerly tube emerging at Raynes Park.

Route H, the extension of the Bakerloo Line to Camberwell, was authorised but later abandoned; Routes J and K were low priority alternatives taking the Finsbury Park-Moorgate trains into south London. Route L would have taken the Holborn-Aldwych line on to Waterloo, again without priority. The remaining Route M was the electrification of the Liverpool Street–Cambridge main line.

Completion of New Works Programme and certain Southern Region improvements were also marked out for early attention.

The priority tasks identified required 79km of new tube construction, a total which would have been doubled with the lower priority works added. With masterly understatement, the Report anticipated that the work would take 20 to 30 years to implement. 'Some regard,' the Working Party averred, 'must be paid to the economics of new railways in tunnel across London.'

ROUTE C

Of all the new items in the list, the one which clearly had the best claim to an early start was Route C. The 1949 Report comments are of some interest:

'This route covers one of the most important in-town sections for local traffic between Victoria and King's Cross. It is considered that the alignment should be via Green Park and Oxford Circus stations rather than via Hyde Park Corner and Bond Street, since this route is likely to carry a heavier traffic, especially outside the peak

Left: **In many ways this is a Southern scene, with an LSWR station building and a concrete footbridge and lamp-posts. However, although latterly managed by the Southern Region, they ran no trains from Richmond towards Gunnersbury. This is Kew Gardens, where service provision was left to the LMR North London-line services, and the District Line. Here, a train of CO/CP stock leaves for Richmond on 21 February 1975, the destination plate already changed for Upminster.** *Kevin Lane*

hours. Satisfactory cross-platform interchange at Oxford Circus with the Bakerloo Line can be provided, but only if the new route is worked with standard-size tube stock, since available space at Oxford Circus is restricted. Besides offering an important new in-town connection, the route will provide additional distribution facilities over the central area from the terminal stations at King's Cross, Euston and Victoria.

'At its northern end, the route can best be used to give the much-needed direct facilities between the Tottenham/Edmonton area and the West End, and will give relief to the overcrowded section of the Piccadilly Line north of King's Cross. It is suggested that the northern terminal must be such that convenient interchange can be provided with the (former Great Eastern) Cambridge main line, which will be electrified. There might possibly be branches on the alignment of the Cambridge Road and from Seven Sisters to Walthamstow. At its southern end, the route proposed via the Brixton Road to Croydon is accepted…no difficulty is anticipated in finding a depot site at the northern end.'

Here, in all essence, is the Victoria Line, which opened 20 years later, between 1968 and 1972. Why did it take so long?

CHAMBERS COMMITTEE
The major problem turned out to be in persuading the Government that it was indeed in their best interest to fund its construction. Attitudes in the postwar era to public transport tended to be hostile; capital was scarce to the point of near invisibility for public transport projects. If a commercial rate of return was being sought, then there were other more attractive investments to make. In vain was it argued that it was London (rather than London Transport) which stood to gain. Various learned bodies looked at the project, among them the Chambers Committee of 1955. This was the year in which statutory powers for construction were obtained. By then the argument was bound up with the peak problem generally. Chambers noted the dilemma posed by the imbalance of peak and off-peak traffic:

'We have every sympathy with the view of London Transport that only as a last resort should they be required to incur very heavy expenditure if it is needed only to provide additional comfort during short periods of peak traffic. The alternative of staggering of working hours would be altogether more acceptable . . .'

So off everybody went on what ultimately turned out to be a wild goose chase, since the staggering of hours had little public appeal.

London Transport thus had a hard time in this period, broken, perhaps briefly, by the Coronation of Her Majesty the Queen in 1953.

THE 'WALL OF NO'
In his autobiography, Sir John Elliot as the then chairman of London Transport, recalled how he broke down 'a wall of no' on Route C. First, the plan was put up for approval in principle but without a firm date for construction. Having received this, work was slowly carried out at points along the line of route as part of the annual renewals programme. In this way, aerial surveys were completed, 70 exploratory boreholes were sunk, and 1.5km or so of experimental tunnelling north of Finsbury Park was excavated and lined by new methods. This was done in 1960, 'to gain practical experience'. Elliot's other gift to Route C was the bestowal of the name Victoria Line.

In the soft clay soil of the experimental section from Finsbury Park to Tottenham, rotating drum diggers were employed. One was of 4.27m external diameter for concrete-lined tunnels, and the other 3.99m for tunnels lined with cast-iron segments. Essentially, the diggers consisted of two drums, one within another. The outer 4.27m drum had a bevelled cutting edge and was driven into the tunnel face as with the Greathead shield. The inner drum of 2.29m diameter was rotated on roller races by hydraulic motors. It had cutting teeth mounted on arms on its outer edge, and cut the area in front of the space between inner and outer drums. The area in front of the inner drum was cut by teeth mounted on an arm across the drum's diameter.

The ram operator was provided with siting guides to enable him to adjust the pressure on the rams to correct any tendency to deviate right or left or up or down from the prescribed direction or gradient. The clay excavated was guided by scoops or paddles to a belt conveyor and subsequently discharged into skips on rails for eventual hoisting up the working shafts.

When the outer shield reached the end of its thrust, a new ring of tunnel lining was added, the rams pushed against the newly installed ring, and the whole cycle recommenced. The process for the cast-iron-lined tunnels was similar, and with both types of lining a far greater speed of excavation was obtained. Some of this was due to the use of cast-iron segments with flexible joints, the new method allowing for each completed ring of segments to be expanded by jacks against the clay outside, and finally wedged firmly in place when the pressure on the jacks

was released. The concrete linings were cast with convex and concave edges to form knuckle joints, and the rings were finally expanded by wedges, the last being ram-driven home at pressure. The methods of lining, which owed their origin to a water tunnel built for the Central Electricity Generating Board, obviated the need for cement grouting. They were adopted for the construction of the Victoria Line proper.

Drum diggers cannot be used where rocky or otherwise obstructive soil formations are encountered, where the only means of winning a passage is the non-rotating shield, mechanical shovel, or even manual excavation. Larger shields have to be constructed for boring the station tunnels, while pedestrian tunnels within station complexes are excavated with hand tools and pneumatic spades. These tunnels are of short length, and shields to excavate them would be uneconomical, as a chamber larger than the shield must necessarily be built in which to erect it. Escalator tunnels are also excavated by hand, as it would be very difficult to control a shield on such a slope as that on which an escalator is built.

WHO BENEFITS?
The long-drawn-out struggle to achieve authorisation of the Victoria Line throughout the 1950s eventually turned to the newly developed science of social cost-benefit analysis. Through this it was demonstrated (rather than asserted) that most of the benefits fell elsewhere and that road users (rather than rail passengers) would be the principal beneficiaries.

Therefore, the argument went, the gains to the wider community were a sufficient and an acceptable justification for building the line, even though it would be a commercial disaster for London Transport should they have to fulfil a commercial rate of return on their investment. How would the Government react?

Benefits of the Victoria Line		
Groups of beneficiaries		*% of benefit derived*
Traffic diverted to the Victoria Line		34
Traffic not diverted: Road users	35)	
Others	17)	52
Generated traffic		14
Total		100

EASTERN END OF THE DISTRICT
Although the Victoria Line saga must have sapped the energies of the Executive, there were other schemes of great importance being undertaken. The District Line services were indirect beneficiaries of the BR Modernisation Plan, which presaged electrification of the London, Tilbury & Southend lines. Hitherto, Underground trains had been part of the general maelstrom of services, each vying for priority. Of the flat junctions for three routes east of Barking station used by 700 trains daily, it was admitted candidly that they caused many delays. So, in the expansive manner of the times, a complex series of flyovers and diveunders was constructed to

provide physical separation of conflicting movements. The plan entailed the complete segregation of services at all points; thus the crossovers from the Tilbury line to the District at Campbell Road Junction, Bow, and the North London Junction at Bromley were also removed.

Down the line at Upminster a new Underground depot was constructed with all mod cons. District Line facilities had never been entirely satisfactory, and the new 34-train capacity depot replaced the inadequate installation at East Ham. Two of the reception roads were given washing machines so that all trains could be washed as they came out of service. All nine roads in the car examination shed were given pits. Overhead conductors, carrying small trolleys with jumper cables to provide power to trains, ran the full length of the pits, as no conductor rails can be installed in such areas. The conductors on the jumper cables are inserted into receptacle boxes on the cars when power is required; this is standard London Transport practice. There was also a small lifting shop.

At that time it was usual for shunters to hand-operate points and hand signal the trains from the ground. A new method adopted at Upminster provided for all points to be power-operated and controlled from the tower. One shunter in the tower would give instructions to drivers via loudspeakers by the trackside, the

position of the trains being determined by reference to a track circuit diagram.

Drivers were given the right to reply with a 'talk back' facility. After giving an instruction to a driver, the loudspeaker automatically switched functions to become a microphone so that the driver could lean out of his cab and respond. All speaker/microphones could be controlled individually by the shunter on duty, but in case of total confusion a panic button was installed to display a red light and, hopefully, to stop everything.

CROMWELL ROAD TRIANGLE

The erection of the West London Air Terminal gave London Transport the excuse they needed to sort out the confusion abounding in the Earl's Court/High Street Kensington/South Kensington triangle. The layout, which stemmed from the separate ownership and operation of the previous century had the fundamental disadvantage of a conflict between eastbound District Line and westbound Circle Line trains at the flat junction east of South Kensington station. Here, the four tracks merged into two. By removing the crossing to a new site west of Gloucester Road and reversing the running direction of the two inner tracks, it became possible to hold a westbound Circle Line train without it delaying District Line services behind it. Furthermore, eastbound passengers who had a choice of two platforms at which to wait would have only one, the more northerly. At that time, non-stopping trains were still in vogue, and these used the inner of the two eastbound tracks. The revised layout was brought into use in 1957.

It did not last, however. The abandonment of non-stopping meant that there was little purpose served by maintaining two eastbound tracks, while the westbound junction could be moved further west with no adverse effects. In 1969 eight platform faces were reduced to five, and South Kensington became one ultra-wide island platform. A new connection west of Gloucester Road allowed all westbound trains to use the former Circle Line platform during less busy periods.

In 1959 a practically new station was brought into use at Notting Hill Gate. Previously there were two stations, one each side of the busy highway. These served the Central and the District/Circle lines respectively, and some 2,000,000 passengers changed between them each year. A sub-surface ticket hall provided access to the two lines, with interchange available by subways at a low level. The eastbound Central Line platform here is 30m below the surface, the westbound partly above it and to one side, while the Circle Line platforms are some distance away but only 8m below ground level. The work was therefore somewhat complex! The old shafts for lifts and stairs were used subsequently for ventilation purposes.

BLACKFRIARS RECONSTRUCTION

The District Line suffered from some platforms being of sub-standard length, and the end cars could be reached only by narrow catwalks. Work at Blackfriars involved lengthening the platforms by 22.5m, the task including the demolition of the existing running tunnel and the construction of a wider covered way for the platforms. It also involved the bridging of the River Fleet, reduced

Below: **An East London Line train consisting of standard District Line stock built in the late 1920s / early 1930s approaches Surrey Docks on 6 June 1970 with a New Cross working.** *A. W. Hobson*

Above: **The Cromwell Road curve was to be the scene of redevelopment for the West London Air Terminal, from which buses were to operate to Heathrow direct. The whole area was rafted over. This view of 28 April 1956 from the south shows a District Line train amongst the construction work which was just beginning.** *Alan A. Jackson*

many years previously from the status of a navigable tidal waterway to an underground sewer, but still carrying a considerable volume of water, and the section-by-section replacement of the roadway above.

The soil along the Thames Embankment is very largely made-up ground and mud. When the line was built, as much as 7m of ruins dating back 2,000 years or so had to be cut through, and the original foundations carried down to 4m below rail level. The general construction then was of brick walls and an arch with a concrete invert, made wider at the stations with girders to support buildings. The rebuilding method used was to excavate trenches outside the existing tunnel walls from street level, and sink piles through the trenches to support concrete bases for the new structure. These bases in turn formed the support for new pre-cast concrete columns, the spaces between which were filled with wall slabs and concrete. Opening the roadway then allowed a pair of cranes to lower the nine new roof beams on to the columns; the placing of each beam was an entire night's work. A concrete slab subsequently formed the base of the new roadway.

Over the Fleet sewer the vertical columns were carried on two reinforced concrete beams.

A further complication was the presence of both a pedestrian and a pipe subway in the area.

With the new walls and roof completed, the old tunnel inside was demolished except for the lower sections of the brick walls, which were then used to form the base of the platform extensions. The work was completed in 1962; similar platform extensions were also undertaken at Westminster.

AMERSHAM ELECTRIFICATION

The last of the 1935-40 projects was the Metropolitan's main-line rebuilding. Whereas the prewar scheme had envisaged the conversion of 'steam' stock to electric multiple-unit use, galloping dilapidation coupled with the growing demand which was apparent by the mid-1950s, secured authorisation for new stock in 1956. Work was thus started on the four-tracking and electrification of the Metropolitan north of Harrow. The scheme was allowed to proceed, as it extended way beyond the Green Belt to areas where development was to be encouraged.

The postwar Metropolitan system was badly in need of relief. By 1955, peak problems were acute; on the main-line services from the City through Baker Street and Finchley Road, 18 train sets and three electric locomotives only were required in the off-peak, but this rose to 50 train sets and nine locomotives at peak times. Peak operation provided many difficult problems; between 17.00 and 18.00, 27 trains carrying 15,000 passengers needed to be dispatched from Baker Street. During this hour, 34 trains approached Baker Street from the Aldgate direction. Of these, 18 were for the main line,

and had to cross the paths of 16 eastbound trains from Edgware Road at the flat junction. In addition, 14 trains left the main-line platforms for the City, making 30 eastbound in total. Parallel working over the junction was thus used whenever possible. The remaining nine trains on the main line northwards originated at Baker Street, for Harrow, Watford or Uxbridge.

Station allowances were varied according to train and station. On the Circle Line the time was generally 20sec, but at Baker Street this was increased to anything between 30sec and 2min to suit the crowded conditions east of the junction. Further complications arose at the City termini, with the Moorgate and Liverpool Street terminating workings all having to cross the westbound tracks. At the latter station, terminus of the locomotive-hauled trains from Aylesbury and Chesham, a spare locomotive was needed to haul the trains out again.

The original modernisation proposals had envisaged the four tracks extending through to the far side of Rickmansworth, but reappraisal cut this back to Watford South Junction, a little to the north of Moor Park station. Similarly, it was decided that platforms need not be provided at intermediate stations on what became the new fast lines. The existing locomotive-hauled stock and the venerable multiple-units would all be replaced with a brand-new design which was to provide for all service requirements on the Metropolitan main line. Physical site work started in 1958, and the changeover to total multiple-unit working took place on 11 September 1961. The widening scheme was not completed until mid-1962.

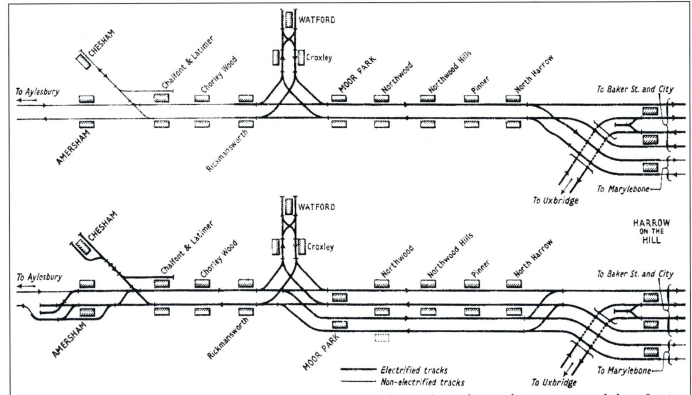

Existing and altered track layouts between Harrow-on-the-Hill and Amersham, showing lines in course of electrification

Legend:
— Electrified tracks
-- Non-electrified tracks

Left: **The Amersham electrification required quadrupling of the track north of Harrow-on-the-Hill to, as it turned out, Watford South Junction and not Rickmansworth as intended originally. There were a number of other works further north, as well as electrification, as this diagram shows.** Railway Gazette, *28 August 1959 / Author's collection*

Below left: **Chesham retained its push-and-pull steam services until electrification. Here, on Christmas Day 1953, ex-GCR Class C13 4-4-2T No 67418 bides its time before departing with the 12.14 to Chalfont & Latimer. It was photographed alongside the water tower at the Chesham terminus. The extensive facilities, such as the run-round loop and the goods yard beyond (further from London) are of note.** N. W. Spinks

TRADITIONAL WORKING

The traditional pattern of working was of six-car trains of 'steam' stock hauled by one of the Metropolitan Railway's Metrovick Bo-Bos to Rickmansworth, where locomotives would be changed. A British Railways ex-LMS Class 4 2-6-4T then took over for the steady climb to Amersham and beyond. At Chalfont & Latimer, the branch connection to Chesham in the bay platform would be formed of an Ivatt 2-6-2T, propelling one of the ancient three-car push-pull sets created out of the 'Ashbury' stock built in Manchester between 1898 and 1900. Other services to Watford and Rickmansworth were formed of the T stock multiple-units. All of these trains were traditional compartment stock, and the transition to saloons with air-operated doors and loss of seating capacity raised howls of protest in Metroland. In reality, saloon vehicles were inevitable, as the Railway Inspectorate was not prepared to sanction new stock without emergency exits through the ends of the cars; the constraint was the single-line tunnels between Baker Street and Finchley Road. Nor were slam doors to be permitted. Experimental rebuilding on two T stock trailer underframes took place in 1946/47, in what turned out to be very preliminary work.

The familiar A stock is described elsewhere. It was not welcomed universally as indeed few compromises are, but especially in view of some of the products bought by British Railways in this period, the Metropolitan Line commuter did rather well. As London Transport said brightly, the A stock 'affords comfort for long-distance passengers as all seating is transverse, but the wide vestibules with air-operated doors in which shorter distance passengers can stand in reasonable comfort,

Top right: **Metropolitan electric locomotive No 14** *Benjamin Disraeli* **is seen at speed with a train of 'Dreadnought' coaching stock on a service for Liverpool Street.** *Author's collection*

Right: **Beyond Chalfont & Latimer station in the far distance, the Metropolitan tracks separate, with the main line to Aylesbury passing below the photographer and the Chesham branch diverging to the left. A clean A-stock train is providing the branch shuttle; the date is 24 October 1977.** *Author*

give the best of both worlds in which this stock has to run'. In all fairness, the A stock was very well conceived.

TRACK WIDENING

The track widening scheme placed the fast tracks alongside the slow lines, rather than one each side as had been adopted earlier south of Harrow. At North Harrow, Pinner and Northwood Hills the additional tracks were built clear of the existing platforms, but at Northwood land was not available on the west side of the existing station so that total reconstruction here, and at Moor Park which became a four-platformed station, was needed. Amersham gained an extra platform, since it was now to be the terminus of all London Transport operations. On the Chesham branch, a bay was let into the (lengthened) terminus platform and a siding was also electrified. The signalbox at Chesham was retained and although certain signals, particularly the down home and up starting signals, were replaced by colour lights, most of the semaphores and mechanical points remained in use.

There were numerous bridge rebuildings. Resignalling was carried out as part of the project, and this provided for standard BR four-aspect signalling on the fast lines (where speeds of up to 112km/h were permitted) and through to Amersham, due to the dual use with BR trains to and from Marylebone. Standard LT two-aspects sufficed elsewhere, although the occasional provision of repeater signals on the same post gave the appearance of four aspects. Following completion of the electrification, London Transport surrendered all interests beyond Amersham or, to be precise, at Mantles Wood, north of a point close to Network Rail milepost 25$^1/_4$ (40.63km), and designated with a boundary marker.

VICTORIA LINE AUTHORISED

At long last, on 20 August 1962, the Government finally approved the construction of the 16km Victoria Line northwards from Victoria to Walthamstow. Not surprisingly, London Transport was well prepared. General principles aimed at in building the new line were:

● the avoidance of curves sharper than 400m radius
● stations to be built on a hump or saw-tooth profile, giving a falling gradient to accelerate a train leaving a station and a rising gradient approaching it
● a tunnel diameter sufficient to minimise air resistance
● the line to be as straight as possible between any two points, not following street patterns above

Below: **Victoria Line 1967 stock in the depot at Northumberland Park on 24 April 1997, the only point where the trains on this line come above ground. Even this limited view gives an idea of the amount of land that a depot will occupy.** *Author*

These ideals had to be modified as necessary to fit the line into the pattern of existing stations, tunnels and sewers, but work could now begin in earnest.

TRANSPORT ACT 1962

The BTC was abolished under the Transport Act 1962 and the London Transport Executive was reconstituted as the London Transport Board. This was a fully fledged nationalised industry in its own right and was responsible direct to the Minister of Transport. The separation from British Railways was all but complete; there were now no revenue pooling arrangements between the two. The Act paid lip service to the need to continue co-ordination with British Railways, but the reality was that each would henceforth go its own way.

Within a broadly similar set of duties, it was the financial duty of each of the new Boards thus created to ensure that revenue was sufficient to meet the costs incurred which were chargeable to revenue, taking one year with another.

The powers of the Transport Tribunal were restricted by introducing a requirement for charges to be reasonable. Fares were thus left largely to the Board's discretion, with a rider that the Tribunal should do nothing to prevent them from levying charges needed to discharge their financial duty. Applications however needed to be published, and the Tribunal was to hold a public inquiry before giving its decision.

Vesting day for the new London Transport Board was 1 January 1963.

CHAPTER SIX

Development of the Underground Train

'The first electric multiple units in Britain entered service on the Central London Railway in 1903.'

The Oxford Companion to British Railway History, 1997

It is time to consider the trains operating on the system over the years, and their development. This covers matters such as construction, the source and application of electric power, performance, technical advances, internal layout and door control, and capacity. This review begins with general considerations, followed by the tube stock and then the surface stock.

THE MOTOR

The electric motor as applied to trains for traction purposes was always of the direct current series type, and commonly mounted on the axle. Stopping has been effected by the friction of the brake shoes on the wheel treads, operated by a compressed air supply. Collector shoes which rubbed on the conductor rails picked up the traction current, which was then fed to the motors and controlled on the multiple-unit principle. All the systems had to be sufficiently developed for the whole to work, but once the nut of multiple-unit control had been cracked, the electric train was able to come into its own. Thereafter, the locomotive had no place in purely urban transit systems. Sprague's invention had enabled two or more motor cars in a train to be controlled from a master controller, with only a small current passing through it and along the train. Each power car picked up its own current from the live rail, and fire and insulation hazards were avoided.

The tube railways used electro-magnetic contactor (switch) control energised by control wires, utilising the 600V dc supply on the British Thomson-Houston system. The Metropolitan used the electro-pneumatic form developed by Westinghouse, with low-voltage electro-magnetic valves controlling air pressure to cylinders, and the pistons working the main switches.

ACCELERATION

In operation, the driver is not faced with a mass of relays, cut-outs or resistances. Just as the driver of a steam locomotive has an ultimate control in the regulator, so the driver of an electric train is concerned only with a single master controller. When he operates the handle or 'winds it up', the following sequence in a traditional installation takes place.

The contactors connect the motors to the current supply, at first in series through starting resistances, where surplus electrical energy which the motors are unable to assimilate is dissipated as heat. As the train gathers speed, an accelerating relay cuts out the starting resistance in a number of steps by the automatic closing of

contactors. When all the resistance has been cut, each motor is working on only half the voltage of the power supply, but is sufficiently accelerated to start absorbing the full line voltage.

The next phase is therefore the regrouping of the motor circuits in parallel, with the starting resistances again in operation. They are cut out in steps as before, until finally the motors are in full parallel; that is, they are receiving the full voltage, being connected directly across the power supply. In the improved type of pneumatic camshaft motor (PCM) control, introduced in 1936, the more sensitive pneumatic accelerator, basically a small air-oil engine operating contacts, replaced the old individual contactors. The stages are as before, but at the intermediate stage a valve operating on the engine forces air against the oil, which in turn moves a piston and camshaft and cuts out resistances.

The third, parallel stage is reached with resistance automatically restored, but at this point the engine operates in reverse and allows the motors full voltage by cutting out resistances. It should be appreciated that these movements, although appearing lengthy and involved when described, take place in the few seconds in which the train is getting under way.

When the driver cuts the power and the train coasts, a 'no-volt' relay in the circuit comes into operation. Its purpose is to prevent the full voltage being suddenly fed to the motors after power is restored, by ensuring that the equipment is returned to its original starting condition and with the complete sequence of operations to follow. The driver may move his controller freely through several accelerating positions or notches, but the accelerating relay ensures that the proper sequence is traversed. Should he lift his hand off the controller handle, the main supply to the controller is broken, current is cut off, and the brakes are applied. This is the safety device introduced in 1906/7 and fitted to all rolling stock to guard against a driver's personal mishap, be it illness or collapse. The colloquial name for this part of the master controller is the 'dead man's handle'.

BRAKING

The braking of trains followed the Westinghouse developments, whereby movement of the operating handle to induce a fall in pressure in

the system results in the brakes being applied. Full exhaustion as a result of the release of the dead man's handle, the operation of the passenger emergency alarms or the activation of the trip cock all resulted in a full emergency brake application. The problem with the Westinghouse brake was the time delay inherent in it and the sequential operation along the length of the train as the brake pipe pressure fell. The electro-pneumatic (EP) brake installed from 1930 used electrically-operated valves to apply the brake in each car simultaneously; the valves allowed compressed air from the main air pipe to enter and leave the brake cylinders. This was henceforth used for service operation, but the Westinghouse brake was retained for safety purposes. The 'Standard' or 'pre-1938' tube stock was all fitted with the EP brake, but only later builds had it supplied as from new.

DOOR CONTROL

The use of gatemen to control entry and exit from the trains was very labour intensive, and this hastened the search for some method of door provision and operation which could be controlled remotely. This was found in the sliding door which, when open, was recessed into a pocket in the body side. Operation was either by hand (as for many years on the surface lines) or by compressed air engine, one to each door leaf, controlled through electro-pneumatic valves.

Opening and closing was overseen by the guard, and a mechanical interlock detected whether the door was properly closed. Later interlocks consisted of a glass bottle, part-filled with mercury and containing a pair of electrical contacts. Every sliding door on a train operates one of these devices, tilting the glass bottle when all the doors are closed, so that the mercury bridges the contacts and the door closed circuit is complete, which then lights the guard's pilot light. The interlocks are extremely reliable, which is just as well seeing that there are more than three million interlock operations every day on the Underground. Only when the doors are all proved shut can the starting signal be given to the driver by means of a bell. One-person operation (OPO), of course, came rather later, but the principle remains.

Various additional safety devices have been tried. The original air-operated doors had a

Above: **The interior of an N-class motor car of around 1930, showing a mixture of transverse and longitudinal seating, in many ways not far distant from more recent practice. The slatted floors were for many years a feature of Underground stock; their purpose was to allow rainwater from passengers' clothing to drain away.** *Author's collection*

Right: **British Rail was also forced to consider some unusual solutions, and this resulted in London Transport's pre-1938 stock being found a new home on the Isle of Wight from 1967, when electrification of the remnant of the island's once-extensive rail network was electrified. This is a VEC+TIS formation headed by No 045 approaching Brading over the single track from Smallbrook Junction on 9 August 1980.** *Author*

pressure-sensitive edge, which if obstructed, caused the door to reopen. This negated the secondary objective, which was to reduce station stop times. The 'sensitive' aspect was quickly abandoned, although a determined foot can still hold a door open indefinitely. To release an item of clothing or a case, one door of a pair when shut can be forced back about 100mm. A further innovation was passenger door control, which conserved heat in the open-air sections that were rapidly increasing as the Underground spread out to the suburbs. Initially, this was not sufficiently reliable, and was dropped until recent years. Indicators which alerted staff to the location of door problems proved difficult to achieve, but this was later solved by the placing of fault-detection lights on the roof of each car.

LONGEVITY

The robustness of some of the early cars was well illustrated by the two cars from the original fleet of 1906 delivered to the Great Northern, Piccadilly & Brompton Railway. This pair of cars was in use for no less than 50 years, finishing their passenger-carrying careers on the not-too-demanding Holborn–Aldwych shuttle. Converted to air door operation in the 1920s, they were further modified in 1930 to work as single units. They were allowed a five-year break during the 1939-45 war when the branch was closed, to be resuscitated afterwards and fitted with electro-pneumatic brakes. They left the

Aldwych branch in 1948 to be used as pilot cars, their last duty being with a flat wagon as a stores train between Acton Works and Northfields depot. Final withdrawal was in 1956.

This, though, was exceptional, and when the initial batches of electric multiple-unit stock needed replacement or supplementation, it was possible to incorporate a number of improvements.

STANDARD TUBE STOCK

The all-steel clerestory-roofed 'pre-1938' stock for the tube lines was built in several batches from 1922 to 1934 to a grand total of 1,466 cars, and was the work of half a dozen different builders. Batches built up to 1930 were replacements for the original stock on the Yerkes tubes, the rest being for the Piccadilly extensions. Despite the name 'Standard', it was not all operationally compatible for some years. Three basic types were produced, consisting of:

● M = (Driving) Motors
● T = Trailers
● CT = Control trailers

Trailer cars lacked traction motors and compressors, but seated 48 passengers or so, unlike the driving motors which lost one third of their seating potential in the equipment compartment behind the cab. However, it did make life much easier for the fitter, who could carry out an inspection from both inside and outside, the latter by raising louvred panels in the coachwork. The frames of these motor cars were upswept at the driving end to give clearance for the motor bogie with its 914mm diameter wheels (all the rest were 813mm in diameter). The control trailers were provided with cabs and driving gear but no motors. They were underused, and several were converted to ordinary trailers.

The final orders for the Piccadilly Line incorporated several improvements. Faster trains

were needed, and weak field control was used. This allowed higher speeds of 80km/h or so on the long open stretches of line, albeit at the expense of additional current consumption. Seven-car trains with three motor cars replaced six-car trains with two. Weight was kept to a minimum by the use of aluminium alloy wherever possible, and by building the steel superstructure of light pressings. External surfaces of the coachwork were rounded off to permit a smoother passage through the car washing apparatus. Inside rearrangement resulted in the guard's control panels in motor cars being built into the end walls, and the addition of power-operated single-leaf doors at each end.

Formations of seven cars became general, made up M-T-T-M and used thus off-peak, with an additional CT-T-M added at peak. Pairs of four-car sets were used on the Central Line to which these trains gravitated later, but their last outpost on the Northern City Line saw a slack-hour formation of M-CT, supplemented with CT-T-T-M at peak times.

NINE-CAR EXPERIMENT

Perhaps the best-known variation of train formations was the nine-car experiment on the Northern Line from February 1938. As a response to complaints of severe overcrowding on the Edgware branch, some platform lengthening was carried out at the above-ground stations. However, this was not practicable, at least in the short term, at those in tunnel. The result was that two trains in the peaks were made up M-T-M+T-T-T+M-T-M, to run between Colindale and Kennington reversing loop. The guard rode in the seventh vehicle.

Elaborate arrangements were made, with the two rear cars on southbound journeys stopping in tunnel and hence not available for entry or exit between Hampstead and Camden Town (inclusive). From there onwards the two leading cars stopped in the tunnel, except at Tottenham Court Road (rear two cars). Northbound, the front two cars were in the tunnel to Leicester Square, then from Tottenham Court Road onwards the rear two. By riding in the seventh vehicle rather than the last, the guard would always be on the platform; it was his job to isolate the door mechanisms as necessary through switches provided.

Perhaps surprisingly, the scheme was said to have worked well, but it was discontinued at the outbreak of war and not revived subsequently. However, the new fleet of 1938 stock was ordered in the expectation that it would

Right: **The 1935-stock trains may have been streamlined, but their appearance is very dated now. This four-car train is made up of two units, resulting in the central position of the route indicator.** *Author's collection*

continue, which led to a major reshuffling of that fleet and new orders later on.

The pre-1938 stock survived in London Transport revenue-earning service until 1966, but a handful of cars saw further use with British Rail on the Isle of Wight until 1989. Five of these cars have returned to London Underground, where they have been united with pre-1938 cars which latterly were part of the engineering fleet. There are hopes that one day it will be possible to form an operational heritage train.

1935 STOCK

Clearly, the available platform lengths were a major problem. Highgate low-level station, opened in 1941, is notably the only one (out of 36!) below-ground Northern Line station which could cope. Another approach was through the trains themselves. The Standard stock, which was in reality anything but standard, had the problem of much equipment being housed above floor level in the ends of the motor cars.

If this could be placed either under the cars themselves, or even below the seats, this would make that much more space available for the passengers. All wheels, including those on the motor cars, would be of such a diameter that the tops could be accommodated in pockets beneath the longitudinal seats.

Thus was born the 1935 experimental tube stock design (four sets of six cars, each made up of three two-car units) and then the production run of the design which became known as the 1938 stock. Of the 24 cars, all driving motors, 18 were delivered with streamlined front ends, the remainder being given an early version of the flat-fronted design which was to become so familiar.

Tube stock has been identified by a year cachet ever since, but it should be explained that actual deliveries may have been spread over a long period, and also that the year may not be that in which the first trains of the type entered service.

1938 STOCK

The decision was made to order sufficient 1938 stock trains to completely re-equip the whole of the Northern Line, and this included the running of some nine-car trains. The new stock offered such a boost to capacity that, in terms of seating, seven trains of 1938 stock could do the work of eight trains of Standard stock. The elimination of the equipment compartments enabled the addition of 12 seats in each of the driving motor cars, while the cars themselves were only fractionally longer at (typically) 15.92m instead of 15.18m.

One new type of car introduced with the 1938 stock was the Special NDM. These were part of the nine-car train intentions, in which the guard needed door controls, but a driving cab would have been superfluous. These cars provided the necessary facility. Thus there were

sufficient to allow 10 nine-car trains to be formed, since two would be needed on each such train.

Not introduced until 1949 were the Uncoupling NDMs, which were intended as a

London Transport 1938/49 tube-stock fleet and compatible vehicles

Year	Type	Description	Total	
1938	DM	Driving motor	644	
1938	T	Trailer	271	
1927	T 58	'58 trailer	58	
1938	NDM	Non-driving motor (include SNDM)	206	
Total, original build:				1,179
1949	UNDM	Uncoupling non-driving motor	70	
1949	T	Trailer	21	
Additional 1949 build:				91
1935	T	Trailer (conversion)	18	
Total fleet, 1938 and compatible stock				1,288

Note: All 20 SNDMs plus two NDMs were converted to form additional UNDMs in 1949. At the same time, 18 streamlined DMs of 1935 stock were converted to 1938 trailers.

simplified DM without a proper cab. This took the place of the normal motor car at the 'coupling up' end of a three-car set. The driving equipment was built into a locked cabinet in the panelling at the end of the car, and for shunting purposes the end window in the communicating door was deemed adequate for the use of the driver. Their principal use was for shunting moves where a three-car unit was to join or be separated from a four-car set during the off-peak. At the time, it was common practice to reduce formations at such times and was an important consideration when planning the make-up of rolling stock fleets.

Given the large size of the fleet, variations were remarkably few. They included a car with glass extended into the upper portion of the doors and which allowed better vision for standing passengers.

The fleet was made up as shown.

A total of 1,288 cars is the equivalent of 184 seven-car trains, which after the war, it was decided were to be used on each of the Bakerloo, Northern and Piccadilly lines, distributed as follows:

Right: **A train of 1938 stock approaches the Stanmore terminus of the Bakerloo Line on 8 June 1975. The Metropolitan Railway-built station is very similar to that constructed a few years earlier at Watford. In both cases, the design allowed the line to continue beneath the station buildings at some future date. In neither case has it happened, and clearly, some tunnelling would be needed in this case.** *R. G. Bradford*

Line	Trains	%
Bakerloo	54	29.3
Northern	115	62.5
Piccadilly	15	8.2
Total	184	100

They were to form the whole of the Bakerloo and Northern fleets, but only a small proportion of the Piccadilly's. Many further changes took place subsequently, but the only additional line on which the 1938 stock was later to be found permanently was the Northern City, between Moorgate and Finsbury Park, while that remained in LT ownership. They were used on the East London Line, 1974–77, and on the Epping–Ongar shuttle, 1957–60.

ENGINEERING

As in the 1935 experimental sets, all control and traction equipment was removed from its traditional home to new positions beneath the floor, thus providing extra passenger space. These were also the first production tube trains to use low-voltage electrical supplies for lighting and other equipment instead of the earlier system of direct supply from the current rails. Motor cars now seated 42 passengers, and additional single-leaf doors were provided. The basic seven-car formations were made up in two semi-permanent sets of DM-NDM-T-DM+DM-T-DM.

The presence of five motored cars out of seven was a recognition that multiple-unit working could also give superior performance characteristics if motors could be distributed intermediately along the length of the train to increase speed and acceleration. Such stock also had the same power/weight ratio irrespective of train length, which could thus be varied to suit the traffic on offer without altering operational performance.

Braking performance was improved. To prevent rates of braking which might produce wheel lock and skidding (and hence wear 'flats' on the wheels), a retardation controller was added. Two tubular rings of glass containing mercury were so mounted that when a certain braking rate had been reached the mercury flowed up one of the tubes and indirectly cut off further supplies of air to the brake cylinder. Should the braking approach a severity sufficient to lock the wheels, the forward surge of the train caused a similar displacement of mercury in the second tube, which released air from the brake cylinder and eased the brakes. The result was that a train could be brought smoothly to a standstill. This was a relatively crude but effective means of compensating for the different weights of empty and heavily loaded trains.

Compared with the pre-1938 stock, the body design had all external corners rounded off, and it was given a semi-streamlined appearance. To each bogie of the five motor cars was fitted one 125kW nose-suspended motor, giving a creditable 1,250kW over the whole train.

Automatic coupling between sets made possible the instantaneous connection of the mechanical, electrical and pneumatic mechanism, no longer needed in what then became the middle of the train.

With their life prolonged by traffic growth, the final trains of 1938 stock ran in Underground service in 1988. Probably the most comfortable trains that have ever run on the Underground, a number were refurbished and reduced to two-car sets for use on the Isle of Wight. Six units only are now in service, having displaced their even more elderly cousins.

A four-car train has now been re-created and forms a vintage train in working order. It can be used on London Underground, but not in general service.

1956, 1959, 1960 AND 1962 STOCK

The 1938 stock was all built by Metropolitan-Cammell or Birmingham RCW, but with the tube stock which followed, BR Derby took the place of BRCW. Following construction of prototypes in 1956, the aluminium-bodied car with rubber suspension and fluorescent lighting became standard. Underframes remained in steel, as aluminium versions would need to be designed too large to fit the restricted space if they were to have adequate strength. A prominent feature was the illuminated roller destination blind, high up on the front of the train so that passengers could see it above the heads of others as the train entered the station.

Mass-produced as seven-car trains for (initially) the Piccadilly (1959 stock) and as eight-car trains for the Central (1962 stock), these cars otherwise followed closely the 1938 design. It had been intended to equip the Central Line with new stock based on the 1960 Cravens design but in the event only 12 motor cars were constructed. Some were used for the automatic train operation (ATO) installation on the Woodford-Hainault line, converted to

Below: **The 1960 stock was to be the answer for the Central Line replacement programme, but a few driving motors only were constructed. This interior view shows them to be generally similar to the 1962 stock.** *IAL*

Bottom: **The 1960 tube stock seen here on one of its regular duties, the ATO shuttle from Hainault to Woodford. A train of 1962 stock is arriving at Hainault from the London direction in 1982, but passengers wishing to change to the shuttle will have to use the subway and hope it doesn't go in the meantime.** *Author*

Above: **The 1959 stock and a few trains of 1962 stock eked out their final years on the Northern, having effectively been replaced on the other parts of the system. Here, 1959 stock arrives at Woodside Park; the signalbox has not been operational for many years, while the goods yard has long since been converted to the car park.** *Author*

Right: **There is no need nowadays to provide for guards on trains; they became obsolete with the withdrawal of the 1959 tube stock from the Northern Line in early 2000. This photograph at King's Cross St Pancras shows the last day of both, the guard dispensing information, as usual.** *Author*

conventional one-person operation (OPO) in 1986. These units were notable for a new type of Wedglock coupler. Unlike previous stock where an 'A' end motor could only be coupled to a 'D' end motor, these cars could be coupled either way. However, this was achieved at the expense of duplicating all the electrical connections.

1967 STOCK

The aluminium alloy car bodies of the Victoria Line trains 1967 stock have a distinctive wrap-round windscreen, without corner pillars. The cars' primary springing is rubber, but the secondary suspension incorporates hydraulic units. Tractive power is provided by 60kW motors driving on all four axles of the driving motor cars. Rheostatic braking is incorporated; this uses the traction motors as generators, dissipating the energy in rheostats and thus exerting a retarding force. Braking combines two systems acting in three stages – rheostatic braking on motored wheels only, rheostatic braking on motored wheels and air braking on trailer wheels, and both rheostatic and air braking on motored wheels and air braking on trailer wheels, all operating in conjunction with mercury retardation control.

For the first time headlights, as opposed to marker lights, were fitted from new. These illuminate the tunnel in front, giving the train operator some idea of the train's movement in the absence of colour light signals, of which there are few. The 1967 stock was also the first to be equipped with public address.

These are now the oldest tube stock trains in passenger use on London Underground.

1972 STOCK

Also built by Metro-Cammell were the very similar 1972 Mk I and Mk II designs, used originally on the Northern and Bakerloo lines, and designed for crew operation. The latter were intended for use on the Fleet Line (an earlier name for what later became the Jubilee Line). The Mk II stock was built with red-painted doors, a first attempt to brighten up the appearance of ageing and pitted aluminium then becoming apparent on the oldest cars. Cars of both types were exhibited in the Lord Mayor's Show in 1981 and 1984, although only on the second occasion did the Mk I driving motor manage to get round the course!

The erstwhile Mk I fleet has now been disbanded. Its vehicles have been distributed between the Victoria Line, to enable the provision of extra train sets, and the Bakerloo Line to make good withdrawals following accident damage. Others have been withdrawn.

1973 STOCK

The 87^1/$_2$ new trains of 1973 tube stock delivered for the Piccadilly Line made provision for extra floor space to accommodate passengers and their luggage travelling to Heathrow; this was achieved by setting back the screens at the doors to offer enlarged vestibules. Car length was also increased, with the six-car train at 107m being about 5m less than the seven-car 1959 stock trains replaced and which were a little too long for the underground platforms. This had the benefit of paving the way for one-person operation, and saved the weight and expense of a seventh set of running gear.

Top right: **The 1972 Mk I stock was built for the Northern Line, a train of which is seen leaving Woodside Park for Morden via Bank on 24 April 1997.** *Author*

Right: **1972 Mk II stock 'at home' on the Jubilee Line at the Charing Cross terminal, awaiting departure for Wembley Park. This stock seems likely to see out its days on the Bakerloo, where it presently provides the services.** *Author*

Right: **More luggage space was provided inside the 1973 Piccadilly Line rolling stock, as seen here at Arnos Grove on 24 April 1997.** *Author*

Bottom: **The variation in profile between sub-surface and tube stock is demonstrated by the District D-stock train (left) and the Piccadilly 1973-stock train (right). The two are passing at Ealing Common. The variations occur all the way up; importantly, and ideally, they need different-height platforms.** *Author*

Fortunately, the curves on the Piccadilly are not such as to make train-to-platform gaps unacceptable with longer cars. A selective close facility for the doors was provided, to enable most of the doors in each car to remain closed at terminals to keep the train warm in winter.

The Westinghouse air brake was finally omitted and replaced by the Westcode electro-pneumatic brake. The guard's controls were repositioned from the rear saloon to the rear cab. Fault finding was to be made easier by the installation of a train equipment panel, but this was apparently more trouble than it was worth. Only 21 three-car units with driving motor cars at each end were provided; the rest had UNDMs at one end. Since the completion of the Heathrow loop, trains are turned in service, and care has to be taken that 'A' ends are always coupled to 'D' ends.

Experiments were also carried out with thyristor control on the Experimental Tube Train (ETT) of 1973 stock. It is also known as 'chopper' control because its action in

regulating current employs a chopper movement. Very basically, the thyristor can be likened to an electronic one-way valve providing an instantaneous current limiter. In this case the control smooths acceleration and reduces electrical losses through that function. Also, the kinetic energy of a train during braking is converted back into electric current, available for use by other trains during their acceleration. However, this works only when such trains are in the same electrical section as

the train regenerating the current, since electricity cannot be stored. Disc brakes were also tried on a 1973 car.

1983 STOCK

The 1983 tube stock was ordered for the Jubilee Line at a time when Underground fortunes were at a low ebb, to the extent that only 15 six-car trains were to be purchased. Subsequent revival led to a decision to re-equip the whole of the Jubilee Line with these units, and builders Metro-

Above: **The 1983 stock was not over-satisfactory. It was ordered in the days when future patronage levels of the system were open to some doubt, and in small numbers. One of the problems was the single-door opening, which takes time to operate and to some extent impedes egress and ingress. A train of this stock enters Wembley Park from the north in June 1988.** *Author*

Cammell constructed another 16½ trains. These entered service in 1987/8.

In many ways, the 1983 stock was a diminutive version of the 'D' stock on the District line, with passenger door control, single-leaf doors and cab arrangements to a similar specification. Interiors were finished in bright colours, contrasting with what are now seen as the dull greys and blues in the units of 35 years ago, but now appearing equally dated. This was the last fleet of conventional trains, but it met with a relatively early demise. The limitations in loading speeds caused by the single-leaf doors were a particular problem, which could be solved only by extensive body rebuilding. The Jubilee Line extension to Stratford required

more trains than this fleet could provide, and it was decided that a new build would replace the existing fleet *in toto*. The last of the 1983 cars were withdrawn from service in 1998.

1986 STOCK

The 1986 stock designs were intended as a real advance in technology, just as the 1935 experimental stock had been a half century earlier. There was a shopping list of items which at least needed examination to see whether change could be supported. Could the costly and heavy underframe be replaced with welded aluminium, and offer revised internal layouts? Was thyristor 'chopper' control yet an economic possibility? Could electric braking which needed all axles to be motored be justified on the basis of cleanliness, if not on performance? What improvements could be made to ride quality, ventilation and noise levels to match rising expectations? Was full automation worth considering?

Some experiments were carried out on service cars of 1972 Mk I stock. Steerable bogies to keep both axles parallel to the rails when

negotiating curves and thus reduce flange wear were fitted to one car, but were not judged satisfactory. Another had bogies of a new type with the motors mounted on the frame instead of being axle-hung, and these were adopted. The 1986 stock consisted of three four-car prototypes, two of which were built by Metro-Cammell, and one by BREL (later ABB Transportation Ltd) of Derby. Electrically, GEC, Brown Boveri and Brush provided equipments. Each prototype train was made up of a pair of two-car units with a cab at one end; they could be coupled in any combination to make a train of up to eight cars.

Doors were mounted externally to the welded (as opposed to riveted) aluminium body shells, and thus no longer slid into a pocket within the body sides when opened. Doors could be both opened and closed by passengers, and an audible signal warned when they were to be closed by the driver. The cab ends were moulded in glass reinforced plastic. Thyristor control and electric braking were provided.

Both types of bogies mentioned above featured in the prototype cars. These had 700mm diameter wheels. Unfortunately, attempts to design for the use of 600mm diameter wheels, which would have allowed the car floors to be completely flat, were unsuccessful.

In terms of appearance, trains were given a red, blue or green prevailing colour scheme for easy identification. The internal design tended to provide more standing space and fewer seats, with a decided 'new look', occasioned no doubt by the employment of design consultants from an early stage. The trains were displayed to the Press in 1987, and provided an experimental service as six-car formations on the Jubilee Line in 1988/9. One of the 'green train' Metro-Cammell cars has been preserved.

1992 STOCK

For the Central Line proper, 85 eight-car trains were ordered from ABB; these were delivered between 1992 and 1995. A further 20 for five four-car trains were ordered for (what was then) Network SouthEast's Waterloo & City line, making a total of 700 vehicles. There are three types of car:

- Type A – driving motor with cab and shoegear
- Type B – non-driving motor with neither cab nor shoegear
- Type C – non-driving motor with shoegear but no cab

It will be noted that all car types are powered; indeed, every axle is motored. Types B and C are also fitted with shunting control cabinets for depot movements.

Cars are semi-permanently coupled in pairs A+B (175 sets) or B+C (165 sets); all types of car have automatic couplers at what might be termed the exposed end of each pair. As a further minor variation, 32 of the cars are fitted with de-icing equipment. Since Central Line trains are regularly reversed via the Hainault loop, operators are no doubt pleased that all types of two-car unit are fully reversible.

The trains feature extensive painted surfaces and bigger curved windows, with each pair of doors 314mm wider than the 1962 stock and push button operated. Doors are hung externally to the body. Banishing under-seat equipment elsewhere (except for the wheels towards the ends of the cars), has allowed the all-longitudinal seats to be set back and thus create wider central aisles for standing. Seating capacity, at 34 per car and 272 for an eight-car set, is 17% less than the 328 of the 1962-stock trains which they replaced. This calculation does, though, ignore the small 'perch' seats at the car ends. The car interior layout allows the possible rearrangement (or even removal) of seats in the centre section of the cars at some future date.

Flooring is of rubber. The heating and ventilation systems are designed to maintain a temperature of 20°C. The ends of the cars have windows to enhance passenger security, and wider interconnecting doors to speed train evacuation in tunnels. Announcements are made by somewhat irritating digitised speech recordings, in female voice mode. Maximum speed is 105km/h and there is a chevron primary and pneumatic secondary suspension system for ride quality.

Technically, there is a monocoque extruded aluminium body shell, which acts effectively as a beam suspended between two bogies. The latter are of welded box-section and of Japanese origin; the suspension system is designed so that the car floor height remains constant relative to the platforms, whatever the passenger load. This is an important feature for access by the mobility impaired, but minimising the height variations helps everybody.

All axles are motored, and thyristor (chopper) control with regenerative braking is fitted. Trains have Automatic Train Control (ATC) and Automatic Train Protection (ATP) and are capable of being operated automatically during the peaks and driver-operated at other times. This has been described as the ultimate development of the Victoria Line system. CCTV is fitted in the cabs, and enables the driver to see the station platform as he approaches and before he departs. The latter is an additional safeguard against anyone being trapped in a door. The PA system allows the line controller to speak to the passengers as well as the driver, and a 'talk back' facility for passenger use is provided. These are 'clever' trains, with on-board performance monitoring and fault diagnostics. All aspects of the new trains are high-tech, and will no doubt bring high-tech problems in their wake, but pre-planning should minimise or at least contain the effects of this.

CHANCERY LANE

It transpired that there was a less 'clever' aspect about the 1992 stock. Accidents of any nature are always regrettable, but London Underground did have an unfortunate day on Saturday 25 January 2003. As a westbound train was approaching Chancery Lane station, the fifth vehicle and the cars behind it were derailed. The train came to a stand, partly in the platform. All passengers were detrained, and about 30 received minor injuries. The train was well filled. According to London Underground, investigations revealed the cause as a traction motor shearing away from its securing bolts, falling on the track and derailing the train.

The result was the suspension of services on the whole of the Central and Waterloo & City lines. Both use 1992 stock exclusively, the latter with slight variations which were required by the then line operator, Network SouthEast. Each type has a total of four traction motors.

Rail services were restored to the Waterloo & City on 18 February and to the Central Line, a section at a time. This started with the section between Leytonstone and Bethnal Green only on 14 March. This was extended gradually, with services through the central area between Bethnal Green and Marble Arch on 3 April, and to all Central Line destinations on 12 April. Shortages of modified stock meant that the full timetabled service was not in place until 30 May. London Underground admitted that corrective action took rather longer than had been anticipated.

The root cause was identified as gearbox failure, which in turn caused the motor to come loose. When the safety brackets failed as well, the motor became detached and fell on the track. It would seem that the whole costly exercise of constructing the 1986 prototypes for exhaustive evaluation and subsequent production was seriously deficient.

The 1995 and 1996 stock trains for the Jubilee and Northern lines are considered later, but it is now time to examine the surface stock from the earlier electric days.

T STOCK

In about 1923 the Metropolitan Railway converted some of its steam stock into motor coaches and regrouped the trailers into multiple-unit trains. The conversion was carried out by Metropolitan Vickers, and the motor cars were equipped with 149kW motors. Subsequently, two of the trains were fitted with larger experimental motors of 205kW, and the successful results led to the introduction of the new T stock. These were the versatile 'brown' Underground trains, which retained that colour for the whole of their long operational lives.

The first batch appeared in 1927, and the 12 motor cars had two motors in each of the two bogies. These cars were coupled to existing trailers and control trailers to form trains for service on the Watford line. The control equipment was situated in a separate compartment behind the cab and not placed underfloor. A second batch of 30 motor cars, 15 trailers and 10 control trailers, was delivered in 1930, and a final delivery was made in 1933 of 18 motor cars, 33 trailers and 14 control trailers. They differed from earlier stock by virtue of their steel-panelled bodies and roller bearing axleboxes. Latterly, the T stock also worked to Amersham, made up into six-car and eight-car trains, with two motor cars in each case. A special three-car formation was used for operating the Chesham branch shuttle after electrification, but before delivery of the A stock.

Below: **Experimentation as to the best internal arrangements which could be devised for the new trains needed for the Amersham electrification began immediately after the Second World War. Here, an open saloon with side corridor which is not partitioned off is seen on a T-stock unit. Several alternatives were tried in service before a decision was made on what became the A stock, which is still in use today.** *IAL*

F STOCK

A remarkable series of 100 all-steel cars was built for the District by the Metropolitan Carriage & Wagon Co in 1920/1. Known as the F stock but nicknamed 'Tanks', these high-performance trains had three pairs of hand-operated double doors on each bodyside, and were adept at clearing huge crowds. In appearance, the 'Tanks' differed from previous and subsequent offerings, for they were fitted with elliptical roofs capped with six large ventilators and two oval-shaped windows placed at each end of all cars. At 2,921mm, the bodies were 279mm wider than previous trains, as a result of which there was an inward slope of the body above the waistline.

Incompatibility with other stock kept the F class apart during its 40 years of service; in the 1950s the class found a new home on the Metropolitan services out to Uxbridge. Here, they were able to exploit their power. During their life, the 'Tanks' became a test-bed for electro-pneumatic braking systems, and were fitted with air doors. Final withdrawal took place in 1963.

Q STOCK

Apart from the F trains, the characteristic American appearance of District Line stock was perpetuated, particularly the clerestory and the straight-sided bodies with large windows. Latterly running under the generic name of Q stock, this class was built as separate sub-groups lettered G, K, L, M and N between 1923 and 1935. In total, 172 motor cars, each with two 179kW motors, and 77 trailers were built, although 36 motor cars were subsequently demoted to trailer status. The cars were built with sliding doors, originally hand-operated on the earlier types, but all fitted for compressed air operation by 1939.

The G cars had a boxy look; this was replaced by a softer appearance with the longer K class cars which had the ends of the clerestory rounded off. A destination indicator was also built in. The L cars offered two-class travel in the trailers, the First class being separated by a glazed screen and a door from the Third; a further division within the First was the separation between smoking and non-smoking accommodation. The M class of 14 motors and 14 trailers was run initially as four six-car sets on the Hammersmith & City; they were the first surface trains to be delivered with air doors, and incorporated passenger door control for the first time on the Underground. They were kept in sets initially due to their incompatibility with other stock, which included their electro-pneumatic brakes. The N cars were all but identical, but came from another manufacturer.

Two G class cars, one to work and one as a spare, were converted to single cars to operate the Acton Town to South Acton shuttle from 1939 until the line closed in 1959. This was the first application of one-person operation on the Underground, albeit in very specialist circumstances. Extra precautions were taken in that traction control could only be obtained

Above: **Q23-stock District Line driving motor No 4248 was built in 1923 by Gloucester as a G-class vehicle with hand-operated sliding doors, later converted to air operation. It is now resident in London's Transport Museum.** *Author*

after the driver had shut himself in the cab, and telephone wires were installed along the trackside as in tunnel sections so that the driver could cut off the current without leaving the train. Alterations to the control circuits limited the speeds which could be attained on the short run. The rest of the Q stock was withdrawn in 1971, its final appearance being on the East London Line.

O AND P STOCK

The 1935 re-equipment programme enabled the replacement of elderly surface as well as tube stock. Three classes of basically similar specification were purchased: O stock cars for the Hammersmith & City, P stock for the Metropolitan, and Q38 stock for the District. A total of 573 cars was ordered from the Gloucester and Birmingham companies, of which 287 were motor cars. However, the trailers were built with conversion to motor cars in mind should the installation of extra power be considered worthwhile later.

The new stock again broke new ground. The elliptical roofs, flush fitting windows and flared body panels, the latter to prevent passengers leaping on the non-existent footboards and attempting to open the air-operated doors on departing trains, gave the cars an extremely sleek appearance. Fittings varied according to the line on which the stock was to be used, and were dictated mainly by compatibility considerations with existing stock.

All motor cars were equipped with two motors rated at 113kW each, one to each bogie. Car bodies were 15.58m long, and seated 40 passengers. The trailers followed the motor cars, but the O and P types were reclassified OP as

being interchangeable. Trailers had a driving cab door fitted but locked out of use. Most of the conversion to motor cars that took place was in connection with the subsequent R stock, but three conversions of P trailers were undertaken as a result of war damage.

Another intriguing reconstruction was of P stock motor car No 14233, which was spliced with Q38 stock trailer No 03167 after both had suffered war damage, to be returned to service after rebuilding in 1941. This car has survived to be preserved.

Unit formations were M-T-M and M-M, and five-, six- or eight-car trains were run.

Dealing first with the motor cars, the O and P stocks were fitted with Wedglock automatic couplers, incorporating mechanical, electrical and pneumatic supplies in one single connection. In cars of the O stock the guard's control panel was in the driver's cab, whereas in the P stock it was in the passenger saloon. Both types were fitted with Metadyne control machines which used a rotary transformer. The Metadyne system offered smoother acceleration and regenerative braking — the feeding-back of the energy dissipated in braking to the power-supply system for other trains to use. It was not an unqualified success, and after one train had been fitted with spare PCM type equipments of the 1938 tube stock type in 1955, the whole fleet was converted. The cars were reclassified CO and CP, the trailers COP.

It would be tedious to relate the problems which resulted from a nearly-but-not-quite compatibility, the 'handing' of cars, and changing ideas on the length of trains and to which lines they might best be allocated. The CO/CP stock had a long life, the last examples being withdrawn in 1981.

R STOCK

The Q38 stock was built for use with the rest of the Q fleet on the District, and the 25 motor cars had resistance and contactor control similar

Above: **The R-stock District Line trains were built piecemeal over a 20-year period, but, as is usual in such cases, all were retired together. Towards the end of its life, a train leaves Ealing Common on 10 May 1978, on the final part of its run to Ealing Broadway.** *Author*

to the existing District cars. Likewise, they were fitted with Ward couplers. However, the rest of the Q fleet needed replacement at the end of the war, and the new R stock was born. Similar in general appearance to the Q38 stock, the new cars were all powered with a single 82kW nose-suspended traction motor in each of their two bogies. There were thus no trailers.

Although there were four sub-classes within the R stock fleet, all cars had features in common. Fluorescent lighting was fitted throughout, the 110V ac supply coming from a motor generator fitted one to each pair of cars. A detector light pinpointed door problems, while a roller blind indicator was displayed above the driver's cab window.

The R38 cars were all driving cars converted from 125 of the 183 Q38 trailers, as had been anticipated when they were built. The motors for the converted cars were installed in the original bogies, after modification, at Acton

Works; the car bodies were sent to Gloucester where the body conversion, which included the fitting of a driver's cab, was carried out. The bogies were refitted at Ealing Common depot. The first batch of 82 cars was converted in 1949-51 to run with the R47 stock; this was followed by a further conversion of 43 cars to run with the R49 stock. In all, 79 were eastward facing cars with Wedglock couplers at the outer end and semi-permanent bar couplers at the inner end. The other 46 cars were westbound driving cars, not normally required to couple at their driving ends and thus only fitted at this end with a Ward coupler for emergency use.

The R47 cars comprised a batch of 143 non-driving motor cars of steel construction built by Birmingham (89 cars) and Gloucester (54 cars), delivered from 1949.

The 90 R49 vehicles were built by Metro-Cammell in 1952/53 and were lightweight aluminium cars, the first to be built in quantity in Britain. The weight saved was in the order of six tonnes per car, and comparative tests carried out between Acton Town and South Ealing confirmed that the increased capital cost was sufficiently offset by reduced current consumption, particularly during acceleration.

Included in this batch were six driving cars, so that some all-aluminium formations could be made up. Fearful of public opposition, London Transport left only one car, and then only one of the lightweight trains unpainted, apart from a thin red band at waist level and with a speed whisker on the cab. However, consideration of the then cost of external painting which was saved eventually won the day.

A further 20 cars were placed in service in 1959. These consisted of seven more Q38 trailer conversions and 13 new non-driving aluminium motors from Metro-Cammell. These last were styled R59 cars. The steel cars were painted silver to match the new cars, and gradually all R stock was turned out in silver, although without the red band.

One of the R59 cars, No 23584, was sent to an exhibition of aluminium stock in Strasbourg in 1960. This was the first time that an Underground car had travelled abroad on business, although many had been built on the Continent.

The R stock survived until 1983.

A STOCK

All the surface stock remaining to be considered is still in service, and has been made suitable for

OPO. The A stock was delivered in two batches from 1961, to provide a complete replacement for what was by then decidedly elderly rolling stock of multiple-unit, electric and steam locomotive-hauled types. This programme was carried out in conjunction with the electrification to Amersham and the cessation of London Transport interests beyond that point. Built by Cravens of Sheffield, the A60 order was for 248 cars in four-car units,

Below: **After refurbishment, the A-stock trains looked like this internally. This was photographed at Baker Street on 17 December 1996.** *Author*

Bottom: **A train of refurbished A stock leaves Chalfont & Latimer in April 1999 on the down grade towards Chorleywood.** *Author*

followed by an order for 216 identical A62 cars for the Uxbridge services.

Two driving motor cars sandwiched two trailers, and the performance was specified to match that of the previous stock. This meant that the traction motors were controlled for two types of running. This was either a high acceleration rate but low balancing speed, suitable for in-town station spacing of 800m or so, or a lower rate with a different motor field strength to take full advantage of the longer outer sections beyond Baker Street. Here, the trains could indulge in 96km/h running.

The A stock was built to the maximum width possible of 2,946mm (thus barring it from most of the Circle Line), and this made 3+2 seating each side of a central gangway possible. The width allowed for each seat was 445mm. The standard eight car formation seated 464 plus 916 standing (total 1,380). By comparison, eight cars of T stock seated 600 at five-a-side in 60 compartments. An extra five standing in each compartment was judged to be the limit but was highly uncomfortable for everybody. That would give a total capacity of 900 passengers – substantially fewer in total, but more would be seated.

To overcome the loss of heat as the doors opened up in the Chilterns on a frosty morning, the A stock saloons were provided with extra powerful heaters.

Bearing in mind the Rickmansworth curve which would turn trains round, automatic couplers were fitted providing full reversibility.

Conversion to OPO was completed in 1986. This work comprised the relocation of the guard's panels in the driving cabs, the fitting of public address, train radio, new windscreen wipers and toughened glass in cabs, and twin headlights. As there is no call for four-car trains other than on the Chesham shuttle and the East London Line, only 24 units have had both cabs converted. This has left the inner cabs on most of the eight-car trains unusable, resulting in some loss of flexibility.

C STOCK

The C stock was again built in two batches. The C69 series of 35⅓ trains of six cars each was for the Hammersmith & City and Circle lines. Ordered in 1968 from Metro-Cammell, it was delivered 1970/1. The second batch, designated C77 and consisting of 11 trains for the Edgware Road–Wimbledon service, appeared in 1977.

Designed for quick loading and unloading, these cars featured no fewer than four pairs of double doors along each side of a car body only

14.93m long. This has meant that, as built, there were only 32 transverse seats, arranged 2+2 in each car. Unusually, all passenger accommodation is identical; the cab in the driving motor cars merely adds an extra 1.09m to the length of those vehicles. Bogie centres were adjusted to minimise overhang on curves for both car designs.

Evaluation of the options suggested that maximum flexibility would be achieved by constructing two car units (M+T) with one cab, three of which would form a service train. This gave the opportunity (never exploited) to run eight-car formations also, but in any case, Hammersmith depot lifting shop could only hold two cars on a road. Automatic couplers are fitted at all unit outer ends. Among their new features was rheostatic braking as on the

Below: **The western end of Farringdon station sees a C-stock train arriving on 5 August 1976, in the days when unpainted aluminium-bodied trains were the norm, and before spray-paint canisters were available. The four sets of double doors per side can be seen. This gives quick movements of people on and off the train, but at the expense of some seating space.** *Author*

contemporary 1967 stock tube cars, a secondary suspension system of rubber-air springing units, and thermostat-controlled blower-heater fans mounted in the roof. A selective door-close facility enables all but one pair of doors in each car to be kept closed at terminals in cold weather. These trains pioneered manual, as opposed to automatic, one-person operation on the Underground in 1984/5.

Service experience has been satisfactory, apart from poor riding qualities blamed on track condition. As built, the trains also offered a low degree of passenger comfort for journeys of any length.

D STOCK

Only three main unit types now provide the whole of the surface stock requirements for the District and Metropolitan lines. The 75 six-car all-aluminium D stock trains made their debut in 1980. As with the Piccadilly 1973 trains, six longer cars replaced seven shorter ones, greatly simplifying formation problems. A total of 65 eastward-facing and 65 westward-facing three-car single-cab units were built (DM-T-UNDM), together with 20 double-cab units with automatic couplers at both ends (DM-T-DM).

Four doors on each car side were again provided, but this time of single leaf only and thus 1,067mm wide as opposed to the 1,370mm or so with double doors.

Door opening was intended to be by passenger controls, released from the cab, but this was of short duration. Any door which fails to close properly can be reopened individually, and all doors can be remotely opened from the cab if necessary. Innovations included coil spring suspension supported by rubber cushions, and motor and wheelset interchangeability with the 1973 tube stock. Traction brake controls were also new, comprising a right-hand 'fore and aft' vertical lever incorporating the dead man device, instead of the previous left-hand rotary-operated controller.

Seating is mainly longitudinal. In the ceilings are concealed fans. These were boosted by additional fans after experience, and this measure, coupled with the installation of opening quarterlights cured the trouble of excessive heat in summer. Modifications have also included the fitting of additional grab handles. These small matters apart, Metro-Cammell's D stock has proved to be most successful. A refurbishment programme has been started, but progress is very slow.

Above: **This is the rear of the Waterloo arrival platform for the Waterloo & City, Platform 26, as the doors open and passengers make a dash for the exit steps. It is the evening peak on 13 September 1983, and car No S59 of the 1940 English Electric stock brings up the rear. Trains painted in dark green or blue, with unpainted ends, never made for a bright and cheerful scene.** *Author*

The newest of the surface lines' stocks is thus a good 20 years old, and badly in need of half-life refurbishment.

REFURBISHMENT

Rolling stock refurbishment became the main occupation of the 1990s. There were two main reasons for this, the first of which was safety. In the aftermath of the King's Cross fire, a general review disclosed a number of changes which were desirable. These included:

- elimination of non-essential use of combustible materials in car interiors or in equipment
- revising the emergency brake alarm system to alert the driver, but not to cause an automatic brake application between stations
- speed control after a driver has had to pass a signal at danger (under the Rules), whether because of signal failure or other reason
- the fitting of public address to all rolling stock
- the fitting of high intensity headlights to make trains more visible to staff on the track
- 'correct side door enable' or, to interpret, a transmission/reception device between the lineside and the driving cab which allows the driver to open a train's doors on the platform side only

The second reason is image. Underground trains have long lives, sometimes almost unbelievably so. Seating layouts for what became the Metropolitan A stock were being tried out as a works mock-up in 1939 and as a series of in-service experiments from 1946. The A stock entered service between 1961 and 1963, and refurbishment of what are basically sound vehicles may require them to remain in service well into the present century. Who today drives a car with that sort of pedigree?

It is hardly surprising if aesthetic tastes have changed over time, as also, it is sad to note, have perceptions of personal safety, whether this is justified or not. Research on test refurbishments has shown much support for providing windows in the car ends to improve visibility through the train, lighting enhancements, a reworking of seating and handrail positions, and a new design of upholstery.

The external painting of the East London Line trains was begun in 1988, at a cost of £5,000 per vehicle. The first A stock trains to be treated featured red fronts, blue doors and grey panels. As the repaint was sponsored by the London Docklands Development Corporation, they also carried the LDDC logo. Several livery variations were tried on the A stock, the C stock and the 1967-72 family of tube stock.

The result was a new corporate livery, which was aimed at offering a much improved appearance over pitted aluminium, that would also be easier to clean if, or perhaps when, it was attacked by the spray can. The new external finishes complemented the interior refurbishment programmes.

Putting this all together resulted in a substantial workload. However, if a train is to last 30 years or more in service, a comprehensive updating at around half-life is surely justifiable. To carry out all the required work on each unit at the same time has its attractions; work has now been completed for some time except on the D stock.

It was also effective, but the general appearance of the fleet is again becoming tatty. This is perhaps inevitable as the age of the assets increases, but one can no longer deceive anybody to think that the refurbished sets are really new. However, the safety work undertaken was a real achievement, and that goes unseen and is therefore not credited.

WATERLOO & CITY

Although not then forming part of the system owned by London Underground, developments on the Waterloo & City tube line are recorded here for the sake of completeness. When the original rolling stock became due for renewal in 1940, English Electric supplied 12 motor open brake thirds with 40 seats and 16 trailer open thirds with 52 seats. These vehicles were only 14.3m long and 2,635mm wide. Maximum speed was 64km/h on the 5min journey between the two stations. Motor coaches were fitted with two 142kW totally enclosed traction motors and weighed 28.4 tonnes; the trailers weighed 19.3 tonnes. The normal formation was two motor cars sandwiching three trailers, but single-car working was envisaged during off-peak hours and the motor cars were accordingly provided with cabs at each end. Their drab appearance was later markedly improved by the application of Network SouthEast livery.

Internally, the motor car floors were on two levels, to provide space below for the switchgear and larger-diameter-than-normal motor bogie wheels. Seating was a mixture of unidirectional transverse in the centre and raised longitudinal at the ends of the cars. Current supplies were altered to the standard Southern Railway outside third, which enabled the cars to run unaided on Southern tracks to and from main depots or workshops, although day-to-day attention was carried out at the line's Waterloo depot. Car

access from the surface was available only via the Armstrong hydraulic lift situated alongside the main-line station, with access below gained from the up line (towards Bank) beyond the end of the platform. The dimensions of the lift precluded the use of any longer stock, although the tunnel dimensions at 3.70m diameter are slightly greater than the standard tube tunnel. By a considerable margin, the Class 487 cars were the oldest operational trains in the London area at the time of their withdrawal in 1993.

They were replaced by 20 cars of a minor variant of the 1992 Central Line stock, from which five four-car trains can be made up. The line was also converted from third to fourth rail electrification. The whole line passed to London Underground in April 1994.

Although a propulsion system based on the use of bogie-mounted linear induction motors operating in conjunction with a reaction rail laid between the running rails was considered, this option was not pursued.

EAST LONDON LINE

The allocation of cars to lines is not constant. The East London Line has had more changes than most over the last 30 years; being self contained, only a relatively small fleet of trains is needed, and the conditions are not such that any particular type of train is required for traffic reasons. Hence, the F stock which had enjoyed a 10-year reign gave way to Q stock in 1963, which lasted a year until it was displaced by CP stock. In 1965 the Q stock was back again for six years, to be followed in 1971 by CO/CP stock. The year 1974 saw the surprise appearance of 1938 tube stock, which lasted until the summer of 1977, after which the A stock from the Metropolitan main line put in an appearance. D stock ran the service from 1985 until 1987, after which the A stock reappeared, this time in OPO guise. It has remained on the line ever since.

Present allocations are shown below.

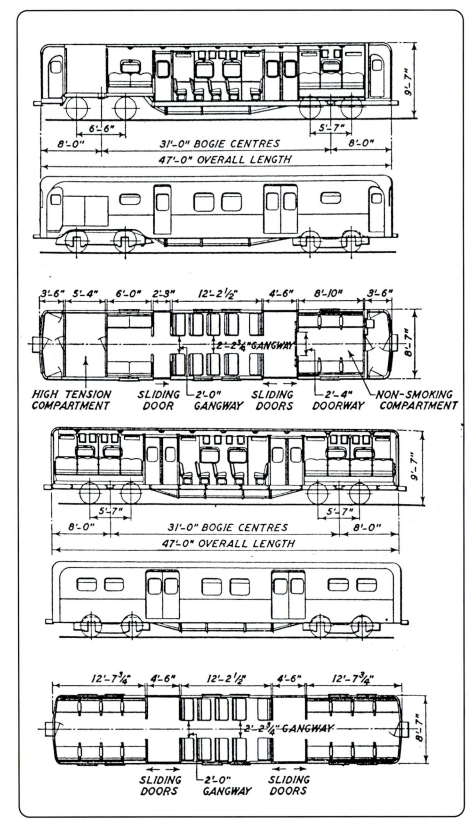

Principal allocations of car types to lines, 2003	
Tube stock	
1967	Victoria
1972	Bakerloo
1973	Piccadilly
1992	Central, Waterloo & City
1995	Jubilee
1996	Northern
Surface stock	
A	Metropolitan, East London
C	Circle, Hammersmith & City, Edgware Road–Wimbledon
D	District (not Edgware Road–Wimbledon)

Left: **An outline diagram of the Waterloo & City replacement stock, including the seating arrangements. Unusually, they had much face-to-back seating, but also a step up from the door area to the longitudinal seats over the bogies.** *Author's collection*

CHAPTER SEVEN

The Underground Station

> 'The station is a shop in which you receive the customer, and there is a lot to be done with this shop.'
>
> *Frank Pick, 1923*

For passengers, the station ranks in importance along with the train in which they travel, since it is here that they access and exit the system, as well as the point where they change trains. Possibly more so than any other railway in the world, the London Underground can demonstrate a range of styles of building and architectural treatment over its century and a half of history which is truly breathtaking in its diversity.

SYSTEM GROWTH

The first stations to be served by the Underground were those on the Metropolitan's initial system, of which none remain today in their original form. However, the chronology is not as straightforward as it might at first appear. Many of today's Underground stations were built originally by the main-line railway companies, for services that they themselves operated. Among the more notable examples are the East London Line stations (first served by Underground trains in the 1880s), and those on the long extensions of what are today the Northern and Central lines into the suburbs.

Most of these stations are now in London Underground ownership, but there are exceptions. Upminster and New Cross are two of the 19 stations managed by Train Operating Companies out of a total of 274 served currently by the Underground. It must be admitted that the total of Underground stations is a little elastic; does the Waterloo & City station at Bank make

the LUL total there now two, and what about Paddington? The Bakerloo and District/Circle lines share the combined station in Praed Street, while the Hammersmith & City platforms are at Bishop's Road, a hike of 250m or so along the main-line station platforms and over a bridge.

Which lines have the most stations? The Underground lines are by no means equal in size (or patronage); a basic measure is perhaps the number of stations each serves, and this is shown in the box below right.

The total numbers of stations shown adds up to considerably more than the actual station numbers, but this is accounted for by individual stations serving more than one line. Thus Holborn is on both the Piccadilly and Central lines, and is counted in both. Nevertheless, the table does demonstrate large differences in extent between (say) the top four and the bottom four lines on the list.

GEOGRAPHICAL SPLIT

The Underground is the predominant means of rail transport in the central-London area, but its influence lessens as distances increase. The table

overleaf shows the number of stations within each fare zone in Greater London, and this is compared with the number of stations at which the trains of National Rail call. Again, there are 10 stations which lie at zonal boundaries and are thus counted as being in each, while some will appear in both lists. The overall result is however of some interest.

This shows that nearly half of all Underground stations are in Zones 1 and 2, as against less than a quarter of the National Rail stations. The latter are much stronger further out. Fare Zones 5 and 6 were originally a single Zone 5, and this in part accounts for the smaller number of stations for both operators.

Another influence is the River Thames, and the predominance of the former Southern Railway electrified lines south of the river, only 33 stations there being served by London Underground.

STATION DESIGN

Station design and construction and, frequently, subsequent modification has to accommodate the varying traffic needs of the individual

Underground lines and stations served		
Line	*Stations*	*%*
District	56	15.5
Piccadilly	52	14.4
Northern	50	13.8
Central	49	13.5
Metropolitan	32	8.8
Hammersmith & City	30	8.3
Jubilee	27	7.5
Bakerloo	25	6.9
Victoria	16	4.4
Edgware Road-Wimbledon	14	3.9
East London	9	2.5
Waterloo & City	2	0.5
Total	362	100

Left: **Newbury Park station retained signs of its Great Eastern origins, and is seen here in 1982 with the embossed glass announcing 'General Waiting Room'. The London Transport signs themselves also look to be from a past era.** *Author*

locations. Whether the architecture is homely or functional, neo-Georgian or the Underground's own style evolved by Pick and his consultant architect Charles Holden, the station has a necessary operational function to perform. If it fails in this it fails completely. The simplest arrangement is a single platform, found today in seven locations – Chesham, Kensington (Olympia), Mill Hill East, New Cross, New Cross Gate, Shoreditch, and the 1986-built Heathrow Terminal 4. This last is placed on the terminal loop of the Piccadilly Line, and is served by trains in the one (clockwise) direction only.

At the other end of the scale, the busiest stations include Victoria, Oxford Circus, Liverpool Street, King's Cross, Waterloo and Piccadilly Circus, each of which sees between 30 million and 60 million passengers joining or alighting there each year. As such, they compare with the 60 million annual usage of Heathrow Airport itself. These Underground stations serve up to five lines, and with only four platforms in the case of three of them. They are large premises: Oxford Circus has 14 escalators, 25 stairways, and 8.8km of platforms and subways. As many as 10 platforms are in use at Baker Street, solely for Underground trains, but the total is inflated due to two dead-end platforms used only for terminating the Metropolitan main-

Stations in each Fare Zone, London Underground and National Rail					
Fare Zone		*Used by LUL*		*Used by National Rail*	
Zone 1	Central area	63	21.6%	21	6.3%
Zone 2	Clapham/Kilburn	75	25.4%	57	16.9%
Zone 3	Ealing/Leyton	55	18.6%	86	25.6%
Zone 4	Southgate/Barking	42	14.4%	75	22.3%
Zone 5	Edgware/Dagenham	29	9.9%	44	13.1%
Zone 6	Heathrow/Uxbridge	28	6.8%	49	14.6%
Zones A–D	Moor Park/Chesham	8	2.7%	4	1.2%
Totals		292	100%	336	100%

line services. Moorgate can also boast 10 platforms, but here four are for the exclusive use of National Rail operators, at two different levels.

OPERATIONAL REQUIREMENTS

What are the operational elements in station design at a busy location? On the passenger side, conflicting flows of incoming, interchanging and

Below: **This wayside station does not immediately shout 'Underground' and indeed it shouldn't. It is the Great Northern Railway's station at Woodside Park, which has been cleaned up and restored, with few changes. This is the northbound platform on 21 March 2000.** *Author*

Below right: **Earl's Court westbound District Line Platform 3 sees a D-stock train arrive with a service bound for Ealing Broadway in March 1983. This is one of the few stations left with a high glass roof; others are Notting Hill Gate and Paddington (Praed Street).** *Author*

outgoing passengers must be kept separated as far as possible, while it is desirable to maintain as many entrances and exits from the premises consistent with acceptable staffing levels. There must be space for people to buy tickets, and ticket queues in stations at main-line termini where many have heavy luggage move noticeably slower than city stations where the majority have Travelcards. Barriers, passages, circulating areas and escalators must have roughly equivalent capacity if bottlenecks are not to form; the inability to clear an area into which an escalator disgorges is a particular danger.

Similarly, there must be a means to shut off platforms if the train service is delayed and the platform becomes overcrowded. Closed circuit television controlled from an operations room can be useful for surveillance, while public address is also helpful. Station platforms on the Victoria Line were built straight or nearly so, to enable the driver to look back down the length of the train, and forwards from the back by the use of closed circuit television. A similar approach was used on the Jubilee Line Extension. One-person operation is now in force throughout the system, with all trains and stations suitably adapted. This requires platform mirrors and as many television monitors as necessary for the driver to be able to view the outside of the whole train properly.

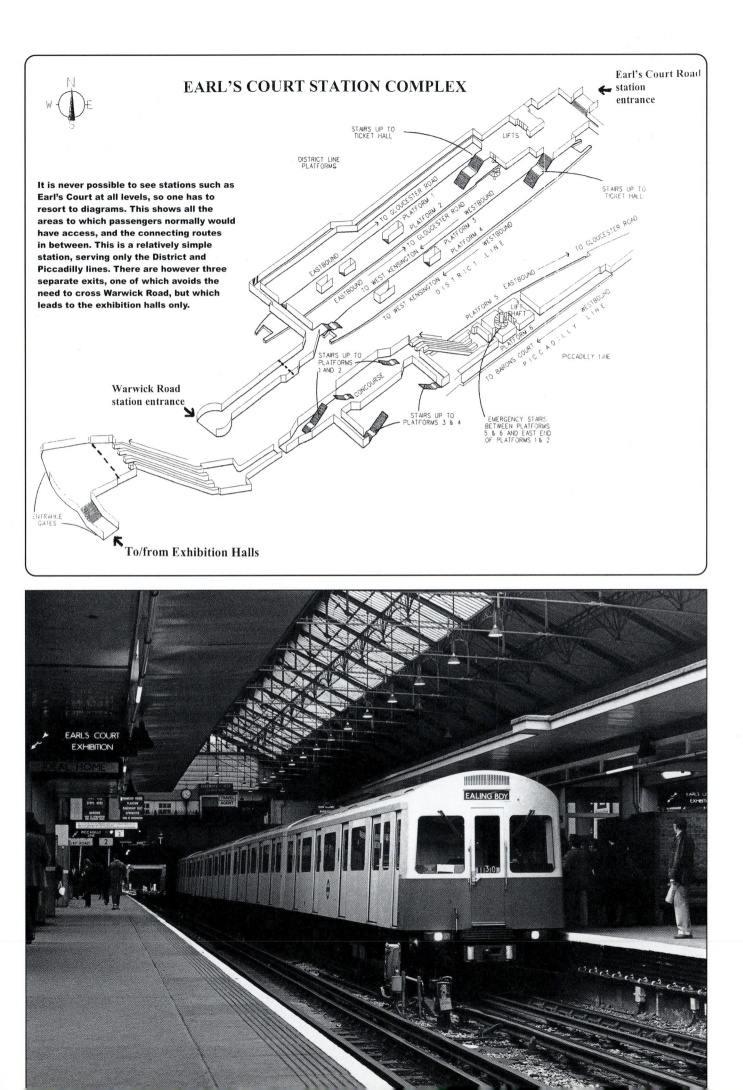

EARL'S COURT STATION COMPLEX

Earl's Court Road station entrance

STAIRS UP TO TICKET HALL

LIFTS

DISTRICT LINE PLATFORMS

STAIRS UP TO TICKET HALL

It is never possible to see stations such as Earl's Court at all levels, so one has to resort to diagrams. This shows all the areas to which passengers normally would have access, and the connecting routes in between. This is a relatively simple station, serving only the District and Piccadilly lines. There are however three separate exits, one of which avoids the need to cross Warwick Road, but which leads to the exhibition halls only.

TO GLOUCESTER ROAD
PLATFORM 1
EASTBOUND

TO GLOUCESTER ROAD
PLATFORM 2
EASTBOUND

TO GLOUCESTER ROAD
PLATFORM 3
WESTBOUND

TO WEST KENSINGTON
PLATFORM 4
WESTBOUND

TO WEST KENSINGTON

DISTRICT LINE

TO GLOUCESTER ROAD

PLATFORM 5 EASTBOUND

LIFT SHAFT

PLATFORM 6
TO BARONS COURT

WESTBOUND

PICCADILLY LINE

PICCADILLY LINE

STAIRS UP TO PLATFORMS 1 AND 2

Warwick Road station entrance

CONCOURSE

STAIRS UP TO PLATFORMS 3 & 4

EMERGENCY STAIRS BETWEEN PLATFORMS 5 & 6 AND EAST END OF PLATFORMS 1 & 2

ENTRANCE GATES

To/from Exhibition Halls

Left: **Shoreditch is not at all an Underground station, having been built by the East London Railway in 1876. Today it serves but a single platform and does not support a UTS gates installation.** *Author*

Centre left: **Fulham Broadway station used to have a large overall roof, and be open at the northern end. This view from the footbridge looks towards Earl's Court with a District Line D-stock train arriving for Wimbledon in 1983. Major redevelopment is now taking place above the station.** *Author*

Bottom left: **The station at Heathrow Terminal 4 was opened in 1986, and was single track in one direction only. A very adequate platform width has been provided here. The dot-matrix 'Next train' indicator seems to be offering two trains simultaneously, but this was early days for such advanced technology.** *IAL*

PASSENGER INFORMATION

Good clear directional information to passengers is most important, and coloured lights over the escalators (follow red for Paddington etc) were a feature for many years. Underground platforms usually carry a comprehensive notice of stations served directly opposite the point where a passenger arrives on the platform. Line and system diagrams are everywhere, and illuminated signs referring to exits, as opposed to interchanges, are colour coded in yellow.

Destination indicators which show the subsequent train or trains are of great value to passengers, especially on lines where there are a number of divergent routes. At Earl's Court westbound District Line platforms for instance, trains may be bound for any one of four branches on the lines to Ealing Broadway, Richmond, Wimbledon or Kensington (Olympia), and it is imperative to know where the train is going. However, the only variation possible on the eastbound Piccadilly Line at the same station is whether or not the train is going the whole length of the route, and the information is of much less value.

Passengers do however like to know how long they will have to wait, and the electronic dot-matrix indicators now widely installed show the next three trains and their estimated arrival times. These indicators consist of a matrix of light-emitting diodes which are illuminated in any combination to show letters, figures or diagrams, so that a wide variety of information and messages can be displayed. Good information brings user confidence, provided it is also accurate.

INTERCHANGE

In a system as old as the Underground, there is rarely an opportunity to start from first principles. New lines have to be meshed in with the existing as best they can, and designed to facilitate arrangements for interchange between lines where this is expected to be heavy. Sometimes, changing from one line to another is a minor marathon. One can walk a long way around Charing Cross (it was once two stations, Strand and Trafalgar Square), while

Above: **Signage at Putney Bridge on 30 January 1981 shows some real period pieces, but their meaning is clear enough.** *Author*

Monument (District and Circle) and Bank (Central) are separated by the full length of the Northern Line platforms as well as stairs and escalators. Bank (Waterloo & City) platforms are also a long subway walk from the Northern Line, but in a quite different direction, while the Docklands Light Railway is at deeper level still, below the Northern.

STATION MODERNISATION

Many stations have been reconstructed or built anew on a different site. This work entails the most complicated of all Underground engineering when such things as subways, sewers, mains and even tunnels may have to be stopped up, diverted or otherwise accommodated. Engineers have not only these things to consider, but they must always make provision in their plans for the continuing daily traffic.

STATION TIME

For the operators, time taken at station stops is non-productive time during which the train is cluttering up the system and not earning revenue; the shorter the stopping period the better. There is a caveat, though, as ideally all station stops are of the same length. If trains consistently spend a longer than average time at only one station due to the numbers of passengers joining and alighting, this has the result of bunching up the service and ultimately restricting the frequency at which it can be operated. Dwell times will vary from a minimum of 15sec off-peak and 20sec peak to 20-30sec at busier locations.

Some of the worst problems of this nature occur at Underground stations serving their main-line equivalents. This can cause very uneven flows of passengers to the Underground platforms, related to when trains arrive 'upstairs'. This will vary the station dwell times achievable on the Underground. Long intervals can easily occur or services can bunch together, especially when a succession of main-line stations is served, as on the Victoria Line. Active management intervention can help, but there is no real solution to this problem.

Overall speeds also depend on the number of station stops; it was to reduce end-to-end journey times and make more productive use of trains and crews that the 'non-stopping' of trains was in vogue during the inter-war period.

A limiting factor in the early days was the method of telling the driver when it was safe to start. Before the ubiquitous door interlocks and bell signals were invented for use with the now universal power doors, a train starting device more elegant than a guard's whistle was introduced. A pair of bare wires insulated from each other was suspended from the roof at one end of each platform. By shorting these wires together with the metal handle of his flag, the guard caused a letter 'S' to appear in lights under the starting signal. A 'reminder' bell near the driver's cab was also set ringing. This arrangement was installed on the District and Metropolitan, and lasted on parts of the latter until the electrification of 1960 finally allowed the withdrawal of the slam-door compartment stock.

TERMINAL REQUIREMENTS

The track layout at terminals is of special significance, since trains spend longer than average at such locations. At an intermediate station, the provision of a central bay as at Putney Bridge (with platform) or Marble Arch (without) keeps the terminating train clear of the running lines, and it does not foul any other train movements when moving to or from that position. The disadvantage of the siding beyond the platform arrangement is that it takes time to detrain all passengers and close the doors before the train can proceed, by which time another train can be waiting behind. The provision of a mere crossover to reverse trains, as on the Bakerloo Line at Piccadilly Circus (southbound to northbound) is too restrictive for general use, while a crossover requiring trains to reverse in tunnel on a running line as at Hampstead is even worse!

At terminals, the usual choice in tunnel is an island with crossovers (Walthamstow Central), or on the surface a three-track multiple-platform arrangement (Uxbridge, Stratford Jubilee Line). Platforms both sides of a track can be useful in separating arriving and departing passengers by judicious use of the door opening/door closing sequence. It can, though, make for cold trains in the winter months.

If it is necessary to speed up the turnround of trains, step-back crews can be employed. By having staff positioned ready to take the train out again after it has arrived, the turnround time is kept to a minimum so the incoming driver does not have to change ends. Terminal loops as at Kennington are not favoured; while there is no need to change ends, neither can layover time be provided as the train cannot be sidetracked. The Heathrow loop is a little different, as there are two platforms available at Heathrow Terminals 1, 2, 3. Loops also introduce the coupling problems of stock reversal which would otherwise be avoided on both the Northern and Piccadilly lines.

OTHER CONSTRAINTS

Other determinants of the capacity of lines are the performance of trains, junction conflicts, signal spacing, gradients and curvature. On a railway, the capacity is determined by the most restrictive element; thus Bakerloo Line capacity was increased by eliminating the use of the Stanmore branch junction at Baker Street when the Jubilee Line was opened in 1979. The capacity was then constrained by the ability of the signalling system to cope with a frequency increase. Beyond that, it might be the speed restriction on the curve north of Charing Cross, which at less than 100m radius is one of the sharpest on the system. Nevertheless, a service frequency of 30 trains per hour should be achievable on most parts of the Underground.

LIFTS

Access to what became known as the surface Underground lines was by stairs, and since the platforms were no more than 5m or so below street level, this caused little difficulty. Even today, Sloane Square is distinctly unusual in having up escalators installed on both platforms. The building of the deep-level tube lines, however, meant that some form of mechanically assisted access became essential. Initially this meant lifts.

The simplest means was used to build the shafts, by assembling the lining segment rings on the surface, undermining them, and letting the whole sink under its own weight. The City & South London Railway used Armstrong's hydraulic lifts, the power from the piston being translated into the movement of the cage by a system of ropes and pulleys. More common were electrically operated lifts, by the Sprague and Otis companies. Lift shafts were commonly built to accommodate two or more lifts, to allow for traffic growth as well as escape from one to another in the case of failure. Lifts were thus not immediately installed in all of them, and some never received their full complement. By 1907 there were 249 lifts on the growing Underground system.

Initially, all lifts were manually controlled by staff, but the first semi-automatic lifts appeared at Warren Street in 1928. It was then but a short step to the fully automatic variety, first seen at Earl's Court four years later.

Above: **Lifts of the automatic type are seen here at the upper landing at Goodge Street, Northern Line, 13 April 1983. In the aftermath of 'Fares Fair', it was not even clear if the investment needed to replace these lifts would be legal.** *Author*

The capacity of a transport system can be increased by speeding up the vehicles, and this is just as applicable to vertical movement. Initially, lifts travelled at 30 to 36m/min, but speeds of 88m/min were reached at Angel and Leicester Square in 1924/5. A speed of 183m/min was attained at Goodge Street in 1937, while Hampstead, the deepest Underground station with a 55m deep lift shaft, had 240m/min lifts installed in 1954. These took a mere 18sec for the journey. In these later installations, time switches controlled movement to provide an evenly spaced service.

Lift safety measures incorporate door contacts so that the lift cannot be started until the doors are properly closed. Speeds are regulated by a governor and an automatic brake to ensure that plunges to the bottom of the shaft are prevented. If a lift becomes stalled in transit, passengers are transferred to another lift brought alongside using connecting doors; as a last resort the slow process of hand winching may be resorted to. A separate staircase, usually spiral, is always provided for emergency use. At school in Hampstead, the author was forbidden to race the lifts; this was only possible when the high-speed versions were not working, as was not unusual.

Although a few of the original lift installations survived until the 1990s at lightly used stations (such as the 1907 Otis manually controlled installation at Mornington Crescent), replacement with escalators or new lifts has been general. Lift renewal is a complex process. First, the old lift has to be dismantled and removed, and new lift guides built for the car to be assembled *in situ*. The machine rooms and landings have to be rebuilt to match the new equipment, following which the ropes and wiring are installed prior to acceptance tests. Physically, the work takes nine months or maybe much more; in the interim passengers often have to resort to the emergency stairs or the station may even be closed while the work is carried out.

Although lift numbers decreased slowly for many years, with 60 remaining in service in 1994, the combination of new stations as a result of line extensions and a more positive approach to those with mobility problems has seen their numbers grow again. At the end of 2002, a total of 103 were in service at 42 locations.

ESCALATORS

The word 'escalator' is an American term dating from 1904. Just as the elevator was used to elevate the passenger, so the new invention 'escaladed' him. For some time, the limitations of lifts had been apparent. Apart from, at that time, the need to staff them, the interruption of the flow of passengers was irksome and could lead to long waiting times. The aim was to find a conveyance which could deal economically with a steady trickle of passengers, and yet could absorb a surge at peak hours without becoming overloaded or causing congestion.

Hence the search for some form of continuous movement, first patented by a Mr Reno. His first moving stairway (albeit without steps!) was installed at Coney Island in New York in 1894, and was moved to Brooklyn Bridge the following year. By 1900, he had gained sufficient experience to build a three-mile-long moving walkway at the Paris Exposition. In London, Reno constructed a pair of concentric spiral moving stairways in a lift shaft at Holloway Road in 1906. They never entered public service, as the Board of Trade was not convinced as to their safety. So it was that the Otis Seeberger design became the first to appear on the Underground system at Earl's Court in 1911.

Being first in the field meant that precedents did not exist, and being a run-on order from elsewhere, nobody objected to the gradient of that escalator being tailored for that precise job. As the number of installations grew, the lack of standardisation of parts was to offer some intractable and expensive problems. These early escalators were of the 'shunt' type, whereby passengers stepped off them sideways. A considerable public education exercise was needed to overcome public unfamiliarity with this new arrival.

Lifts still had their place at the deeper stations, since with a vertical rise of more than about 25m two flights of escalators with an intermediate landing are needed. But such was the escalator's general superiority with two escalators being reckoned to do the work of five lifts, that new lift installations stopped altogether after a couple of years. Raised cleats on the steps, which ended in a 'comb' at the landings to trap debris, became universal after Otis bought out Reno and his patents. The first cleat/comb escalator was installed at Clapham Common in 1924. All 'shunts' were then removed.

A 30° gradient became the standard. A great variety of machines was constructed, later substituting aluminium for much of the woodwork used originally and, much later, shown to be a fire hazard. Indeed, the 1936 Moorgate installation made a virtue of its use of wood panels veneered with samples from trees growing all over the British Empire. For the record, the greatest vertical rise can now be found at Angel (27m). The shortest is at Chancery Lane (4.6m). The maximum number found together is five, at Canary Wharf.

OPTIMUM SPEED

Experiments over the years have sought to determine the optimum speed. This rose rapidly from the 27m/min until 55m/min was reached, but it was found that understandable hesitancy by some passengers actually reduced the capacity. Since then, the maximum speed has been set at 44m/min, and this can handle 10,000 passengers an hour comfortably. Lesser speeds to conserve energy at times of light traffic may also be set.

Safety devices include the obvious plungers for emergency use, and these will stop the escalator in about 1.2m; these activate the brakes, which will also operate if the electricity supply fails. Detectors are installed to stop the machine should a drive chain break.

During the 1920s an extensive programme of station improvement and modernisation was undertaken, and this often included the replacement of lifts by escalators. The problem was that the slope required by an escalator shaft would not join the existing ticket office with the existing below ground passages. Typically, the remedy was to construct a new sub-surface ticket hall underneath a road intersection. Escalator shafts from there lead to landings above tube level since the tracks are generally too closely spaced to allow direct access to platforms. A short stairway joins the two. Since then, few stations in the central area have had more than a series of subway entrances to mark their presence. This kind of work is tremendously expensive: replacing the four lifts at Angel with two sets of three escalators (with an intermediate landing in between) cost £25 million.

Escalators, too, need renewal, and a prolonged major effort has restored escalator availability to a much higher level than that experienced generally in recent years.

FLOODING

The water table under London is rising, and with it comes the increased risk of flooding of the system. Exceptional rainfall or the breaching of water supply or sewerage pipes can also result in the discharge of water into the Underground system – where it is not welcomed. Without a satisfactory means of dealing with water, the Underground would quickly resemble one massive sump.

About 700 pumps are installed at 350 sites throughout the system. This includes a key installation next to the westbound Circle and District platform at Victoria, which deals with up to 5.5 million litres of water in a 24hr period. One of the biggest tests of the maintenance men came in July 1987 with the rupture of a 1,067mm Thames Water Authority main at Euston. An estimated 82 million litres of water poured into the station car park and on into the Underground. The torrent surged across the booking hall and cascaded down the eight

Right: **Wood was introduced for escalator treads around 1926. It provided a rigid surface under foot and was generally satisfactory. Aluminium was introduced around 1963 as a more durable material, which allowed a closer-fitting comb. Synthetic rubber was then used from around 1971, but was removed following the King's Cross fire of 1987. Here, an early wooden tread with its comb may be seen – and walked on – in London's Transport Museum.** *Author*

escalators, rendering them instantly unserviceable. Water filled the lower machine chambers, ran on to all six platforms, spilling on to the track and into the tunnel, filling the track inverts. According to the track gradients, it then followed the tunnels; on the Victoria Line, it was quickly demonstrated that it is downhill to Warren Street! The pumping out operation, which took three days, was at one stage removing more than 4,500 litres/min from the station to the car park and into the sewer.

Such incidents which involve prolonged suspension of services are exceptional, but it is only constant attention that keeps the Underground as remarkably dry as it is.

VENTILATION

A problem as old as Underground railways themselves is that of ventilating the tunnels adequately with economy, and without causing discomfort to passengers or creating nuisance for residents near ventilation shafts. It was an insoluble problem in steam days, but there were so many other inconveniences associated with horse-drawn surface travel that many were resigned to the smoke and dirt. The problem was much reduced with the end of steam traction, but even so the residual difficulties have taken many years of research to overcome. The Central London Railway installed 'ozonisers' which were meant to purify the air, and some of the ducts at stations can still be spotted. The ozonisers certainly sucked air into the stations, but apparently the tang clung about the person for some time afterwards, and finally condemned the experiment.

Modern practice is to exhaust spent and heated air from the tunnels by means of powerful fans discharging into special ducts, and to admit fresh air through the natural channels of station entrances and escalator shafts. To augment this incoming flow, fresh air is also pumped through shafts enclosed in staircase wells, or through shafts sunk specially for the purpose.

An earlier method, still employed, works on the exhaust fan principle. Between Bounds Green and Finsbury Park three of the numerous shafts used during construction were retained to act as air extraction ducts. Below ground, two galleries and headings connected the shafts to the running tunnels. A later example is at Notting Hill Gate where a stairway shaft, no longer used, was extended to the roof level of an office block over the station site. All this adaptation and new construction has proved worthwhile, and the experience of having positively to force one's way against the rushes of air in passageways as fast moving trains approach a station is now forgotten.

A further aim has been to keep the air temperatures in the Underground at a reasonable level, since heat is created faster than it is dissipated through the tunnel segments and into the surrounding clay. With the help of over 100 fans, the temperature underground is kept to an annual average in the region of 23°C.

STATION GARDENS

Most of the Underground's stations are on the surface, but even so it is not the most obvious organisation to run a garden competition. An event of long standing, it was early justified 'by

adding greatly to the cheerfulness of the railway', to the extent that management were prepared to pay for 25p worth of seed at each location. In spite of all the obvious difficulties, a challenge cup is awarded annually, with the gardens being judged on visual impact, health and vigour, choice and care of plants, design, and site problems overcome. Theft, vandalism and sheer thoughtlessness are problems to be coped with, but the efforts are appreciated by many.

TICKETS

A ticket represents the means by which an acknowledgement is given by the railway for a fare tendered, and confers on the passenger an authority to travel within the terms of the contract which has thus been made. It follows that the ticket and the means of obtaining it are all important parts of the organisation. Besides being a more-or-less foolproof way of collecting revenue, tickets provide a record of where a passenger entered the system. Without a ticket it is not possible to charge fares graduated by distance, which is a severe limitation. In London, the best known examples of flat fares were the LSWR's Waterloo & City (which had only two stations anyway), and the Central London Railway which opened its doors in 1900 with the commercial policy which gave it the popular nickname of the 'Twopenny Tube'. However, most of the other tube lines also opened with a flat fare.

Until recent years, the issuing methods used were almost entirely traditional, save for a little relatively unsophisticated mechanisation (none the worse for that, one might add), and some ill-fated experiments. Even the *Underground Official Handbook* of 1988 admitted that most of the previous attempts to improve the issue and control of tickets, coupled with an effort to reduce fraud and increase ticket office security, had been unsuccessful. Before examining current developments, though, it is useful to consider the history.

Thomas Edmondson invented his system of pre-printed and numbered card tickets, dating press and storage rack in 1836, and this was universally adopted by British railway companies. When the Metropolitan Railway commenced operations in 1863 it saw no reason to differ, but the tube railways in this as in other matters, had more allegiance to North American transit operations in their more individual approach. Besides flat fares collected at turnstiles, Bell Punch tickets were issued by conductors, and the

use of roll tickets of various colours was commonplace. On the CLR, tickets bought at the office were surrendered on entering the system. Edmondson tickets were a rarity.

By 1907, however, competition from buses was beginning to bite, and this forced the Underground companies into ever more complex ticketing. Flat fares were too easily undercut: 2d (0.8p) was probably less than some were prepared to pay for the 9km from Shepherd's Bush to Bank, but it looked distinctly expensive for what the advertising industry in a later generation called 'short hops'. And although the physical interchange between lines was far less satisfactory than it was later made, the lesson for the companies was clear: they had to make the system a lot more attractive to the user. This move was linked to the establishment of the London Passenger Traffic Conference, and the later coining of the word 'Underground' to market the companies. Graduated fares and through ticketing between the lines were introduced and, with them, Mr Edmondson's familiar product.

The City & South London Railway had tried to help its ticket collectors by matching the ticket colour to the destination station, of which it had 15 by 1907. That the company was hard pushed to find sufficient means of distinguishing the Edmondson cards is evident, with red, reddish-brown, pink, lilac and purple all being used. Return tickets were even more colourful, as each half was coloured according to its correct code! Others used various overprints, but the complexity was beginning to get out of hand.

A BUSY SYSTEM

What did distinguish the Underground from the main-line railways was the sheer volume of journeys made. In 1875, with less than 16 route km of track, the Metropolitan was calculated as issuing 20% more tickets than the whole of the Great Western Railway. With the proliferation of through booked tickets which ensued after 1907, the situation quickly became untenable, given

also the number of stations on the network and the possibility of different classes of travel on the Metropolitan and District railways.

This culminated in the gradual introduction of so-called 'scheme' tickets from 1911, when all stations available at a given fare were listed on the back of the ticket instead of requiring separate prints for each. This facility applied only to stations within the Group, and through tickets to any railways not included in the Conference still retained separate issues. The reason was as much to do with the apportionment of receipts between companies as anything else, but the range of bookings which were (and were not) available always contained many idiosyncrasies, and has persisted thus ever since. Even then, there were a number of different ticket types to be contended with, and among the less obvious nowadays were workmen's tickets, those for the military and police, to say nothing of 'Dogs and Folding Mailcarts'.

MECHANISATION OF ISSUE

Mechanisation of ticket issue was of high priority. By the time the 'Rapidprinter' machines which printed, dated, guillotined and ejected a ticket on the press of a button by the ticket clerk arrived in the late 1920s, the Underground Group was issuing around 270 million tickets a year. Other mechanical help took the form of change-giving machines, and various dispensing devices for office use containing pre-printed tickets. However, most clerks became sufficiently skilled at their work that they could usually work quicker than the customer whom, it may be said, also benefited from research. A new design of brass plate with an upward curve was introduced, to make it easier for passengers to scoop up their tickets and change. A test at an (unidentified) Underground station in 1930 revealed that 663 tickets could be issued by a clerk from a single window in the half-hour period from 07.00 to 07.30, at a rate of 22.1 tickets per minute – or 2.7sec each. Such dexterity was an indication both of traffic

Left: **A rather self-conscious demonstration of a ticket being issued by the clerk hitting one of a series of keys behind the window and the ticket being ejected for the passenger to pick up without the clerk touching it. Also of note is the change machine. Most tickets, it is clear, were still Edmondson card issues, as seen in the rack on the right.** *Author's collection*

Right: **A 'passimeter' booking office in which the clerk sits in the middle, showing also the barriers provided on each side. The location is not known.** *IAL*

volumes and the speeds which passenger-operated ticket machines would have to match.

The earliest slot machines of the 'pull bar' variety appeared in 1904, dispensing pre-printed tickets, but free-standing electric machines did not appear until 1937. By then the problems of change giving had been solved, and machines of the period also sorted mixed coinage placed in them by means of the 'bunch hopper'. They were installed at all the principal stations, and covered the main fare denominations. At the busiest locations, they accounted for up to 70% of ticket issues, or 30% systemwide since small stations had none. The fare for each machine was shown on an illuminated panel, which also contained the names of all the destination stations covered by that fare. Tickets were printed from a roll of blank card in similar fashion to the 'Rapidprinters' and the simpler 'Miniprinters' in the ticket offices. The machines had to be filled with ticket rolls and change, and emptied of cash, as well as having the date adjusted and the meters read each night. The sound of mountains of loose coin cascading into the collecting boxes wielded by the late shift clerks is one which now belongs to the past.

The 1950s saw the introduction of the 'Station of Origin' ticket, which conferred the right to travel for any journey from the originating station to any other where the fare was that shown on the face of the ticket. There matters stagnated until the automation phase of the 1960s as embodied by the Victoria Line, for there was a lot wrong with the ticketing system. Barrier checks were cursory, particularly for ingoing passengers, adequate staffing became ever more difficult, and it became clear that a large amount of revenue was being lost by fraud. What could be done to automate the process?

TICKET GATES

So began the installation of mechanical barriers, through which all passengers would have to pass both to gain entry to and exit from the system. Special yellow tickets with an oxide backing were issued to operate the barriers, and all machines had to be adapted to encode the tickets on issue. A contemporary account described how the Automatic Fare Collection (AFC) system was used:

'The four-door gate has two sets of twin doors. When the passenger inserts his ticket into a slot, the first pair of doors opens, allowing him to step through, and as he does so, the second pair of doors opens and the first pair closes behind him. The whole process can be carried out at normal walking speed, and if there is a continuous stream of passengers inserting valid tickets one after another, the door will remain open, giving an unimpeded flow. The (alternative) tripod gate has a three-armed turnstile which is released by the insertion of a valid ticket and allows one passenger at a time to pass through. At inwards barriers the ticket is returned to the passenger, but at outwards barriers, at the end of the journey, the ticket is

Above: **Stratford gate barriers were installed as part of the rebuilding for the Jubilee Line, and are seen here from the footbridge which connects them to the platforms. The North London Line platforms prevent any other means of getting to the trains.** *Author*

retained in the gate. Both types of gate are operated by tickets with a magnetic oxide backing on which the journey details are electronically encoded. When passengers place their tickets in the slot, these details are read by electronic equipment in the gates, which open only if the ticket is valid.' LT Annual Report, 1968

But it quickly became clear that the system aspects had not been thoroughly thought through. If manual barriers were to be dispensed with, all passengers had to have encoded tickets, and this included those issued at the smallest stations on the Underground system as well as the large numbers of BR stations from which barrier-free transfer was available. What sort of costs might be incurred in a comprehensive installation? In 1977, the cost of adapting and enlarging the ticket hall at Bank station for AFC was put at around £1 million, compared with £5,000-£10,000 for a small suburban station. In the meantime, few of the public could be bothered to use the barriers, especially if they were carrying luggage. With technical problems to contend with as well as several changes of plan, the vision faded and the outward barriers, followed by the inward, gradually fell into disuse.

DECIMALISATION

The adoption of decimal currency on 15 February 1971 posed a few problems for London Transport, which had favoured the £ Sterling being halved in value and divided into 100 pence — what today might be termed a '50p pound'. With their extensive use of coin-operated machines, the Board took strong exception to the proposed introduction of $\frac{1}{2}$p

coins, the lack of any coin between 2p and 5p and the lack of a close relationship of old values and coins with the new. It was all too difficult, and it was indeed at London Transport's behest that the sixpence ($2\frac{1}{2}$p) was retained in the coinage for the time being.

UNDERGROUND TICKETING SYSTEM

Rebirth of automatic ticketing came in the 1980s, with the Underground ticketing system (UTS). The objective had now expanded to improve the control and issue of tickets and security for the staff. It also represented a return to first principles; the previous systems had developed gradually from the early days, and modernisation had always been piecemeal. The main features of the new system were:

- Self-service ticket machines which issue a wide range of daily tickets and give change
- Automatic ticket checking on entry and exit at Central London (Zone 1) stations, in which 80% of all journeys start or finish
- Creation of 'open' no-barrier suburban stations without regular ticket checks, but with more roving inspectors able to levy penalty fares
- Secure 'wall' ticket offices for staff, whereby all machines can be serviced without leaving the office
- Data capture to provide centralised accounting reports and management information

A credit-card-sized ticket was adopted as standard, with a magnetic strip on the back for encoded data. Encoding takes place on issue, together with visual printing of station at which issued, fare paid and other details.

Right: **The Underground ticketing system produced its own range of tickets; seen here is an adult fare from Aldwych on the day of the line's closure in 1994, the minimum (child) fare from Ongar at that line's closure in 1994, a Zone 1 single from King's Cross and an issue for British Rail travel from Moorgate.** *Author's collection*

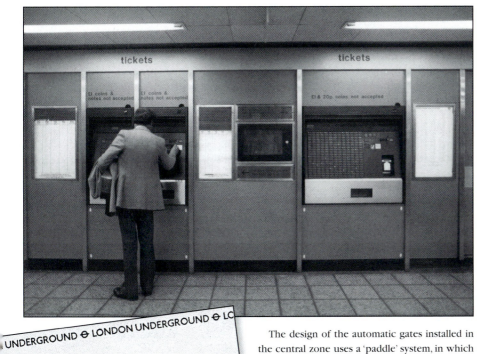

Left: **The passenger-operated machines as originally supplied for the Underground ticketing system (UTS). The photograph is not dated, but notices state that the machines cannot accept £1 coins or notes, or 20p coins.** *Westinghouse Cubic*

Below: **The UTS barriers at Uxbridge in February 1983, with passengers gaining access to the platforms.** *Author*

were installed, replacing a maximum of 10 manned booths.

Each station was controlled by its own computer, and linked to a mainframe installation at Baker Street. Stations were also daisy-chained together so that they were not cut off by a failure of the main link. Through this interconnection, the control centre could update the fares at individual stations. Data on fares and usage was extracted by the control centre. Installation was completed in 1989, and linked to the compatible British Rail system. UTS featured many enhancements over what had been intended previously, such are the advances in micro-electronics. It took less than a second for gates to perform 64 checks and rewrite the magnetic stripe. Thus the new ticket readers were able to detect irregularities in ticket use through time, history, geography and price tests. The acid test though was its acceptance by the public and the staff who had to use and run the system respectively. This was achieved and eventually UTS became all but universal.

JOURNEY PLANNER

One of the most well-known manifestations of the Underground is the map, diagram of lines, journey planner or what you will. Since 1933 the

The design of the automatic gates installed in the central zone uses a 'paddle' system, in which the paddles are kept closed electro-pneumatically. Tickets have to be inserted and collected from another slot before the gates will open; photo-electric cells detect the presence of a passenger so that the gates remain open while the passenger passes through. The gates open automatically in the event of power failure, or by the operation of emergency buttons. The minimum number of gates at any one station is one inward, one outward and one reversible gate. At busy stations such as Oxford Circus as many as 26 gates

93

map has appeared regularly, having twice undergone major redesign at the hands of new cartographers, and with minor (or occasionally major) adjustments made at each reprinting. It has always been available in a poster edition as displayed on station platforms, and as a pocket edition, but it has also appeared on T-shirts, mugs and carrier bags, on postcards and in diaries, as a jigsaw, on trays and as a tea towel. Recognised all over the world as an icon of London, it also happens to be a useful guide for those wanting to use the system!

As time went by, firm proposals for line extensions were incorporated and shown by dashed lines as 'under construction' or 'to be electrified'. This was fine, as long as the work was eventually completed, but the Northern Line became less extensive with every edition during the postwar years until it regressed to the position reached in 1941.

In 1955 a grid was superimposed and keyed to an index of the 272 stations then extant. Minor changes continued, such as an improvement in the typography, the indication of which stations had car parks, and the closure of the South Acton branch. By this time Beck's map, with its curved transitions from horizontal to vertical and limited use of the diagonal, was judged passé, and Harold F. Hutchison's 1960/1 map took its place. In contrast, this used lines at 45° wherever possible, and eschewed all curvature. Perhaps it was meant to reflect the spirit of the times, but in truth it was heartily disliked. When Paul Garbutt, the LTE's Chief Secretary, doodled a more rounded replacement, his ideas were enthusiastically taken up. The first Garbutt map appeared in 1964, and its descendants, which have had to cope with the Victoria, Jubilee and Docklands lines, are still with us. Only one physical feature has ever been shown: the River Thames, which over the years, has been twisted this way and that.

There have always been major trouble spots for would-be designers, the City being the most intractable. Hutchison's design was weak here, the main problem being the need to enlarge the area significantly to get all the lines in without unbalancing either the appearance or distorting relationships. Interchange between lines presents problems for which compromise is often inevitable, and a couple of examples are examined here.

Hammersmith consists of two completely separate stations on different sites, the walk between them requiring the use of a public subway to cross the road. Should they be shown separately, or as an interchange? The present convention is interchange, but it has not always been so.

BRANCH LINES

Branch lines may be shown as divergences from their main lines or as separate lines from their junction station. Today, the distinction depends on the way in which the service is operated. If the line is always self contained (Waterloo-Bank), interchange is shown. If through trains

are operated as part of the basic service (Finchley Central-Mill Hill East), it is a divergence from the main line. If sometimes one, sometimes the other (Chalfont & Latimer-Chesham) it is shown as interchange. Should it also show a broken line connection indicating, in this case, 'peak hours only'? At one time, yes, nowadays, no; today you see a note 'For Chesham, change at Chalfont & Latimer on most trains'.

Many other conundrums have had to be resolved over the passage of time. How many of Network Rail's lines should be shown? To what extent should weekend station closures and peak-hour-only operations be covered? Does the walk between Fenchurch Street and Tower Hill count as interchange? What about one-way working as on the Heathrow terminal loop? Is it helpful to anticipate future events such as additions to the system, or does it serve only to confuse? An answer has to be found to all such questions.

LINE COLOURS

Most of the line colours are long established, though subtle changes have taken place over the years, certainly in terms of the exact shade of the colours used. Old versions of the diagram can still surprise; as late as 1946 it was reproduced using only five line colours in total. These were red for the Central, blue for the Piccadilly, brown for the Bakerloo, black for the Northern, and green for all the surface lines. In those days the Metropolitan also was green, like the District, and the Inner Circle was not yet shown separately.

Subsequently, the Metropolitan reverted to purple and the Circle Line became yellow. The Victoria Line of 1968 was rendered in light blue, while the separation of the old Bakerloo into two lines in 1979 resulted in grey being adopted for the Jubilee. Further changes came from new line management structures, and in 1990 the East London Line was re-coloured orange, and the Hammersmith & City salmon pink. The 1994 acquisition of the Waterloo & City introduced turquoise to the journey planner.

POSTERS

While the Underground map is a well-known feature of every station platform, that area would not be the same without the display of posters which nowadays is taken for granted. It was not always so. Some posters may be displayed by the undertaking's management, to inform about the services offered. Others may have the intention of stimulating travel, with artist's drawing of places in London worth visiting – by tube. Most,

though, merely advertise a commercial product. As such, they are useful earners of revenue for the owner of the sites, who is thus tempted to cover all the available space with them, and so it had come to pass in the early years of the tube.

However, posters also compete for attention with the really necessary information for the passenger on the train – the name of the station at which the train is arriving. To distinguish the station nameboards and make them stand out, what now became the universally recognised Underground (and, indeed, London Transport symbol) was devised – the bull's eye. (An earlier version had solid red half circles). Even then, the lettering styles available at the beginning of the 20th century were seen as seriously deficient. The upshot was the commissioning by the Underground companies of a new typeface. This was to be in a simple sans-serif form, with the objective of being clear and open, and also modern. It was to be used to present information from the company, as distinct from the typefaces used on ordinary commercial advertising.

JOHNSTON TYPEFACE

The net result was a revolution in the appearance of the Underground. For this, the Group's then Traffic Manager, Frank Pick, was largely responsible. It was he, too, who commissioned Edward Johnston to design both the bull's eye and the lettering form which still bears his name. The Johnston typeface was first used in 1916. One of the earliest examples of a modern sans-serif, it was originally called Underground Sans.

In 1979 LT commissioned the New Johnston family of typefaces, by extending Johnston to take full advantage of developing technology. Ownership of the Johnston typeface is now vested in Transport *for* London. It is fully protected by copyright law, which is enforced. Today, New Johnston is intended to give the organisation a distinctive and uniform image, very much as it has always done.

New Johnston has been designed for reproduction in small sizes, in cramped conditions, and for laser printing. The range is

Right: **The roundel and some of the other ways in which the Underground or its parent organisation has been represented over the years. Transport *for* London seems only to require the 'for' to be in italics.** *Author's collection*

Below: **New Johnston typeface is used widely by the London Underground.** *Author's collection*

Our Customer Charter
Our commitment
London Underground aims to deliver the best possible service for all our customers. You want a quick, frequent and reliable train service, a safe, clean and welcoming station environment with up-to-date information and helpful, courteous staff. This means a continuous, demanding programme of improvements to meet rising expectations.

Underground symbol c 1907

District Railway station nameboard c 1908

Underground sign at Tooting Bec station 1926

London Passenger Transport Board symbol c 1934

London Transport roundel as used in the 1930's

The London Underground roundel

The London Transport roundel

The LRT mark

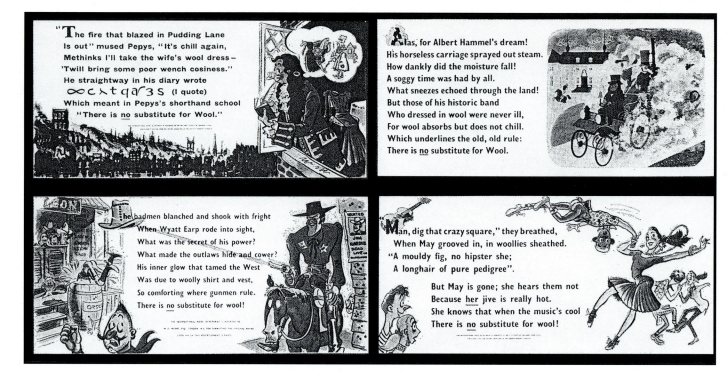

Above: **A selection of the 'wool' rhymes produced for the International Wool Secretariat in the postwar years and used as car cards on the Underground and also buses. Each shared the last line: 'There is <u>no</u> substitute for wool!' Many of the verses were contributed by the public.**

intended to preserve flexibility and continuity in the production of corporate material, in which the typefaces are the keystones. To the present writer, the lower-case letters 'i' and 'j' are good clues; if the dot at the top is rendered in a diamond shape, the likelihood is that it is New Johnston.

CAR CARDS

Besides stations, advertising extends to the trains, and particularly to the car cards. Most are displayed landscape-format in a line above the car windows, designed to be read by those sitting opposite.

In the postwar austerity world of the late 1940s, one of those to use this medium was the International Wool Secretariat, now The Woolmark Company. This was encouraged by the contemporary paper shortages, which limited the use of newspapers for advertising. The result was a series of cards which appeared at intervals over the next 15 years or so, brightening up the daily lives of travellers. The cards themselves gained what might now be described as a minor cult following. The advertising agency was Dorands. Some of the original ideas were submitted by members of the public, who became members of the Guest Rhymesters Club. It was the first manifestation of what much later became 'Poems on the Underground'.

Thus, with a decidedly contemporary feel to it:

'The problem in a satellite
Is where to put the cat at night;
For if you want your mind at ease
How can you let poor pussy freeze?
The answer reads on your computer –
'A woolly overcoat will suit her'.
From sheep to Bleep, all know the rule
There is <u>no</u> substitute for wool!'

Sadly, few car cards survive; another series from those years was that of H. J. Heinz in 1957. Each of their (nominally) 57 varieties formed the subject of a numbered car card and they ran a competition in which one had to 'collect' the name of each product featured. For those like the author at school at the time, this meant hurtling down the inside of a 1938 tube stock car, pausing only to note the essential information, and if possible getting into the next car before the doors closed and the train restarted.

Heinz must have considered the promotion a success, since in 1958 the company repeated it in a slightly different form. However, this happened to coincide with the disastrous London Bus strike, which lasted for 47 days. Antics such as those described above must have been a sore trial to other passengers in the overcrowded tube conditions of the time.

LISTED STATUS

It is perhaps unsurprising that Underground stations and structures have increasingly been listed for their architectural interest; today they number at least 50. Examples from the earliest times include the Thames Tunnel and its entrance portals at Wapping and Rotherhithe (Brunels, father and son, 1843) and the original Metropolitan Railway Platforms 5 and 6 at Baker Street (John Fowler, Engineer, 1863). Later examples include Fulham Broadway's train shed (John Wolfe Barry, Engineer, 1880) and the street buildings and arcade at the same station (Harry Ford, 1905).

From the first years of the tube lines is the surface building at Kennington with its domed roof (Thomas Philips Figgis, 1890) and Mornington Crescent station with its fine surface building featuring the dark red tiles sometimes referred to as ox-blood in relation to their colour (Leslie Green, 1907). In similar vein is the entrance hallway with its Underground mosaic, staircase and ticket hall at Maida Vale (Stanley Heaps, 1915).

Dating from the inter-war period come the Clapham Common entrance building (on the Morden-line extension) and, indeed, all the other stations to South Wimbledon (Charles Holden, 1924-6), while Piccadilly Circus is listed for its sub-surface ticket hall, concourse and bronzework at subway entrances on the pavements (Holden, 1928).

No fewer than 15 stations on the Piccadilly Line west of Hammersmith or north of Finsbury Park now have listed status. These all date from the 1930s when the Piccadilly was breaking new ground in the suburbs, and some of the older stations were being rebuilt. First of these was Sudbury Town (Holden, 1931), a large load-bearing brick box with a flat concrete roof. It was followed by the broadly similar Sudbury Hill and Acton Town (both Holden, 1933). The drum shape appeared first on the northern extension, as at Arnos Grove (Holden, 1933) and at Southgate (Holden, 1934). The design for Southgate was integral with a bus station.

A rather different style may be found at Loughton on the Central Line, which was reconstructed by the LNER before the advent of the Underground (John Murray Easton, 1940).

Finally, the headquarters of the Underground group at Electric Railway House at St James's Park had become increasingly inadequate, and it was resolved to replace them. The result was the building known today at 55 Broadway (Holden, 1929), which became the headquarters of the London Passenger Transport Board in 1933 and has fulfilled that role for the Board and its railway successors ever since. It too has listed status.

CHAPTER EIGHT

Operations and Control

'No matter how good the timetable may be, it is of little use if passenger needs are not met.'

H. Samuel, Railway Operating Practice, 1961

Many regarded the prewar London Transport as reaching a high-point which has never been attained since. Indeed, as folklore would have it, declining traffics, staff shortages and unreliability were wholly phenomena of the 1950s onwards. But what was the London Underground capable of 60 years or so ago?

CORONATION, 1937

One of their largest tasks was the transport arrangements for the Coronation of King George VI on Wednesday 12 May 1937. It is perhaps worth looking at this operation in detail.

In those far-off days with no television and few cars, there was little alternative to public transport. The success or otherwise of such an event depended upon the adequacy of the planning and operation by the transport providers. There had been some recent experience of major Royal occasions, notably the Silver Jubilee of 1935, but even so these could not match the intensity of movement in the first part of May 1937 around the West End.

This started with Cup Final day on 1 May. Subsequently traffic rose daily; the last of three dawn rehearsals of the Coronation procession on 9 May had over a million spectators.

Pre-planning decided that there was a need to operate all-night trains on the Tuesday night on all lines; for Coronation day itself some stations on the processional route would be closed or partially closed to assist in crowd control. Some stations in the outer areas were also closed, but in these cases to economise on running time. It was not just the procession, attraction though that was; crowds of sightseers were expected to throng the streets to view the decorations and illuminations. At key stations, a special system of barrier control was instituted, with bell signals or telephones between platforms, ticket halls and subway entrances. Gates were erected to enable the passenger flows between platforms to be regulated to match accommodation available. This required substantial augmentation of staff, and the 6,000 employees were supplemented by no fewer than 1,319 'extras'. Some were recently retired staff, but all had to be instructed in their duties and perhaps receive some training. Over 600 regular staff received temporary promotion.

Below: **There was no more isolated spot on the Underground than Blake Hall, Central Line. According to some sources, this was the least-used Metro station in the world. A glance at the landscape does not suggest that the potential for custom was high. It is seen here on 1 March 1977 with a 1962-stock train leaving for Epping.** *Author*

When the Underground opened for business on the Tuesday morning, it was to run continuously for 46 hours. At Charing Cross (now Embankment) alone, 6,530 trains worked through the station, which handled 467,000 passengers. These were part of the 5,669,000 carried in this exhausting traffic day. Not having overnight breaks in service avoided huge influxes at the start of operations, and the peak was reached, incredibly, at 05.30. This perhaps indicated the success of warnings to the public to be in good time, seeing that the procession did not arrive at Westminster Abbey until 11.00! The police request to close some stations partially backfired as it merely put undue strain on the rest. Nevertheless, a continuous 30 trains per hour was successfully maintained during this time on all lines. Included in this were 17 specials run for 10,000 schoolchildren, 1,000 troops and 2,000 dignitaries.

Weather always plays an important part. May 1937 was cold and foggy, with some rain. Consequently, return journeys tended to be earlier than anticipated, and by 16.15 queues totalling 580m long had formed outside St James's Park station. Traffic levels fell away after 01.00 on the Thursday morning, the service finally ceasing at 02.15. The respite was brief; over three million passengers were carried on each of the following three traffic days, which was approaching twice normal levels. There are numerous statistics to illustrate the magnitude of what was achieved, including the 12-tonne weight of tickets issued during the week.

Operationally, it would seem that a state of near perfection was achieved, with no instances of failure causing appreciable delay or inconvenience to passengers on Coronation Day itself. Only minor problems were encountered on other days.

Whatever the cost, it was excellent public relations. 'The manner in which the (Underground workers) have carried out their task must excite universal admiration,' enthused the *Morning Post* (later amalgamated with *The Daily Telegraph*). 'When it was inevitable that human beings should be packed like sardines, the sardines have at least been made to feel that the packers regretted unfortunate necessity along with them.' The editorial went on to suggest that if the Underground could cope with such a massive influx of passengers, the nation would do well to develop the network further as a solution to London's ever-growing traffic problems. This support for the public network was all the more encouraging as, although the trams and trolleybuses were running, the buses were absent at the time due to a strike.

TIMETABLE PLANNING

Few travellers on the Underground need to give any thought to the timetable, most probably assuming that trains run on some sort of continuous basis. In reality, the timetable is constructed carefully to extract the maximum out of the resources which are available. Any railway service can only be as good as its

Above: **The busy Underground is epitomised by this view of the yet-to-be-rebuilt Mansion House, on 24 September 1983. At this time, there were 31tph in the peak. A westbound Circle Line service of C stock arrives, this being after the previous train had been failed and disgorged its human contents onto the platform. However, there is still room to read a newspaper, so the platform isn't *that* crowded!** *Author*

timetable, and given the things that can go wrong, the performance is usually a little below what has been planned. Arguments have raged over whether timetable compilation is an art or a science; the consensus seems to be that it is a science, but one in which the art of the specialist gives the result the final polish.

The timetable is the written expression of the formal plan of action, which confirms what is being offered to the passenger and summarises what the organisation expects of its staff. It also indirectly commits the resources which are necessary to provide the service advertised. Before the timetable compilation is attempted, therefore, the volume and pattern of traffic must be known or assumed, and the resources available must be assessed.

The decision to revise a timetable may stem from a number of reasons as well as shifts in the pattern of demand sufficient to affect the service levels to be provided. Technical changes involving the trains, track layouts or signalling, and the availability of staff, are all matters to which the compiler may need to address his skills. A thorough knowledge of the physical characteristics of the line and the performance capability of rolling stock is also needed.

The journey time is the summation of the individual start-to-stop timings for the inter-station distances, with an addition for station dwell times. These need to be adjusted according to whether the period is the peak or

off-peak, or whether the stop is in the central area or the suburbs. Too long an allowance and the train has to wait time, which results in a slow and inefficient operation; too tight, and chronic unpunctuality quickly ensues. The number of trains required to operate the service is determined by taking the round trip time plus the layover at each terminus and dividing it by the service frequency.

In putting a timetable together, the requirements at the different times of the day need to be blended with each other. It is obviously undesirable to proceed directly from a 10min off-peak service to a peak frequency of perhaps 2min between trains. Given also differential running times, the trickiest part of the job is to achieve a gradual change in frequency without causing large service gaps.

RESOURCE COMMITMENTS

The Underground lines are unequal in their resource requirements. The accompanying table shows how many trains are needed to operate the maximum timetabled service, by line.

There is also a great difference in the service required at different times of the day. While the number of trains on the network drops during the mid-day period to 393, and also at weekends, the result is remarkably constant, at 387 trains during most of Saturday and 379 for the Sunday maximum.

The ability to supplement or reduce the service level depends on any physical constraints; in particular, this includes conflicting moves at junctions and waiting for platforms at termini. A basic principle is that trains should run at even intervals, but this always becomes difficult where lines diverge, as does for instance the Central at North Acton. It is perfectly possible to run trains in a ratio of two to one destination and one to the other, but not to do this and maintain even intervals throughout.

To these sorts of problems, which are repeated in one form or another all over railway systems, there are no perfect solutions. The difficulties, however, are those of mathematics rather than unresponsive or reluctant management. The best single answer, which is feasible only if the business so justifies, is to run an intensive service. One third of a 30-trains-per-hour service is still 10 trains per hour, or a train every 6min.

CONNECTIONS

Timetables also determine service connectional possibilities, and obvious problems arise if the services to be connected do not run at similar intervals. Sometimes it is only possible to make one set of connections; thus it may have to be decided if the Chesham shuttle from Chalfont & Latimer is sufficiently important for the whole of the Metropolitan main-line timetable to be constructed around connections into and out of both up and down trains at Chalfont.

The timetable also has to return the trains at the end of the day to where they will be wanted the following morning. This is not necessarily back to their starting points, since outbased trains stabling in sidings overnight have to return to depots for periodic routine examination. At intervals, they also require both internal and external cleaning.

Generally, operational control can be made more effective if services are self-contained between specific terminals where possible, such as running Arnos Grove-Rayners

Above: **The District and Central lines at Ealing Broadway can operate entirely independently, but there is a connection between them as seen to the right of the arriving train of D stock. This does give some flexibility, especially for engineers' trains. In the background of this 1982 view are three cars of withdrawn CO/CP stock. The Central Line service is provided by 1962 stock, right.** *Author*

Lane and Cockfosters–Heathrow on the Piccadilly Line. All trains, though, should pass common crew-change points.

The above summarises the main constraints and methods, but in addition special timetables need to be devised for sporting and other events. Junction working can produce parallel movements which do not interfere with each other, or conflicting ones which do. Trains on several lines can get themselves reversed as on the Northern Line's Kennington Loop, which can lead to stock marshalling difficulties. Uncoupling to run shorter trains during the off-peak is no longer practised, but when it was a feature of Underground operation a major practical difficulty was that, on splitting, there would be two trains but only one train crew.

NON-STOPPING OF TRAINS

'Non-stopping' of Underground services through lesser used stations used to be quite widespread practice. Nowadays it really exists only on the Metropolitan Line north of Finchley Road and on the Piccadilly west of Hammersmith. In both

Number of trains and Underground cars needed to provide timetabled morning-peak services, 2003

Line	Trains	Cars per Train	Car Total
Bakerloo	32	7	224
Central	72	8	576
Circle/Hammersmith & City	30	6	180
District (main)	67	6	402
District (Edgware Road–Wimbledon)	8	6	48
East London	6	4	24
Jubilee	47	6	282
Metropolitan	43	8	344
Metropolitan Chesham branch	1	4	4
Northern	90	6	540
Piccadilly	76	6	456
Victoria	37	8	296
Waterloo & City	4	4	16
Total	513		3,392

of these cases, the Underground takes on more of the attributes of a 'proper' railway.

The practice of more general non-stopping, which came to an end in the late 1950s, was discontinued because:

- it tended to confuse the public and, sometimes, the staff as well
- it made service regulation difficult, in that trains which were nominally 'non-stopping' were in practice often held up by the previous 'stopping' train
- service frequency at the stations omitted fell to an unacceptably low level in the evenings and on Sundays

Today, there are only some sections of line which close early, eg Woodford–Hainault at 20.00, and some stations which are closed at certain times, eg Cannon Street at weekends.

NORTHERN LINE PROBLEMS

The aborted Northern Line extensions, whatever problems they may have given to those who might have benefited, would certainly have caused major problems for the operators. The Northern would have become a complete railway in its own right, and the service provision correspondingly complex.

Today, the Northern has what might be called $2\frac{1}{2}$ termini at the northern end, two routes through central London via both Charing Cross and Bank, and one (only) south from Kennington. To run a frequent service from each of High Barnet, Mill Hill East and Edgware, via both in-town routes, and for them all to proceed to Morden, is just not possible. Compromises have to be made, and even then operating a reliable and regular service is far from easy. To give but one example, running *all* Edgware branch trains via Bank and *all* High Barnet and Mill Hill East trains via Charing Cross eliminates delays as a result of conflicting moves at the Camden Town junctions. On the other hand, it

Below: **Elephant & Castle Bakerloo Line platforms sported these 'Next Train' indicator, once common on much of the system. It was important to know from which platform the next train would depart, especially if one wanted a destination north of Queen's Park. A 1938-stock train arrives on 13 April 1983.** *Author*

also creates a lot of forced interchange for people who otherwise would have a through service.

COPING WITH GROWTH

Consider, then, the extra problems which the proposed extensions would have brought. In its 1938 proposals, the LPTB would have operated the services listed in the box on the right.

The operational difficulties are apparent, but coupled with them are the differential running times between the same points by different routes. Where they have a choice, passengers are likely to choose the quicker route, and the service pattern must try to cope with this.

This has a direct link into the service capacity which is needed and how its provision on each segment of line is determined. Ideally, trains should be full (but not over-full) at all times. This then leads on to what is meant by such terms, and is moving well outside the scope of this volume. However, the general principle is that the best use possible should be made of the available line capacity and that of the trains themselves.

But does that total capacity match the total demands placed upon it? If not, no amount of

service tinkering will overcome this. The best that can be achieved is going to be an uneasy compromise, and general dissatisfaction amongst the passengers. It is also true that using every last bit of resource, in the sense of 'can we squeeze another train in?' is also unwise. In such circumstances even the smallest delay due, for instance, to a train door sticking, will have a disproportionate effect on the operation. The challenge of operating the timetable must have a reasonable chance of success, day after day after day. Staff can and will make a special effort from time to time, but it is not reasonable to rely on this merely to operate the scheduled service.

DEPOT REQUIREMENTS

This leads also to the depot accommodation which was needed. The Northern Line has a history of amalgamation and expansion, and the push to the Northern Heights courtesy the LNER was further growth. More route kilometres meant more trains, and more trains means more maintenance depots and siding accommodation.

In this, the Northern was not well provided, with very cramped premises at Golders Green and a larger depot at Morden. But these on their own would not be adequate for the expanded service provision, and while lines forming part of the new empire such as the Northern City between Moorgate and Finsbury Park had premises at Drayton Park, these too had severe shortcomings.

Given the size of the Northern operation as intended, with 40% more route km than there are today, the construction of a large new depot was seen as essential. So far, so good, but what sites were available? Recent experience at Cockfosters, where the depot is as much as 1.35km long from end to end was a practical demonstration of the land take needed. The only available plot which met this and other requirements, including width, was that at Aldenham, at the far end of the proposed extension.

However, even this was less than ideal, for completely different reasons. Thus the High Barnet services – and all those to Moorgate via Finsbury Park – would not in the usual course of events come nearer Aldenham than Finchley Central, at best. This was no less than 9km distant, and thus implied a considerable degree

of expensive and essentially unproductive empty running when anything other than stabling in sidings was needed. But trains do require regular examination, with external and internal cleaning and other attention as necessary.

There are ways of making almost anything work, but this was not perhaps one of the best-thought-out plans.

STAFF TRAINING

Three million passengers daily entrust themselves to the care of the Underground, and the staff require training in their own tasks and

the work of the railway in general. In 1963, the railway training centre at White City was opened. Instruction covered the duties of operating apprentices, stationmen and stationwomen, booking clerks, station foremen and guards; all entrants to these grades received background and theoretical training in the school, with practical work at stations and on trains. To enable suitable staff to qualify as ticket collectors, guards, motormen, signalmen, station foremen and station supervisors, there were training courses, varying from four days for ticket collectors to 36 days for station supervisors. Special courses were organised also to train railway instructors, traffic controllers, divisional inspectors and other senior staff. The centre had 11 teaching staff.

The White City school was claimed to be the most comprehensively equipped railway training centre in the country, with an intake of 3,500 students each year. The facilities were designed so that practically all out of course incidents and failures could be reproduced. These

Below: **This picture of the tube-stock driver at work with his right hand on the 'dead man's handle' appears straightforward enough, but the print has in fact been doctored to provide a more acceptable view through the window! Quite what it might have shown originally is not known.** *IAL*

arrangements were aimed particularly at control grades, so that they could be set to unravel, practically, a number of difficult situations.

One room contained a full-size section of an Underground station, with running track, platform, tunnel entrance and various ancillary equipment. Incidents could thus be simulated, while the 'passengers' were kept informed by public address. A 600V traction supply was laid on, and a device to reproduce current arcing was installed. Elsewhere, there were working electro-pneumatic and Westinghouse brake mechanisms, and electrical control apparatus and automatic couplers. A cutaway 1938 stock tube car demonstrated the air-operated door mechanisms and the guard's panel, and also the Drico (Driver-Controller) communication equipment. Lift and escalators were not forgotten, while a fully fledged booking office was fitted with ticket issuing and change-giving machines. Role playing incidents were staged on the mock platform.

The White City school is now closed permanently and a smaller facility at Lillie Bridge has taken its place.

UNDERGROUND SPEEDS

The fastest section of the Underground is on the Metropolitan Line, which has signalling between Harrow and Amersham spaced on the assumption that steam-hauled vacuum-braked trains (with quite long braking distances) are still sharing the tracks. However, in the late 1980s, when the 96km/h A60/62 stock trains started to experience considerable mechanical troubles with their traction motors, an investigation was made to see how fast the trains were actually running. This showed that top speeds were normally reached by northbound trains passing under the North Circular Road bridge at Neasden, having come all the way downhill from the viaduct over the North London Line at Kilburn, at full power.

Unfortunately, a combination of deteriorating track condition and concern at the condition of the traction motor pinions and corresponding wear on the axles resulted in an 80km/h speed restriction being imposed. The problems have since been attended to, in the sense of:

● bogie rebuilds, with considerable portions renewed
● traction motors performance problems resolved
● gears and pinions renewed and the restoration to the original dimensions of the suspension sleeve, which was wearing out

It would thus be possible to restore higher speed operation over new track. This includes the trackbed, with the aim that once completed the track can be kept in a condition for high speed at an acceptable cost. Older track on limestone ballast tends to need a lot of attention to keep it sufficiently level to give a good ride at speed.

For test trains, the fastest section is down the hill from Chalfont & Latimer to Rickmansworth (passenger trains have the fun spoilt by the stop at Chorleywood). There are several reports of 130km/h being obtained on this section, the peak speed being reached as the train passes under the M25 bridge. Usually, such events are not formally recorded, as most Underground equipment is not really designed to go this fast.

On most lines, speeds are quite low, with very few trains hitting 80km/h even on the longer downhill station-to-station runs. With the higher performance trains now available, and providing the signalling allows, there are distinct possibilities. From the passengers' point of view the most noticeable feature will be the higher acceleration of the train out of stations, regardless of loading, and sustaining this high rate for much longer. This helps the running of a more frequent service in the peak, as trains will clear the platform significantly quicker.

This will speed up the service considerably, with at least a 10% reduction in the journey time. This is not wasteful of energy, since modern trains are considerably lighter than those they replace, and a regenerative brake dissipates the kinetic energy when slowing down, which may be used by other trains.

Resignalling is the key requirement, but there can be other factors. The Underground was never able to make use of the full performance potential of the District Line's R-stock trains, as they would merely catch up the Q or CO/CP stock train ahead of them. This is one of the limitations imposed by using more than one type of stock on any given line and is a feature of many of the surface-line operations.

SIGNALLING

Signalling is the means of enabling the railway to run frequent trains at speed on potentially conflicting courses but with safety of operation. The complexity of the signalling system is related to what is expected of it; thus the capacity of a line is dependent in part on the signal spacing, which determines the minimum gap between succeeding trains. As a safety back-up, additional devices come into play, should either the human element or mechanical defect intervene. The most important advance in safety was the adoption of automatic signalling, whereby each train alternately protects itself and clears the road behind by completing and breaking certain electrical circuits in its passage.

The traditional 'block' system with the 'blocks' being defined as the distances between the stations and with one train only allowed in each at any one time sufficed for a while with steam traction. Semaphore signals were quickly supplanted by colour lights (although the last semaphores used by Underground trains survived

Right: **Three-aspect semaphore signals were used on the Central Line in the 1920s and 1930s in an attempt to reduce headways; they are broadly the equivalent of multiple-aspect colour-light signalling as used widely today. One has survived in London's Transport Museum in working order, as shown in this sequence of pictures. The instructions are, respectively, Stop, Proceed and All-clear.** *Author (all)*

at Richmond BR until 1980), but early tunnel signals were operated electro-mechanically, having moving spectacles illuminated from behind with an oil lamp! Growing weights of traffic and electric traction required a more flexible approach to signalling which was not conditioned by the station spacing.

AUTOMATIC SIGNALLING

Automatic signalling is no new invention, since it was adopted by the Metropolitan and London Electric Railways in 1905 and 1907 respectively, and earlier still on some of the main-line railways. The system works as follows. The running rails are divided into lengths which are insulated from each other electrically. The signal

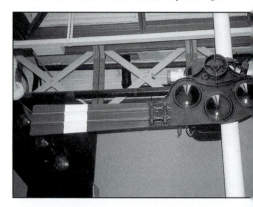

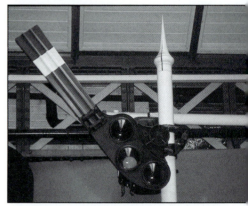

current passes along the rails on one side of a section of track, through a track relay, and then back through the rails on the other side. When current is flowing through the relay, its contacts are closed, and this completes the circuit for the control of the signal and causes it to show a proceed aspect.

When a train passes the starting signal and thus enters the track circuit section which the signal protects, the wheels and axles bridge the running rails and short circuit the signal current. This de-energises the signal relay which causes the signal to show a red aspect. When the train clears the track circuit section by passing another signal plus a further short section or overlap beyond that, the short circuit is removed. The signal relay is re-energised, and the normal green aspect of an automatic signal is restored, allowing the following train to proceed.

The length of the overlap is designed to be sufficient to enable a train travelling at maximum permitted speed to stop short of any obstruction using an emergency brake application. With several automatic sections between two signalboxes which retain non-automatic control as at junctions, trains can follow each other safely without further intervention. As all trains on the Underground system are now of multiple-unit stock, the variation of acceleration and braking characteristics as found on an all-purpose railway is missing, and the signalling can be specified and designed that much more precisely.

TRACK CIRCUITS

The track circuit depends upon the presence of a train to short circuit the running rails, but on little-used sidings or crossovers a build-up of rust could prevent this from happening. This is dealt with in two ways: 'rusty rail' workings are deliberately introduced into the working timetable so that as many lines as possible see a train during the normal course of events, and secondly a narrow wavy band of stainless steel is welded to the head of the rails. This ensures that rust does not prevent electrical continuity being maintained.

Should a driver ignore the signal aspects, a second line of protection is brought into play. The automatic train stop apparatus alongside the rails will apply the brakes, taking control out of the driver's hands. Normally, the arm on the train stop lies clear of the trains, but it is raised automatically by air pressure when the signal turns to a danger aspect. In this position, the arm position is pre-set to make contact with a trip cock on the train, and if contact is made the cock will open and release the compressed air supply in the train pipe and apply the brakes, causing the train to stop within the overlap distance. The raising of the train stop is detected by the preceding stop signal which will remain at danger until the fault is rectified; this 'fail safe' approach is always apparent in railway signalling matters, and it will be realised that a loss of current in the track circuiting device already described will always cause the signal to display a red aspect.

Above: **Crowd control can become a major preoccupation, even if the weather is fine and everybody is good-natured. Events such as this have to be anticipated (if the operator isn't told in advance), and they have to be managed. This view is of the outside of Colindale station, with passengers waiting to join their Northern Line trains home after an air show.** *Author's collection*

On the Underground system, two-aspect red/green signals are sufficient for most purposes; yellow is used as a repeater for a red aspect in advance where the sighting distance is limited. Exceptions include the sections where Underground and National Rail trains use the same tracks as happens north of Harrow-on-the-Hill, where four-aspect Network Rail signals provide additional braking distance.

Automatic signals cannot cope with junctions, and here semi-automatic signals are installed which have to be cleared each time for the route selected, although they will restore themselves to danger automatically after the train has passed. It follows that they normally display a red aspect. Usually, such signals can be set to full automatic operation when all trains are to take the same route. Junction signals will normally feature the 'lunar' lights, a series of three white lights placed at an angle above the signal head as a visual indication to the driver of the route setting. Lack of any indication indicates that the 'normal' route is set.

For slow-speed operation, the theatre-type indicator is used. This can display various numbers, each of which indicates a separate route, through the illumination of a pattern of light bulbs. It will usually be found above a ground or shunt signal controlling the entrance to sidings.

SPEED CONTROL

Signalling may also be used to control train speeds rather more directly than just displaying large numerals to denote speed restriction signs at the side of the track. A specific problem was the southbound run from East Finchley on the

Northern Line. From entering the tunnel, the gradient falls steadily at 2% (1 in 50) for the two miles to Archway station, outside which there is a sharp and therefore speed-restricted curve. Two timing points were therefore arranged on the section. The first controls a signal about 180m beyond it, which will not clear if the train exceeds 64km/h over the timing length. The second section controls a signal about 90m beyond it and 230m from the curve, which will not clear to any train exceeding 48km/h over the second length. In this way, the speed has been reduced so that the curve cannot be taken too fast, since if a speeding driver should attempt to do so, the automatic train stop will come into action.

Later refinements but with a similar end in mind have been applied to approach control systems, where the speed of an approaching train is assessed by the current it generates in coils situated with magnets under the rail. The detector now consists of a 3.7m length of dummy positive current rail adjacent to the home signal, with a stainless steel surface; beneath it are 12 permanent magnets and coils, in which a current is induced by the positive shoes of the train making contact with the inductor. This causes a small alternating current

a cost involved, and the standards must be consistent with the fulfilment of the basic *raison d'être* of the organisation. One issue that has raised its head several times is the procedure to be followed when a driver encounters a signal at red and which resolutely refuses to change to a proceed aspect. In order to keep the traffic moving, the stop-and-proceed rule was devised which, after a 1min interval, allows the driver to 'trip' past it and, after resetting the trip cock on the train, to proceed at a speed consistent with stopping short of any obstruction that he may encounter, or at the next signal.

The obstruction may be no more than a failed train stop which, as noted, will cause the signal

Left: **The headway clocks, whose hands revolved anti-clockwise, measured the time in minutes and seconds since the preceding train departed. This told the driver how much he was behind the train in front, and whether he should make as much speed as possible or hold back. It also recorded on paper the time each train departed.** *Real Photographs*

Below: **The Metropolitan always had to share tracks with the Great Central northwards along the main line from Harrow-on-the-Hill. Assuming compatibility problems are overcome, train regulators still have the problem that trains 'disappear' from their system while they are in the care of another party. Will they 'reappear' on time or 30 minutes late? The 14.38 Marylebone to Nottingham is seen near Chorleywood on 6 April 1963 behind 'Black Five' 4-6-0 No 44665.** *Gerald T. Robinson*

to be generated in the coil, its frequency proportional to the speed of the train. A related relay responding only to alternating current below a given frequency is connected, and only when the relay operates does the signal clear. Measurements correct to 0.8km/h are said to have been achieved, the advantage being that the detector makes constant checks as the decelerating train's pick-up shoes pass over the inductors. Speed control of this nature allows trains to enter platforms where the signalling would normally demand that they be detained in the running tunnels as, of course, the time taken in the platforms will allow the next train in front to proceed further.

Another application is in the approach to dead-end platform tunnels underground, following the disastrous accident at Moorgate in 1975. Here, for reasons never fully established, the driver of the train failed to stop in the platform. Instead, he carried on and the train hit the end of the tunnel with the loss of 42 lives.

It is always easy to be wise after the event, and railway safety has had a century and a half in which to develop. This has led to rail becoming one of the safest forms of transport available, since the whole operation takes place in a strictly controlled environment.

STOP AND PROCEED

One must never lose sight of the purpose of the railway, which in the case of the Underground is mass movement. Safety is important, but there is

behind to remain at red. However, it may be a failed train, in which case the normal procedure would be to push it until such time as it can be diverted to siding or depot. So far, so good, and any other arrangement would be far more disruptive.

Nevertheless, the safety of this operation depends upon the driver of the second train continuing with care and attention to what he is doing. On 8 April 1953, this did not happen. A damaged train stop caused a signal between Stratford and Leyton on the Central Line to display a permanent red aspect. Eleven trains passed the signal according to the rules; the twelfth was in the process of doing so when it was struck heavily in the rear. The Inspecting Officer commented on the damage, 'which greatly exceeded that ever experienced in any previous damage to tube stock. The leading driving cab of the first car (of the rear train) was wrecked and the headstock was forced down with such violence that the whole end of the car was lifted and became jammed between the track and the roof of the tube, buckling itself in the process.

'This had two results – first, the whole of the energy of the train was dissipated at that point instead of some, at least, being expended on pushing (the preceding) train further forwards; and secondly, the lifting of the front end caused the rear end to be lowered, enabling the buffer of the second car to ride over that of the first car and to telescope into it for a distance of 1.8m.' The accident took place during the rush hour and was, at that time, the only really serious accident in the history of the Underground. It resulted in 12 deaths, with the cause being a lack of care, or misjudgement by the driver.

There have been a number of other accidents from the same basic cause, both before and since, but none with such devastating results. In the last analysis, no safety device can replace the skill and vigilance of the staff.

TUBE AND SURFACE STOCK

The railwayman deserves all the help he can get, and an anticipated hazard concerned the two major types of rolling stock. Those for surface and tube operation respectively have totally different cross-sections, and the extensions of the 1930s and the years following brought with them increased opportunities for both types to share the same tracks. Sometimes, this sharing also encompassed the main-line railways, whose goods trains continued to run long after the passenger services had been ceded to London Transport. The risk thus arose of a surface or main-line train being diverted in error towards a tube tunnel of 3.65m diameter, against which the signalling would not provide protection. The solution was first to detect surface trains and then to stop them.

The method chosen was to suspend a series of three mercury-filled glass tubes from an overhead gantry, clear of tube stock but obstructing larger trains. Breakage of the tubes returned the signals in advance to danger, with their associated trip-

Above: **Bus services replacing trains, even if only temporary, need supervision and signing. This display could be found outside Leytonstone station in June 2003.** *Author*

cock mechanisms. The first installation was at Hammersmith in 1932, to prevent District Line trains entering the eastbound Piccadilly Line tunnels at Barons Court. Other detection methods have also been used.

On the Central Line eastward extensions it was necessary to distinguish between electric tube trains and BR services. Electric trains were required to 'prove' their presence through the pick-up shoes making contact with a length of specially installed conductor rail on the opposite side of the track to the positive rail. Traditionally, each junction location was controlled by its own signalbox, featuring a miniature lever frame. This mirrored main-line practice, with each lever controlling a separate set of points or a signal. The first was installed at the present Acton Town station in 1905, and the following describes the Aldgate 'box, which controlled the triple triangular junction at the eastern extremity of the Circle Line.

ALDGATE 'BOX

'In the cabin a long power frame of miniature levers is worked by signalmen who handle at peak periods as many as 120 trains per hour.

'Above the frame an illuminated diagram gives a picture of the various tracks and the position of trains moving over them. Trains are advised to the cabin on a train describer panel, and are described on a transmitter as they are dispatched away from the controlled area. Signalmen receive trains by "pulling off" a signal after setting the road where necessary. These signals are of the semi-automatic type, and are restored to danger by the passage of the trains past them. The signal cannot clear again until the signalman has restored his lever to normal and "restroked", or reversed it. The levers have both electrical and mechanical locking as safeguards against irregular movement.

'Back-locking relay apparatus prevents a signalman from inadvertently replacing a lever and resetting a road once a train has accepted the signal, and mechanical locks block the movement of any lever, other than the one pulled, that could set up a conflicting movement. Below the cabin is a room housing 266 relays in glass-fronted covers to protect them from dust and damp. More than 85km of wire was needed to complete the circuiting in this room when the equipment was installed.'

The first change was to consolidate the movement of a number of levers, so that each performed a series of functions and set up an entire route. Local control remained possible, through the expedient of switching the box back into the system. Next, remote control of the levers from an adjacent location by push-button was introduced, using compressed air to activate them. Push-buttons conferred a number of advantages, not the least of which was that the signalman could remain seated. Routes no longer needed to be reset after use, and it became possible to pre-select the following route which was required and which would then be set up automatically. The status of each route, whether it was clear, pre-selected or at danger, was shown by panel lights. The first of these installations was commissioned at Ealing Broadway in 1952.

Hitherto, the signalman had initiated the movements, albeit over a wide area; the next step was to use the trains themselves through the working timetable to set up their own routes. At simple facing junctions, the automatic train describers can be used to control the junction points; at trailing junctions, signals can be arranged to pass trains on a first-come first-served basis.

PROGRAMME MACHINES

In 1955 the first programme machine or 'pianola' was installed experimentally at the complex Camden Town junctions on the Northern Line. This contemporary description nowadays reads like a combination of a primeval computer and the music rolls used by steam-driven fairground organs! But this is not to mock the real advance which the development represented:

'The programme machine carries a plastic roll about 8ft [2.4m] long and 8in [0.24m] wide, on which is recorded the day's train service in terms of the train time, the reporting numbers, and their destination. Each entry is in the form of punched holes in the roll which forms a unique code. Feeler arms on the machine press against the roll, and as the roll advances the holes come into position and make various contacts.

'These are sufficient to initiate the setting up of the route for each train. As each train proceeds, the programme machine roll is automatically stepped to the next entry. Checks ensure that the train being described is that which should be approaching according to the timetable, in which case the route will be set at the correct time. (This could involve the much troubled "Positive Train Identification" system, whereby each train confirmed its identity automatically.) If a train is late by more than a pre-set time, the machine may "ask" for a supervisor to decide on the course of action or, if trains arrive at a converging junction out of order, the machine may automatically step forward to deal with the train that has arrived first, storing the route details in its memory until the missing train arrives.

It should perhaps be noted that the programme machines did not directly operate points and signals, which was carried out as previously. There was thus no safety connotation. The machine took the place of the signalman in his decision as to what action to initiate next.'

COMPUTERISATION

The inevitable move into computerisation of such tasks is proceeding concurrently with resignalling schemes. The first use of computers was for track circuits, and allowed the elimination of the insulation joints in running rails. These could be replaced by impedance bonds, the track circuit being tuned to a particular computer detector. Trials began with electronic versions of the programme machine at Watford in the 1970s, subsequent installations covering Heathrow and the northern part of the Piccadilly Line. The Metropolitan and Jubilee lines followed.

With increasing sophistication, the need for signalmen to be able to identify trains on sight disappeared. Consequently, the headcode was also phased out, and from the 1959 tube stock build onwards, marker or headlights only were carried. Underground codes were related to destinations, and the juxtaposition of which out of three, four or five lights (according to type of stock) formed the code. The Metropolitan's electric locomotives had three locations only.

Early headcodes were provided by positioning oil lamps, an anachronism on an electrified railway. Amazingly, though, oil tail lamps continued to be carried by the CO/CP and R stocks into the 1980s, as only one fuse was fitted to the electric tail lamps.

CONTROL OFFICES

Although signalling was originally carried out locally, centralisation has gradually concentrated the task into the hands of train regulators in single locations. But regulators, signalmen and programme machines alike require supervision from some kind of control organisation which is in a position to take a broader view of what is happening on the network.

Control offices can be traced back to the early days of the District Railway, when the telegraph office at Earl's Court was notified of breakdowns and failures, following which orders were issued to maintenance chargehands standing by at various key points. Signal fitters at Aldgate East, electrical linesmen at Victoria, and locomotive

foremen could thus be summoned to deal with any emergency, whilst a chief inspector stationed at Earl's Court was responsible for train working throughout the District system.

Complex track layouts may offer some flexibility, but in general they are a curse on the operators. The 'keep it simple' school of thought, based on the maxim that the more there is to go right, the more there is to go wrong, has something to commend it. With a high degree of service interaction, even a quite trivial delay at one location can have consequential effects out of all proportion to its inherent significance. The problems are clearly worse when lines are being run at or near their capacity.

The example of Earl's Court on the surface lines shows some of the problems. In the peak hour, the westbound District Line at Earl's Court has to deal with services from Embankment in the east and High Street Kensington in the north, bound for four separate destinations west of the station. In addition, there is a need to mesh in with the Circle Line services in both directions. Most of the junctions are grade separated and there are two westbound platforms available at Earl's Court itself as well as two terminal platforms at High Street Kensington. Nevertheless, given also the

Below: **Southgate station on the Piccadilly Line incorporates a bus station, as seen here. This is another Holden station; internally, it is one of the few that retain uplighters on the escalators.** *Author*

Above: **Leaving Surrey Quays is a northbound A-stock train for Shoreditch in June 2003; in the background is the mouth of the tunnel which will take it to Canada Water.** *Author*

Right: **The 'Press to Open' button and the 'Keep Clear' notices were part of the 1938 tube stock, although passenger-opening doors have had at best a chequered history. The driver has over-riding controls anyway, and it is rare for them not to be used. The problem is the fumble factor; any slowness by passengers increases the stop time delays.** *Author*

interfaces elsewhere with the Hammersmith & City and the Metropolitan lines, the huge scope for out-of-course running is apparent.

'NO DRIVER AVAILABLE'

Problems which fall to the controllers to deal with include those which local management has been unable to resolve, such as no driver being available to take over a train when it arrives at a crew changeover point. This can be doubly disruptive to the operation, since there is not only a potential gap in the service but also a train without a driver holding up the system. Other commonplace events include train, signal and track failures, or actions by passengers or staff. The job of the controllers, who are organised on a line basis, is to keep an eye on all that is happening, and to anticipate and to minimise the effects of unwanted events on the train service. The principle is that of intervention when needed; if everything is running perfectly, the controller has nothing to do.

To undertake the control task effectively, a flow of incoming information is required, together with an intimate knowledge of the track layout, rolling stock characteristics, station facilities, the timetable and traction and other current supplies. The objective is to minimise the causes of delay and to contain such delays as cannot be prevented to the smallest possible geographical area.

In the event of disruption, the controller has to decide on the appropriate action. This may include turning trains short of destination, ensuring train crews are available, reducing the service interval, organising a replacement bus service, calling out engineering staff and, of course, restoring the service to normal. The controller has an information assistant who can use the selective public address facility to inform passengers of operational problems, whether they be irregular running or the non-availability of lifts at a particular station. It has to be said that such public announcements are not always audible, and often seem to be largely irrelevant.

At all times, the safety of staff and passengers alike must take top priority. For major incidents, the line controller can turn to the Headquarters Controller, who would normally summon the public emergency services.

COMMUNICATION EQUIPMENT

Effective control depends upon effective communication, and the traditional telephone, useful as it is, has serious drawbacks — notably that it cannot be used to or from a moving train. Along the walls of all tunnel sections may be seen two bare copper wires. Their primary function is to discharge the traction current, which is carried out by pinching the two wires together to make contact. This is essentially an emergency measure, to counteract any fusing or arcing which may arise.

Right from the earliest days of tube railways, drivers were also provided with a telephone which could be clipped to the wires, which has the same discharging effect. It also enables the driver to talk to the substation control room and pass messages through those staff to the line controller. Unless instructed otherwise, the traction current will be reconnected by the substation control after a short interval. This can be overridden by the driver in emergency, and always if passengers are to be detrained and walked to a station, by placing short circuiting bars on the rails.

Detraining is to be avoided if at all possible, as it can take a long time for passengers to be led through the entire train and out through one of the cab doors and then along the track to the nearest means of exit. At the very least, there are likely to be some bills presented for dry-cleaning! Tunnel emergency lighting is automatically switched on.

Such communication is really for emergency use only, and the Drico system dating from the 1950s allowed direct speech communication through speakers in the cab and the control room. Contact was made through attachment to the same tunnel wires; again the train had to be stationary, and there was no facility for control to call the driver.

For the Victoria Line, which was built for automatic train operation (ATO), carrier-wave contact through the conductor rails was used to transmit messages between the driver and the regulator. Although this system could be used while the train was in motion, it suffered from interference and could not be used if short circuiting devices had been put down after the current had been discharged. It was thus likely to be useless in the event of a real emergency when communications were most needed. The 1967 Victoria Line stock was the first to be built with a public address facility.

With driver-only operation (DOO) in mind, train radio was developed to overcome this rather unsatisfactory state of affairs. Train radio allows communication while the train is moving, unlike the previous cumbersome system which required the driver to stop and attach the telephone handset. Priority has been given to train radio since it benefits the whole operation of the railway, and a high premium is attached to its reliability, providing as it does the front line communication between train and control.

Train radio is operated by means of a continuous leaky-feeder cable through the running tunnels, transmitting to and receiving from fixed on-train equipment. Radio also allows contact with supervisory and management staff, who are out and about on the system. Station staff also benefit, and principal tunnel stations now have radio contact with the surface. These personal sets are effective on trains or immediately adjacent to the track. Initially, development was hampered by the allocation of an insufficient number of radio frequencies.

The provision of direct contact at all times is one of the prerequisites for driver-only operation. STORNO train radio is fitted to all DOO trains, and this allowed the Drico equipment to be discarded.

Below: **To be successful, one-person operation needs the driver to be able to see back along the whole length of the train. Mirrors are one method, and CCTV another. More recently, CCTV monitors have been mounted in the cab rather than at platform ends. Here, the cab view using a mirror on an eastbound train at Royal Oak on 24 May 1984 shows how good the definition can be.** *Author*

CHAPTER NINE

Engineering the System

Without the engineering function, there could be no Underground. This chapter takes a look at some of the many areas in which the engineers contribute to the operation of the system.

The term 'asset' is considered to encompass whole systems, sub-systems and components. 'Infrastructure assets' encompass fixed track, signalling, electrification, plant and telecommunications equipment and structures. 'Mobile assets' cover the trains and other powered rail vehicles.

There are 394 route km served by Underground trains, of which 32km are in 'cut and cover' tunnels, 142km are in tube tunnels, and 220km are in the open. In 1971/2 distances were officially re-measured in kilometres; while the location of the zero point for the system is really academic, the choice of the now defunct Ongar sand drag for this honour seemed a little quaint.

On an electrified railway, there are two main interfaces:

- wheel – rail
- third/fourth rail – shoegear

Both of them need to work if the train is to go; otherwise it doesn't, and that is an important contractual matter as well as highly exasperating for all concerned.

PERMANENT WAY

The track and its support is the literal foundation of the railway: it has to be strong and resilient enough to withstand the weight, speed and frequency of rail traffic to be run upon it. It must also be sufficiently stable to offset the worst that climate and weather can do, and needs to wear well and minimise the requirements for maintenance and, ultimately, renewal. For the sake of good relations with the surrounding property owners, it must also offer reasonably unobtrusive running, particularly in terms of the noise generated.

The purpose of the running rails themselves is to act as hard and unyielding surfaces on which steel wheels may run, without causing abrasion or rutting to either. They also act as beams to transmit the weight of the train to the sleepers, and to interact with the wheel tread and flange to guide the direction of the train.

For many years the standard running rail on the Underground system was of 47kg/m bull-headed section in 18.3m lengths, secured by oak or steel keys to chairs in which the rail was seated, which were coach-screwed to the sleepers.

Early days saw much experience being gained the hard way. On the Bakerloo, it was decided to

'The definition of good engineering is achieving more with less; the emphasis is on getting the most out of what we have.'

Andrew McNaughton, President, Permanent Way Institution, 2003

Above: **The Underground's battery locomotives are fitted with driving positions at both ends and are constructed to tube gauge. Battery operation is necessary only when the traction current is switched off. No L18 heads an engineers' train consisting of flat wagons and personnel carriers out of Lillie Bridge during August 1978.** *Author*

lower the rails into the tunnels down vertical shafts, turning them at the bottom to reach the trackbed. This meant that 11m was the longest rail length that could be accommodated. The Central London Railway opted for 45-tonne locomotives to haul their trains. These 28 machines were built by the General Electric Company of America, and were of the double-bogie type, with a centrally placed cab and sloping front and rear ends.

They were quickly blamed for vibration in the properties above. Investigation narrowed the problem down to a relatively flimsy track construction combined with a high proportion of unsprung locomotive weight. Rebuilding of the locomotives reduced the nuisance, but the solution was the adoption of multiple-unit operation. Recommendations which followed from this incident included enlarged tunnel

clearances in future construction, and deeper rail sections to give added stiffness.

The corrugation of running rails was also discovered as a source of noise nuisance for passengers, and this 'roaring rails' phenomenon can still be found occasionally. Part of the solution in this case was the introduction of regular rail grinding to restore the rail profile to a smooth surface. In any event, Underground travel tends to be noisy for passengers as the tunnels reflect the noise back into the train.

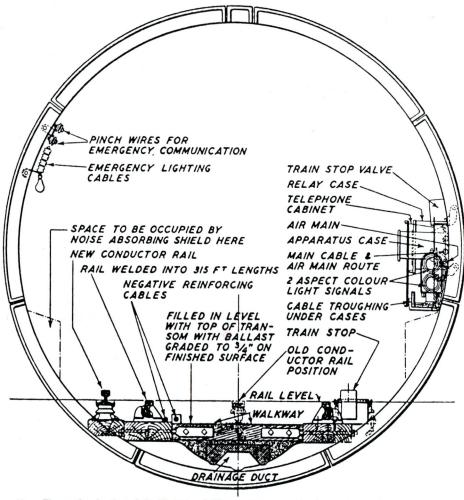

PINCH WIRES FOR
EMERGENCY, COMMUNICATION

EMERGENCY LIGHTING
CABLES

SPACE TO BE OCCUPIED BY
NOISE ABSORBING SHIELD HERE

NEW CONDUCTOR RAIL

RAIL WELDED INTO 315 FT LENGTHS

NEGATIVE REINFORCING
CABLES

FILLED IN LEVEL
WITH TOP OF TRAN-
SOM WITH BALLAST
GRADED TO ¾" ON
FINISHED SURFACE

TRAIN STOP VALVE
RELAY CASE
TELEPHONE
CABINET
AIR MAIN
APPARATUS CASE
MAIN CABLE &
AIR MAIN ROUTE
2 ASPECT COLOUR
LIGHT SIGNALS
CABLE TROUGHING
UNDER CASES
TRAIN STOP
OLD COND-
UCTOR RAIL
POSITION

RAIL LEVEL

WALKWAY

DRAINAGE DUCT

Above: **The modernisation of the Waterloo & City Railway in conjunction with new rolling stock was a major Southern Railway project. This 1940 diagram shows the main infrastructure work. There were of course also new trains, the second of only three types which the line has had since it opened in 1898.** *Author's collection*

Right: **The 'throw' of rolling stock as it traverses curves or, as seen here, pointwork, is amply demonstrated by the platform edge at Parsons Green on 17 February 1981. A D-stock train for Wimbledon is arriving. The close-fitting platform on this otherwise straight piece of track will minimise the stepping gap to the train, but problems like this have to be dealt with, and there isn't much choice as to the action taken.** *Author*

Experimental use of asbestos sprayed on tunnel walls in the 1930s did work. Thankfully, it was found too costly for general adoption, since it had to be expensively removed in recent years for health reasons. Relief was eventually forthcoming by the installation of sound-absorbent screens at below-car-body level, and the introduction of rail welding to reduce the number of joints. Eventually, track construction and electrification systems were standardised.

SLEEPERS

Wooden sleepers have many attributes, among them the relative ease of handling compared with the heavy concrete variety. Jarrah wood, a costly hardwood imported from Australia was universally used in tunnel sections, with sleeper ends held in concrete to prevent track

movement. Track 'creep' could, if not prevented, lead to clearances between trains and tunnels being fouled. In the open sections, creosoted fir or similar wood sleepers at rather closer intervals was the standard.

The weakest part of the rail is at the joint with the adjoining rail, and this is always supported by closer spacing of the sleepers. However, rails become worn and are subject to

cracking at joints, and moves were made to extend rail lengths. Standard rails are welded into 91m lengths at the permanent-way depot and transported to site on trains of bogie bolster wagons. Once on site, the wagons are withdrawn and longer lengths are then welded together. Constraints to the process include the allowance needed for rail expansion (of little import in the tunnels as the temperature remains fairly constant), and the insulating joints giving electrical separation within each running rail, required for signalling purposes. For the rails themselves, flat-bottom section is now standard.

Much of the trackwork now needs thorough renewal from the foundations upwards. Track fires in tunnels need to be eliminated, and involve more people than just the Civil Engineer. Work under consideration includes:

- screeding all ballast
- use of non-flammable rail lubricants
- eliminating the hydraulic handbrake on trains and its propensity to drip oil
- train-mounted transponders to detect conductor rail gaps and cut the current without sparking
- thermo-energy cameras on trains to measure temperature changes
- perhaps in the long term laying fibre-optic cables in the tunnels able to detect to the nearest metre local rises in temperature of 2°C.

TRACK GEOMETRY

What is permissible in terms of track geometry will affect the speeds attainable and the type of rolling stock which can be run; furthermore, it is the most restrictive of the curves or junction layouts on a railway which is the determining factor. One of the advantages of a light rail system is its greater ability to accept these constraints, but for the Underground a maximum gradient of 3.3% (1 in 30), and curves

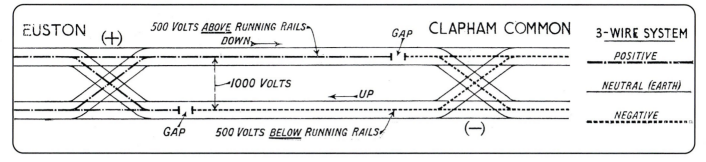

EUSTON (+)   500 VOLTS _ABOVE_ RUNNING RAILS.
              DOWN →   GAP   CLAPHAM COMMON   3-WIRE SYSTEM
                                                                       POSITIVE ▬ ▬ ▬
              ┌1000 VOLTS   ← UP   NEUTRAL (EARTH) ────
                                                                       NEGATIVE ∙∙∙∙∙∙∙
       GAP   500 VOLTS _BELOW_ RUNNING RAILS.   (−)

Above: **The three-wire electrification system used on the City & South London Railway between Euston and Clapham Common.** The Railway Handbook, *1943-44 / Author's collection*

of not less than 400m radius are desirable. At junctions, curvature is eased as far as possible, but space constraints in older tunnels frequently result in less than ideal situations. In any event, trains need to clear junctions as quickly as possible to keep the throughput of traffic moving, and in this sense 'clearance' is what the signalling system will accept.

Points and crossings all receive heavy wear, as the wheels passing over them deliver a series of blows. The tougher manganese steel is used in busier locations, since its use is justified not only by the capital cost but also by the disruption caused by replacement or by welding repairs. Wearing of all rails, particularly on sharp curves, may also be eased by the use of rail lubricators which use the wheels of passing trains to spread a film of grease for distances of up to half a mile.

Points are operated by compressed air. Movements actuated by the signalling apparatus complete a number of electrical circuits, one of which opens a valve to admit compressed air to the cylinder of an air engine placed alongside the points, and the ensuing thrust of the piston moves the point blades across. This gives rise to the characteristic 'hiss – crash' which can be observed when points are changed. Air supplies are contained in the piping which is present on the walls of all running tunnels. Facing points, that is where the approaching train has the choice of route, must be locked in position to prevent their movement during the passage of the train. Those which are always trailing to the direction of traffic may be unworked, with the blades being pushed across by the leading wheels. Some electrically operated points are now being installed.

NOVEL ELECTRIFICATION SYSTEM

As a rule, live rails on which shoes run have their surfaces above that of the running rails. On the City & South London Railway of 1890, however, the third rail was below, and on the Waterloo & City it was at the same level. This was done to get as much clearance as possible below the underframes, which came down rather low and no more so than on the C&SLR locomotives. Where turnouts existed, wood inclines were inserted and the live rail broken off a distance back, so that the shoes were carried up and over where running rails crossed. In the first scissors crossover at Stockwell, movable conducting bridges were worked from the signalbox and interlocked to provide a continuous path.

The C&SLR used a third-rail system from its opening in 1890. The third rail, carrying a

potential of 500V dc, was laid *between* the running rails, 305mm from one of them and offset to one side to keep the pick-up shoes clear of the couplings. The return current used the train wheels and the running rails.

The City & South London Railway was thus operated on the straight third-rail system, with the third rail fed directly from the Stockwell power house. With the 1900 extensions, a new power station was built and the line converted to the three-wire method of working. With this, the third rail on the southbound track was positive and that on the northbound was negative. At 500V dc, there was thus 1,000V difference between them, with the running rails forming a neutral intermediate point and being earthed.

Current passed through the trains in one direction on the southbound line (third rail to running rails) and in the reverse direction on the northbound (running rails to third rail). To avoid complications at the scissors crossovers at each of the two terminals, Euston and Clapham Common, each of these was arranged wholly on one side of the system (that on which trains would depart). This is shown in the diagram above.

Before a train reached the home signals at a terminal, it went over a gap longer than the locomotive, breaking the traction supply to it. As it passed from one polarity to the other, the lights went out for a brief interval.

The transmission system to the substations was on the five-wire principle, with 2,000V across the outlets. The substations also included large accumulator batteries, which were especially useful during emergencies; the whole installation was unique in tube railway engineering.

The Central London Railway adopted a true centre-third-rail system 10 years later, while the Great Northern & City went for a four-rail system, but with the two current rails outside the running rails, one on each side.

STANDARD FOURTH RAIL

In 1898 the Metropolitan Railway decided at last that it would electrify its lines, after 35 years of steam operation underground. The means by which the choice of system was made has been related; here it is necessary only to record that the use of the fourth-rail system reduces electro-

Below: **This view of the Jubilee Line north of West Ham shows the curious manœuvres necessary to accommodate this and the former Great Eastern North Woolwich line, right. Both are electrified, one fourth-rail, the other third – although this is now disconnected from the third-rail Southern network!** *Author*

magnetic interference and stray currents, and the ability of the latter to corrode pipes and cables.

The arrangement placed the positive rail outside the running rails, usually on the far side from the platform face in stations to minimise the risk of accidents from people falling on the track. The return rail is located centrally between the running rails. All the other underground lines were either built or later converted to this standard, although on the CLR (today's Central Line), the changes in curvature in the tunnels still require a limited repositioning of the positive rail to maintain clearances.

North of Queen's Park on the Bakerloo Line and on the Richmond and Wimbledon branches of the District, Underground trains run over lines electrified on the third-rail principle. The fourth rail here is effectively a dummy, provided to accommodate the shoes of Underground trains. It is bonded to the running rails, through which the current is returned via the wheels and axles of third-rail National Rail trains. The Bakerloo was built with the polarity of the conductor rails reversed; this was altered when the line was extended.

A disadvantage of using relatively low-voltage dc traction current is the need for frequent substations by the lineside. The heavy currents involved and the cost of equipment were among the reasons that British Railways eventually adopted ac overhead traction supplies in the 1950s, but clearances in any case would have been insufficient in the Underground tunnels. One wonders how Messrs Ganz would have fared if given the chance!

Appendix IV summarises the electrification systems.

CONDUCTOR RAILS

The function of the conductor rail is to enable the moving train to collect traction current which is generated in a fixed substation. On the train, it is fed to the traction motors via the control system.

Top-side-contact conductor rails as used on the Underground were of 64.5kg/m rectangular section in tube tunnels, and 74.4kg/m flat-bottomed section elsewhere. They are made from low-carbon steel. The outer conductor rail carries the positive traction current and will be found on the side furthest from the station platform wherever possible; the centre conductor is the return. Both are, of necessity, supported on insulators. Potentially, aluminium conductor rails offer lower electrical resistance and hence less waste of power.

The fourth-rail system is not without its problems; old tunnels can be wet, in which case they are likely to deposit muck on the conductor rail from above. Ice is also a well-known problem; when the temperature hovers around freezing, it produces freezing fog and arcing. The difficulty with oil-based de-icing fluids is that they cause rail damage and reduce conductivity; oil is poor at transferring current and causes arcing. It is electrical wear, rather than mechanical wear, which is the primary difficulty.

Arcs can also be caused by gaps in the conductor rail, as at pointwork. They result in damage to both the pick-up shoe and the rail. Who pays for the damage? Are good rails being wrecked by the shoegear, or *vice versa*?

Despite the above, in the event, the fourth-rail dc system has worked superbly well. Its only real operational vices for urban applications are the susceptibility to frost and snow, and the potential safety hazard.

LILLIE BRIDGE AND RUISLIP

Track maintenance nowadays is highly mechanised, and the main depot for the whole of the Underground system is at Lillie Bridge, west of Earl's Court. Despite space limitations, it is well situated at the geographical centre of the system which minimises the valuable time taken to run works trains in non-traffic hours, though it is no longer connected to the Network Rail system via the West London line. Appendix III gives details of the connections available.

Recent remodelling of the premises has provided a new points and crossings workshop, a new railway track layout to separate road and rail movements in the depot, the rationalisation of storage facilities and the installation of a new maintenance area for battery locomotives. Part of the depot has been covered by an elevated raft supporting a new exhibition hall for Earl's Court.

Rail welding is carried out at Ruislip. Flash-butt welding consists of placing the rail butts, or ends, together and passing high-tension current through them. The rails are drawn apart slightly during the operation to create an arc, and when this has been done a few times the butts become so hot and soft that when pressed tightly together they fuse into one.

Below: **At Ruislip, a green-livered 1962-stock vehicle is being lifted on 15 March 1997; it is for use on engineering duties, having been withdrawn from passenger service.** *Author*

TRACK MACHINES AND CRANAGE

A fleet of wagons for track maintenance purposes is retained. These include ballast hoppers and flat wagons for carrying pre-assembled sections of track. Of interest are the specialist vehicles, which includes four cranes. The movement of a crane to any part of the Underground system imposes severe limitations upon design if it is to negotiate tube tunnels successfully.

The limitation was overcome in 1955 when two Taylor Hubbard cranes, each weighing 36.5 tonnes, were put into service. Previously, over 160km of Underground open track could be reached only by long detours or not at all. The cranes had to be capable of slewing a complete revolution and to have a tail radius which would effectively clear cable posts and platforms with the minimum of obstruction to traffic on parallel tracks when working. They also had to operate within tube gauge, while axle loading was not allowed to exceed 12 tonnes. This required some design ingenuity, particularly in the articulation of the foot of the jib, which is necessary to negotiate curves in tube tunnels. The articulation is automatic when the jib is lowered on to the jib carrying wagon, and the re-engagement of the foot of the jib when raised for use is also fully automatic.

A five-car tunnel cleaning train was built at Acton in the 1970s, and acts as a giant vacuum cleaner in tube tunnels during non-traffic hours.

A fleet of tamping and lining machines from the Austrian firm of Plasser & Theurer carries out by machine tasks that a few years ago were left to careful observation and measurement followed by hard physical work. To find out where this work is most needed, a new Track Recording Train entered service in 1987. It consists of an instrumented 1973 stock trailer, specially modified by British Rail at Derby, between two 1960 stock pilot cars. Other pilot

cars for ballast trains and moving trains or parts of trains around the system other than under their own power are formed from old passenger driving motor cars.

TRACTION FOR HAULAGE

Traction for engineers' trains was provided by the fleet of retained steam locomotives after passenger train haulage passed to the LNER in 1937. These locomotives eventually wore out, and it was curious that just as the British Railways publicity machine was being cranked into action to extol the advantages of modern types of traction, Britain's most completely electrified system should issue a confession of faith in steam, albeit for very specialised purposes only.

In 1957 the Underground acquired Western Region pannier tanks Nos 7711 and 5752, renumbered them L90 and L91, painted them in lined maroon livery and set them to work on miscellaneous duties. According to London Transport, the minimal use to which the locomotives were put meant that retention of steam was a viable proposition. Battery locomotives were considered, but their cost and the practice of working them in tandem told against them. So, replacement with WR surplus steam was proceeded with until a maximum of 11 pannier tanks was in service. They were finally withdrawn in 1971, being replaced by three Sentinel diesels (themselves now defunct) and more battery locomotives…

Above: **The Great Western provided both the first and the last locomotives for the Metropolitan. The fleet of 0-6-0PTs acquired by London Transport extended to 13 locomotives, although not all at the same time. No L89 was built at Swindon as GWR No 5775 in 1929, and went to LT in 1963. It was retired from LT service in 1970, when it was sold to the Keighley & Worth Valley Railway. It is seen here in London Transport livery at Kensington Goods, BR, on 2 July 1969.** *D. A. Idle*

Right: **The battery locomotives came from several builders; this batch of seven was from Pickering of Wishaw, but with the equipment supplied by other builders.** *Railway Gazette, 20 July 1956/Author's collection*

Most haulage around the system is now provided by the battery locomotive fleet, usually placed one at each end of their trains to speed reversal. All are of 'tube' loading gauge to enable them to pass anywhere without restraint, and have variable height drawgear to suit both 'tube' and 'surface' stock coupling heights. Wherever possible they operate on current obtained from the conductor rail, during which time the batteries (on the more modern locomotives) are recharged in readiness for use where no live supply exists. Charging time is about 1hr for each hour of discharge. A fleet of 32 such locomotives is seen as about right; built by various manufacturers over the last 50 years, they cost about £2.5 million each.

In some years, winter weather precautions are hardly needed. Sleet locomotives were used to help in solving the current collection problems during winter weather by the use of antifreeze solution, liquid sprayers and wire brushes on the conductor rails. Electrically operated pneumatic control actuated the valves controlling the de-icing fluid, and the cylinders which lowered the

Above: **From the engineering fleet, battery locomotive No L25, a 1965 build by Metro-Cammell, newly turned out in yellow livery and seen at Ruislip in 2000.** *Author*

brushes and ice-cutting rollers to the rails. These locomotives were built out of redundant CLR motor cars of 1903 vintage, but have now been replaced by equipment on a number of passenger cars. Night-time heating of conductor rails was tried as a frost precaution; the method used was to short circuit the negative and positive rails so that their resistance to the 600V dc traction current being passed through them raised the rail temperature and melted any snow or ice. This method could only be used out of traffic hours, but once trains started to run, their passage was usually enough to keep the current rails clear. In 1963, 27km of track on rising gradients on the Metropolitan, Piccadilly and Central lines were being treated thus.

AUTUMN LEAVES

The autumn has always brought the problem of falling leaves, and various methods of removing them before they are ground to a slithery paste on the rail have been tried. This included water cannon, but in 1983 a Unimog tractor and trailer which could run on road or rail was acquired to vacuum up the leaves as they fell. The tractor unit had a cabinet containing a centrifugal fan, and a flexible hose with suction nozzle to draw up the leaves from the track into the cabinet. They then passed into the trailer van where they were collected for disposal. This unit was kept at Chalfont & Latimer station high in the Chilterns, where many of the worst problems are to be found, and made night-time sorties. However, it was found that Unimogs could not be relied upon to operate track circuits at all times; this is a serious deficiency on vehicles intended for use on the running lines. The two which remain are now restricted to depot shunting purposes only.

No precautions were possible for the night of 15/16 October 1987, when hurricane-force winds swept southern Britain, after which over

600 trees had to be cleared from the tracks. The more serious damage was to signal cables, cut by falling debris, while the stability of some embankments previously bound by tree roots had to be attended to in the longer term. Even the Epping-Ongar line, which had 60 fallen trees to itself, was back in business three days later.

WORK ON THE INFRASTRUCTURE

In practical terms, very little infrastructure work can be achieved when passenger trains are running. The prime time for this work is thus during the night hours, which are strictly limited.

Below: **A Unimog tractor-and-trailer combination was delivered at the end of 1982. It is basically a lorry powered by a Mercedes-Benz engine, with road/rail capability. This was an attempt to deal with the autumn leaf problem; the leaves were sucked up into a 16cu m tank on the trailer, collected by flexible nozzle heads between the two. It was numbered TMM774 (motor) and TMM775 (trailer).**
Photographed at Neasden, 24 April 1983. Author

On the London Underground network, every part of the system is designated either as part of the Line-Clear Area or Line-Safe Area. This excludes non-electrified track, and that within depots and sidings where traction current is normally switched on at all times. In general, the Line-Clear Areas include all sections of line where clearances are very severely restricted, as well as those in tunnel (tube or otherwise). Line-Clear Areas include, for instance, the whole of the Circle Line, the Northern Line south of the East Finchley/Golders Green tunnel mouths, but also the Burroughs Tunnels at Hendon. The Line-Safe Areas refer to the rest of the system.

Each day is divided into Traffic Hours, during which traction current is switched on, and Engineering Hours, when current is switched off. The times at which Engineering Hours begin and end vary according to location and day of the week. Roundly, Engineering Hours cover the period from 01.00 to 05.00 on Monday nights/Tuesday mornings to Friday

Right: **The Underground made much use of compressed air for power. This air grid at Moorgate station carried high-pressure air in steel tubes for working points and signals.**
Stewarts & Lloyds Ltd, 1956

nights/Saturday mornings, 01.00 to 06.00 on Saturday nights/Sunday mornings and 00.30 to 05.00 on Sunday nights/Monday mornings.

In the Line-Clear Areas, access for engineering activity of any sort, including routine inspections, may be made only within Engineering Hours. In the Line-Safe Areas, minor activities which do not affect the safety of the trains may be undertaken within Traffic Hours, subject to making suitable staff protection arrangements.

The exceptions are the undertaking of major works, such as bridge reconstruction, as realistically these cannot be achieved within a series of night-time occupations and must be undertaken as one continuous job over (say) a weekend. In such cases, extended Engineer's Possessions are arranged specially, and bus replacement services or similar are provided for passengers.

The short time available for engineering work, and the unsocial hours during which it must be carried out, means that it is costly. It is also difficult to make full use of labour during the limited hours available on each shift. Getting men, equipment and materials to work sites can only be achieved after the traction current has been switched off. This accentuates the importance of optimising the pathing of engineers' trains from Lillie Bridge, Ruislip and Neasden, meeting the following criteria:

● allowing maximum time at the site concerned
● avoiding delays to the start of (or imposing an early finish on) other scheduled engineering work on the route which they need to traverse
● avoiding disruption of the operation of passenger trains

PRODUCTIVE USE OF MEN AND EQUIPMENT

It will be seen that the problem is not merely that of funding and the commitment of resources but also the limited opportunities available to use them productively. This has in turn led to a rather more protracted series of line closures than would take place in an ideal world. The most serious of these was the total closure of the East London Line from 1995 until 1998. While other factors had a hand here (notably the Grade II listing of the Brunels' under-Thames tunnel from Wapping to Rotherhithe, just hours before work was due to commence), this does not disguise the fact that the upkeep of ageing infrastructure is a major problem. The use of low-maintenance forms of track and other assets is a sensible step in the right direction, but the key difficulty is the lack of sufficient Engineering Hours during the course of the day.

While the relentless pursuit of efficiency will continue to make a necessary and welcome contribution, market projections envisage an increasingly busy Underground system as the years progress. But this also means more wear and tear, irrespective of any outstanding backlog of maintenance work.

One possible solution is to reduce Traffic Hours by perhaps an hour every night, with a corresponding increase in Engineering Hours, but this would no doubt be resisted fiercely by the customers whose last trains would depart that much earlier. There are also the effects on traffic revenues to be considered. More weekend or longer period closures seem increasingly likely in the future.

POWER GENERATION

The early tube railways began the tradition of self-sufficiency in power generation, and the City & South London Railway built its own power station at Stockwell when it opened in 1890; the Central London Railway's establishment was at Wood Lane. The electrification of the Metropolitan and the Metropolitan District Railways spawned coal-fired power stations at Neasden and at Lots Road, Chelsea respectively in 1905. By this time, the District and three of the tube railways were under the unified control of Yerkes, and Lots Road which was then claimed to be the biggest power station in the world, provided power for them all. Later, the power station at Greenwich was added, after being released from its former role of supplying power to the LCC tramways and, later, trolleybuses. Supply is now standardised at 630V dc on all lines, using the fourth-rail system.

Lots Road was built on the banks of the Thames. It burned about 6,100 tonnes of small grained 'pea' coal a week coming in by barge. Bucket conveyors transported the coal to bunkers over the 32 boilers in the basement. These were fed mechanically, and the draught for the fire raised by the four 84m chimneys and assisted by fans. An agreeable description referred to 'the old warm, gently roaring power house with its glowing, slowly moving chain grates; its glistening rows of humming generators; and its parquet-floored control room, all knobbly with polished dials and instruments with, above, thin plumes of smoke drifting from its tall chimneys.'

Each boiler produced about 23,000kg of steam each hour, used to turn the nine turbo-generators arranged in two rows above the boiler basement. Their output was electricity at 11,000V, three phase at $33\frac{1}{3}$Hz. Jutting out into the river bed were the two water intake pipes of 2.74m and 2.29m diameter respectively, supplying cooling water at up to 41 million litres each hour. After passing through screens to remove debris, the water was passed over the condensers to cool them, and returned to warm up Chelsea Creek. The condensed steam in the boilers was then recycled, and any losses were made good after purification by supplies from artesian wells.

All this was swept away in a modernisation programme in 1968, with natural gas or oil taking the place of coal as the primary energy source. Neasden was closed at the same time,

Above: **This fireless locomotive was built by Andrew Barclay of Kilmarnock in 1930 (No 1989) and was used at the NorthMet power station at Brimsdown, whose roundel it bears. It is named** *Lord Ashfield.* **Looking a little the worse for wear, but, one trusts, not for ever, as it is now in the Manchester Museum of Science & Industry.** *Author*

and provision made in the investment programme for supplying power to meet the needs of the expanding Underground system. Lots Road was re-equipped, with six vertical oil-fired boilers serving new turbo-alternators. The voltage generated was now 22,000V at 50Hz, and the total capacity of the plant increased by 7% to 180,000kW. Shortly afterwards, in 1972, Greenwich was also re-equipped, but with gas turbine alternators and a 103mW capacity.

POWER SOURCES

The Underground uses about 900 million units of electricity a year. Although outer sections have been fed by the National Grid for half a century, constituting about 25% of the total, the principle of generating the base requirement of electricity was not challenged until recent years. However, a number of failures of power supplies for technical reasons served to bring trains to an abrupt stop all over the system. In October 1979 an explosion in one of the boilers at Lots Road blew out the other two which were in use at the time. As this happened at 14.30 when Greenwich was not operating, this caused a complete power loss in the central area. Although Greenwich came on load within a couple of minutes, this was not sufficient to prevent a shutdown. Supply was restored in 20min, but it took more than an hour to get most of the trains running again, with disruption lasting for the rest of the day.

Industry sources were highly critical of the Underground's generating policy. 'London Transport has two choices – find an alternative source of economic electricity to operate in parallel with Lots Road, or go on taking the risk of

spasmodic shutdowns' said the *Electrical Times.* 'Its problem is that one of its power stations is specifically designed for base-load operation and the other for peak demand. It could overcome some of its difficulties if it improved the efficiency of one or two of its gas turbine sets at Greenwich and ran them continuously in parallel with Lots Road.' However, it turned out that internal power supplies were not necessarily any more secure than the Grid could offer or, as it happened, any cheaper.

Further incidents in 1993, which crippled the Central Line and up to five others for extended periods, were traced to three separate faults. These were in an earthing cable at Lots Road, a cable failure between Mile End and Greenwich, and a transformer failure at Newbury Park. They demonstrated both the vulnerability of the Underground to power supply problems (with a bill estimated at £2 million for repairs, lost revenue and passenger compensation), and the importance of adequate investment in the largely unseen infrastructure.

A review of long-term requirements and the cost of running power stations and installing new generation plant every 30 years or so came to the view that Lots Road should be decommissioned. This formed part of a PFI deal in August 1998 between SEEBOARD Powerlink Ltd (SPL) and London Underground. SPL operates, maintains, finances and renews the Underground's high-voltage power distribution network under a 30-year contract worth more than £1bn.

Under the terms of the deal, SPL was required to complete a major programme of capital works, which included the installation of equipment to provide emergency supplies to the railway in case of a major power failure, replacement of existing power control systems, and renewal of the Northern Line's power distribution system. The company is also responsible for distributing high-voltage electricity supplies to every Underground station and 400km of track. London

Underground's payment is made on the basis of an availability charged for the services provided.

Lots Road power station was finally switched off formally on 21 October 2002 by John Spellar, Transport Minister, following which all Underground power was derived from the National Grid. (In practice, this had been the case since 8 October). Supplies are delivered to the Powerlink network at the bulk supply points of Lots Road and Aldgate, together with an existing point at Neasden. Back-up battery systems installed at the stations are capable of powering emergency lighting, PA systems and train radio.

Greenwich has been retained but is restricted to providing emergency cover. Four gas turbines at Greenwich are supposed to be sufficient to insure against a total power failure in southeast England; they can be brought into use within a quarter of an hour to take over from the batteries and to provide power for tunnel and station lighting, ventilation, pumps, lifts and escalators. This allows passengers to be evacuated from tunnels, but there is insufficient power to provide for traction purposes. However, none of this could prevent a 34min power loss over more than half the Underground system on 28 August 2003, due to Grid failure.

SUBSTATIONS

The function of substation equipment is to receive high-tension current, step it down to the traction voltage and rectify the supply from alternating current as generated to direct current at 630V, as required by the traction motors. The current then flows through track feeders to the conductor rail, each length of which is bonded or welded to its neighbour to minimise voltage drop.

Over the whole system there are approximately 100 substations owned by London Underground or, in some cases, by Network Rail. The substations are unmanned, and use mercury arc or silicon rectifiers. Current can be cut by the operation of relays in the substation which trip the track breakers; all stations have the facility to do this in emergency, as have train drivers when underground by pinching together the tunnel wires.

Each section of track is fed by the substation at each end (double end feed), apart from terminal sections (single end feed). Electrified sections are discrete, and separated from each other by gaps in the conductor rails; in the event of a failure a section can be neutralised without affecting nearby parts of the line. If a section in advance of an approaching train is dead, a triangle of three red warning lights alerts the driver to an approaching train. The driver should attempt to stop short or, if this is not possible, to ensure his train is completely on the dead section. Otherwise, he will bridge the section gap and render the section in advance live, which could endanger persons on the track or otherwise exacerbate the incident which caused the current to be discharged in the first place.

Substations also provide current for ventilating fans, lifts, escalators, lighting and pumps.

CONNECT

This Private Finance Initiative (PFI) Connect contract outsources the provision of radio and transmission services to the Underground over a 20-year period with Citylink communications. Copper cables are to be replaced with an integrated radio system, supported by a new fibre-optic transmission system. The whole will help staff keep in contact with each other, exchange information to co-ordinate passenger flows, and respond in case of service disruption. A side effect is that passengers will be able to use mobile phones throughout the tunnelled parts of the network.

ACTON WORKS

Acton Works, for many years the central railway overhaul workshops in west London, was opened in 1922. As such, it was responsible for the cars of the District, both the Bakerloo branches and the Piccadilly Line. The overhaul capacity was in the order of 16 cars per week, and motor cars were expected to put in an appearance about every 50,000 miles; this equated roughly to their annual mileage. The overhaul requirement for trailers was less, at 70,000 miles.

Subsequent expansion was intended to increase the throughput to 60 cars per week and add body repair and painting to the tasks undertaken. The works was also to cater for all the lines, though not at that stage the Metropolitan which was then a separate concern.

At its maximum extent, Acton Works occupied a 20ha site to the south of Acton Town station and provided facilities for heavy overhaul and reconditioning of all London Transport's railway rolling stock as well as supplying reconditioned

Below: **Although lifts and escalators take most of the attention, there is a need to maintain emergency staircases at many stations. This shows the commendable degree of lighting and general cleanliness at Regent's Park in June 2000.** *Author*

wheels and other components to the running depots. Acton Works is no more, and the site is now being used for much more modest purposes. This description of the progress of Underground cars through the complex, taken from an early edition of this book, has been retained for its interest.

CAR PROGRESSION

The works are arranged so that cars for overhaul are first drawn up at a platform alongside the trimming shop, where the seats are removed. The seats are either washed or retrimmed and then stored ready to go back to the cars after overhaul. Cars can then proceed to the lifting shop. Here, the car body is lifted off its service bogies or trucks by means of a 30.5-tonne overhead traversing crane and placed on special accommodation bogies. These are old bogies built up with raised transverse beams so that the body sits much higher off the track than usual, giving additional working space beneath.

After the car bodies are lifted on to accommodation bogies, the service trucks have their traction motors and current collection equipment removed and are drawn by chain into the truck shop. Down one side of this large building is the dismantling track or road, along which the trucks are slowly moved and progressively stripped down to the bare frames.

On the far side of the shop is the truck assembly line and across the wide space between pass all the various components on a series of conveyors. On their journey across the shop, the components are cleaned, inspected and reconditioned or renewed as necessary.

The truck frames themselves are now removed from the line and come under close scrutiny for defects, such as rivets working loose, which may occur under the stress of continued running.

WHEELS AND WHEEL ASSEMBLIES

All that is now left of the service trucks on the dismantling road are the pairs of wheels and

axles and these are moved to the extreme end of the truck shop, known as the wheel area. Here the wheel assemblies, comprising either wheels with gear drive mounted directly on the axle, or plain wheels and axles, are subject to very close examination for wear and faults.

Wheel axles, approximately 125mm in diameter, sometimes reveal faults during a special testing process. If so, they are tested on an ultrasonic flaw detector. Should there be any suspicion of a crack on an axle, the wheels are pressed off and subjected to a test on a magnetic particle tester. In this, fluorescent ink containing particles is sprayed on to the axle, which is then electrified. The particles are thus attracted magnetically to the opposite poles of any crack, which thereupon reveals itself as a black hairline.

Overhauled wheel assemblies are conveyed to the assembly line, and then begins the building up of the bogie, which continues as the bogie slowly moves along the line in the reverse direction to that in which it entered. The completed trucks are now ready to return to the lifting shop.

MOTORS

The motor shop overhauls traction motors, compressors, alternators and a variety of other machines such as lift and escalator motors. Motor overhaul is a specialised business and can vary from superficial attention and cleaning to complete rebuilding from the shaft upwards. Three of the processes involved are the stoving of reconditioned armatures to drive out moisture and ensure good insulation, the banding of armatures to prevent the copper bars from rising due to the high rotating motor speeds, and the armature insulation tests at 2,000V – or double if the armature is rebuilt.

These high-tension tests are carried out within a special raised enclosure to keep out unauthorised personnel during testing. Modern traction motors use better insulating materials, so the number of machines rewound because of insulation breakdown is decreasing.

CAR BODIES

The car body overhaul starts when the car is moved from the lifting shop to the blow-out enclosure, where compressed air jets unsettle dust and dirt from the equipment and underframes, while induced draught sucks all this debris away. The car body then travels by traverser to the main car body shop.

Compressors and motor alternators are then removed to the motor shop, and all electrical and mechanical equipment on the cars, such as brake valves, door engines and traction control equipment are removed for attention at specially equipped benches and then refitted.

Overhaul of the car structure and fittings also takes place here. After this process the car body is sent through the paint shop and then returns to the lifting shop where it is lowered on to its service trucks. Roads with pit facilities are provided for inspection and testing on

Above: **A signalling and CCTV installation at Cockfosters, Piccadilly Line, with a 1973-stock train approaching, in May 2002.** *Author*

completed cars. The cars are then coupled into unit formation, the seats refitted, and a final test run performed.

NEW METHODS

Even in this description, the seeds of change can be detected. Overall, maintenance requirements were decreasing, and further economies were foreseen. For example, if the vehicle bodies needed to be lifted from their bogies less frequently, this would be of little value if the lifting was still needed to remove the wheelsets so that they could be machined periodically to restore their correct profile.

Underfloor wheel lathes to re-machine the wheels, but without removing them from the vehicles, were first introduced in 1947. These lathes dealt with the flanges only, but in 1961 a new machine was put into service at Northfields depot which could machine the entire profile. This used rollers pressed against the inner faces of the wheels to rotate them, while hydraulic jacks supported the axleboxes and hence the vehicle's weight. The copying tool to cut away the surplus metal was then moved across the wheel flange and tread, following a master profile. Using this method, it was not even necessary to uncouple the vehicles, and a complete four-car set would be drawn progressively across the lathe by winch.

Armature rewinding was being replaced with the use of better insulation techniques. Painting of aluminium cars with plastic-faced interiors was not necessary. Wheel changes were being extended from one year to every four years, and heavy overhauls from every four to every nine years. Heavy mechanical work was being replaced with increasing requirements for electrical and electronic work.

For modern rolling stock with nine years adopted as the basis for heavy overhauls, the half-life overhaul at 18 years has similar work content to previous half-life overhauls. However, the nine and 27-year overhauls are much lighter, with some items removed for repair but most

equipment being subjected only to a clean-up and test. For example, the cars in a train no longer need to be separated, let alone have the bodies lifted off the bogies.

TRANSFER TO LINE DEPOTS

Given the age of much of the equipment at Acton, the upshot was the decision in 1985 to transfer all car overhauls to the line depots, with equipment removed from the vehicles maintained at a new facility at Acton or by outside contractors. The new Acton unit concentrates on seat retrimming, wheel maintenance, sub-assembly work, electrical and electronic maintenance and machining. None of these required a rail connection, since the plan was to bring the parts for overhaul in by road. Meanwhile, Acton was allowed to tender for other work, such as the conversion of the Metropolitan Line A stock to one-person operation.

Golders Green was the first of the line depots to take on this work in 1986, and was quickly followed by others. These main depots have always dealt with day-to-day cleaning, inspection and maintenance. A lifting facility and inspection pits both beneath and at the side of the cars were also part of the standard provision, and do of course aid the new tasks. One should not assume that the facilities are always new; Hammersmith depot still remains largely as built by the Great Western Railway on a very restricted site. This does limit the work which can be undertaken there.

TRAIN EXAMINATION AND MAINTENANCE

What do the trains need in the way of care? Requirements vary according to the type and age of the train, but the following is a general guide.

Examination and maintenance are carried out at several levels. First, daily train preparation. The aims here are to check that a train is in a safe and proper condition when offered for service, and to ensure that defects reported by operators are acknowledged and corrected. This is essentially a systems check, covering items such as the trip-

cock, dead man's handle, door pilot and passenger alarm. The next level up, at 14 days, is the detailed examination of brake blocks and mechanical parts, the door operating mechanisms and the current collecting equipment.

Then there are periodic examinations, which have a fuller agenda, *viz*:

- to ensure trains remain in a wholly serviceable condition
- to examine elements of the train not accessible in normal usage, for damage and degradation
- to check and adjust wearing parts and consumable items to ensure they remain serviceable within defined limits
- to check secondary protective structural devices

The intervals between successive car examinations are determined by the rate at which consumables wear out, and the time it is considered prudent to run trains before having a good look underneath. In short, the aim is to make sure that nothing falls off, as happened at Chancery Lane. With consumables, the time between replacements can be increased, but it must be recognised that the rate of wear depends upon the use made of the train. Thus, if a brake block is not fully worn when it is replaced some wastage will result, but this is unavoidable on a time-interval rather than usage-based system.

A detailed examination of all equipment is carried out at 30 weeks; more extensive overhaul work is performed at 4- to 4½-year intervals.

Additionally, trains returning to service following maintenance need to be tested. The minimum testing and inspection requirements need to be defined, to ensure the train is fit for service. This is to guard against matters such as the incorrect renewal of wiring, which could induce wrong-side failures.

CHAPTER TEN

Twenty Uncertain Years

By the early 1960s the age of the Underground was beginning to cause some concern. The approval of new lines is only a partial solution: the existing infrastructure must be maintained in good order and, indeed, upgraded to meet modern expectations as nearly as possible. It was such areas that were shown subsequently not to have received as much attention as they might have done.

UNDERGROUND CENTENARY

It was now 100 years since the Metropolitan Railway opened its doors to the public in 1863, and a major display was staged at Neasden for a gathering of invited transport officials from all over the world. They were to be shown the modern system at work and, in contrast, part of its history in review. The description provides a

> 'A new Underground railway [can] provide approximately five times more capacity for passenger movement than a four-lane motorway.'
>
> *London Transport Board, Annual Report, 1963*

snapshot of the Underground of 40 years ago. A plaque commemorating the centenary was placed outside Baker Street station.

Essentially, this was a Metropolitan occasion, which was reflected in the exhibits. The parade of 15 trains took place at Neasden depot on 23 May 1963. The first comprised Metropolitan Railway Class A locomotive No 23 and two contractors' wagons. No 23 was built in 1866 and survived in traffic until 1948, when it was withdrawn after 82 years of service. The

locomotive was subsequently restored externally to its 1903 condition and resided in the (then) British Transport Museum at Clapham. The two contractors' wagons had been doctored to resemble the vehicles used by Smith & Knight, builders of the Paddington-Euston Square section of the original Metropolitan Railway, to

Below: **The Centenary Parade of 23 May 1963 saw 'E' class 0-4-4T No L44 heading a train consisting of a Metropolitan milk van and coaches from the turn of the 19th century.** *IAL*

Above: **The Underground of 1982 tended to be fairly basic in its amenities. This is North Acton, with an eastbound train of 1962 stock for Epping arriving at Platform 2. The station was reconstructed as part of the Central Line works of recent times, and an additional running line was in turn built to turn the platform on the right into an island. The new Platform 3 is normally used for eastbound services, and Platform 2 for trains terminating from central London.** *Author*

convey a party of VIPs along the still unfinished line on 24 May 1862. Twenty-four members of the LT Musical & Dramatic Society, attired in period costume, re-created the scene. Cheating slightly, the entourage was propelled by battery locomotive No L76.

The train was followed by Metropolitan Railway 0-4-4T No L44 with milk van No 3 and four bogie coaches. No L44 was the first of the Class E locomotives to be built at Neasden Works in 1896 for the extension of the Metropolitan's services into the Chilterns. The milk van was built at the same time by the Birmingham Railway Carriage & Wagon Co and was used in passenger trains on the outer sections of the Metropolitan until 1936, when it was transferred to the engineers' department for use as a tool van in the breakdown train. The four passenger coaches were built between 1898 and 1900, and were not withdrawn from revenue service until the electrification of the Chesham branch in 1960. All these vehicles survive in preservation.

Third in the procession was electric locomotive No 1 *John Lyon* with a six-coach train of 'Dreadnought' stock. This was the first of a batch of 20 which replaced the original 1905 locomotives in 1922/3. They were employed primarily on through London–Aylesbury trains as far as Rickmansworth until 1961. At this time, four were still in use for shunting.

First in the line of multiple-units was a three-car train of compartment T stock. The Metropolitan preferred compartment stock for

its longer-distance trains, due to its greater seating capacity compared with saloons. It was followed by a four-car train of District F stock, by then confined to the East London Line services.

Next came a three-car train of P stock with Metadyne control, which had replaced early Metropolitan electric trains on the Uxbridge line just prior to World War 2. This stock was still in the process of being converted to normal resistance control with PCM equipment. To bring the surface stock story right up to date, the P stock was followed by a single unit of silver A stock, built by Cravens of Sheffield in 1961.

TUBE STOCK

The inclusion of some tube stock in the parade was justified by the projection of Piccadilly Line trains to Uxbridge and the Bakerloo extension to Stanmore, a former Metropolitan appendage. Pre-1938 stock was used initially on both these extensions although it was by then fast disappearing; it was compared with the 1938 tube stock with its increased carrying capacity due to the PCM control equipment being placed beneath the floor. A few of these trains were then in service on the Piccadilly, but they monopolised the Bakerloo, albeit with one trailer of pre-1938 stock in each train.

An example of the 1959 aluminium successors for the Piccadilly Line was then shown, which was eventually to oust all the pre-1938 rolling stock and, with the similar 1962 stock, most of the 1938 stock as well.

ENGINEERING TRAINS

Attention next turned to Metropolitan 'F' class 0-6-2T No L52 with an engineers' train. No L52 was one of four engines which were built in 1901 for use on freight trains on the Aylesbury and Uxbridge lines. In 1937 they were transferred to engineers' duties, with No L52 being the last survivor and about to be superseded by a further arrival of 0-6-0PT locomotives from BR's Western Region. Pannier

tank No L98 was shown on a cable-laying train, with special wagons carrying drums of new power or signalling cable. One end of the cable was fixed to a convenient point by the track and the wagon pulled slowly along, paying out the cable which was supported on brackets at the side of the track.

Locomotive No L57 used battery power while the current in the conductor rails was switched off and the crew of the long welded-rail train which it was hauling gave a demonstration using 122m rails. When being transported from the depot to the working site, the rails – up to 18 rails may be loaded at a time – are secured only to the middle wagon; with the ends free to move, the rails bending with the train as it goes round curves. Further lateral movement is prevented by the stanchions located along the sides of the wagon. The whole then resembles a gigantic leaf spring. The assembled guests were then shown the ease with which these rails, weighing over $4^1/_2$ tonnes each, are handled. To load a rail length, the end is winched up and placed in a roller mounted in a hinged frame on the rear wagon. The whole train is then propelled under the rail, until the last 6m overhangs the roller. This is hauled on by the winch. Both loading and unloading operations were carried out by the eight-man crew, the entire manoeuvre taking 10min.

Also on view was the Chief Mechanical Engineer's Instruction Train. This consisted of five yellow-painted ex-Bakerloo Line 1920 Cammell Laird trailers of 1920 vintage, which had been fitted out as a mobile school. These were the first production tube cars to have air doors from new. Using adapted pre-1938 motor cars as power, the train was taken from depot to depot to give instruction courses on new train equipment and refresher courses to staff responsible for maintenance work on Underground trains.

BARBICAN DIVERSION

The 1960s was the age of the big holes in London, when the scars left from the bombing of World War 2 were finally healed. The Barbican was one of the largest construction projects, and at the behest of the City of London, London Transport diverted the Metropolitan Line to a straighter and more southerly route between Aldersgate (now Barbican) and Moorgate.

Centre right: **What was then Aldersgate & Barbican station had an overall roof, but wartime damage led to its demolition. On 9 October 1954 the station is seen in its complete form, with the Widened Lines on the right and the electrified Underground lines on the left. It is now Barbican.** *D. E. Shepherd/Author's collection*

Right: **The reconstruction of the railway between Barbican and Moorgate on a new alignment allowed major building works to take place, including at Moorgate station, which itself was roofed in. An eastbound train of CO/CP stock arrives at Moorgate from the rerouted section of line with a Whitechapel service in the 1970s.** *IAL*

This work first entailed the moving of the Widened Lines. The 450m of new railway were constructed by the 'cut and cover' method, reinforced concrete being used both to enclose the line and support the Barbican development above. This work was completed in 1965.

EXCAVATIONS AT VICTORIA

Progress with Victoria Line construction saw the work of the shields cutting the running and station tunnels complete by September 1966. The earlier experimental work with a 'drum digger' shield and a groutless method of installing the tunnel lining had proved useful and had been adopted for the main construction. During 35 months, this had involved 44 different tunnel drives starting from 21 shafts sunk for that purpose, the last drive breaking through an already completed tunnel section near King's Cross. There remained only a few short sections of running tunnel to be excavated without the use of a shield. The whole of the line is underground apart from the depot, located at Northumberland Park.

At Victoria, the ticket hall for both the Victoria and District lines was sited under the existing forecourt of the main-line station. The Victoria Line's platforms lie 18m below; beyond, to the south, there were four sidings, two of which subsequently formed the start of the Brixton extension.

The Network Rail station was largely built over a filled-in canal basin. It was necessary to stabilise part of the thick stratum of water-bearing sand and gravel to permit deep mining beneath it, by injecting chemicals through a large number of narrow pipes driven 11m into the gravel over the affected area, to harden it.

A large part of the land south of Victoria down to the Thames was ancient low drainage ground, referred to as early as the year 951 as Bullinga Fen, into which the River Tyburn is thought to have drained. This once open river is now either non-existent or reduced to a subterranean trickle, but it is roughly beneath and along its alignment that the Victoria Line now runs. This is northward to cross deep under The Mall opposite the Queen Victoria

Memorial, then beneath Green Park to the station of that name.

The Victoria Line platforms lie just to the west and above the Piccadilly Line station, connected to the latter (and now also to the Jubilee Line) by a subway and to the new ticket hall by a bank of three escalators. From Green Park the line, having crossed the Piccadilly Line roughly at right-angles, runs north again beneath Mayfair to Oxford Circus for interchange with the Bakerloo and Central lines. It has climbed steadily to follow the land contour rising from the Thames, but is still 21m below the surface.

Tunnelling here was a major job, as the tubes swing out to flank the Bakerloo on both sides, thus providing the ideal cross-platform interchange. Building this composite station below ground took longer than any other along the line, and the only visible surface evidence of the day and night activity going on below was the 6,700-tonne steel 'umbrella' bridging the whole of Oxford Circus itself. This carried all the street traffic 1.06m above its former level. Below the Circus is a large circular ticket hall and below that are five escalator shafts, separate Victoria Line station tunnels, subways, passages and concourses linking it all together, including the Central Line at right angles.

At Oxford Circus, the engineers were faced with an unusually intricate task in underpinning part of a large store and transferring the load from its foundations to the southbound Victoria Line station tunnel. Below the third basement, the building's columns were underpinned with massive pre-stressed concrete, the bottom layer cast in weaker concrete. Later, the tunnel shield drove beneath a saddle shape cut in the base of the concrete, and finally the station tunnel segments were expanded by jacks to produce the necessary stresses in the ground.

The line continues north, cutting diagonally across a grid pattern of the streets above to Warren Street. Along the route the northbound tunnel was made to roll over the southbound and continues thus to the station 27m below ground level. New escalators connected the Victoria Line platforms with the existing escalators to the Northern at an intermediate landing; there is no low-level connection between the two.

APPROACHING THE MAIN LINES

The tunnels then swing northeast to Euston, another deep-level underground complex which provides interconnection between the Network Rail station above, and both the City (via Bank) and West End branches of the Northern Line. The reversed tunnels emerge into a combined, one-level, double-island Euston station, with the northbound tunnel on the right and the southbound tunnel on the left. Across their respective platforms are the northbound City branch trains to Camden Town and the southbound City trains to King's Cross. These platforms are unusual in that trains run in opposite directions on each side of them. One mildly odd result is that to travel from Euston to

King's Cross one can catch either a northbound Victoria Line train or a southbound Northern Line via Bank service. Pedestrian subways give access to Northern Line-via-Charing Cross trains.

The line rises gradually to King's Cross, a congested maze of tunnels between which the new line and its platforms had to be threaded. A complicating factor was the brick arch of the Midland curve, now used by Thameslink services. This had to be removed and replaced by a new structure of reinforced concrete so as to provide room for a subway. Lower down, part of the Victoria Line's station tunnel crown is positioned a little below the foundations of the Midland curve and the Circle line tunnels. As these are in brick with either no inverts or inverts of varying depth, an extra robust tunnel shield was employed here to exert great pressure in the ground at its working face during excavation. Finally, extra heavy steel tunnel lining was expanded against the ground

Below: **Seen in 1978, these tunnels are on the north side of Southgate station, Piccadilly Line; the emerging train of 1973 stock is bound for Cockfosters. The bell mouths are to counter the rush of air as a train enters at speed, which can otherwise result in ears popping in the front vehicle.** *Author*

by powerful jacks and steel wedges, so as to maintain at all times equilibrium of ground stresses and prevent settlement of the brick tunnel foundations.

King's Cross is currently the only 'four-tier' station on the Underground system. The work here included the excavation of two horizontal tunnels, one 3.66m and one 4.57m in diameter, both of them for draught relief and each about 23m long. They connect the Piccadilly and Victoria Line stations to a vertical air shaft. The Victoria Line is above the other tube lines but below the Metropolitan. At ticket hall level, the River Fleet sewer had to be diverted and re-contained in a new concrete ring and box construction, which at one point nearly obtrudes into the ticket hall. All this work had to thread between existing tunnels and shafts in deep earth, without any visual means of pinpointing obstructions as would be the case above ground.

NORTH OF KING'S CROSS
Beyond King's Cross the tunnels curve and ascend to follow the rising ground to Highbury & Islington, providing interchange there with what was then the Northern City Line and later became part of the West Anglia Great Northern electrics.

About halfway along this 2.43km stretch, the running tunnels resume their normal positions by the southbound crossing over the northbound. The old Highbury station was rebuilt extensively both above and below ground, and a joint station building was constructed to serve also BR's North London line. The northbound Northern City platform became the Victoria Line southbound; the other pair of lines use new tunnels and platforms. The result was a very positive improvement to interchange facilities.

The running tunnels continue a further 1.93km to Finsbury Park, where the old Great Northern & City and the Piccadilly stations, opened in 1904 and 1906 respectively, were utterly transformed. The below-ground works here involved building step-plate junctions around tunnels through which trains continued to run, building underground crossovers, and ultimately switching trains from old lines to new. This resulted in southbound Piccadilly and Victoria Line trains using the old GN&C former terminal platforms, while the northbound trains of both lines used the former Piccadilly station. Again, the result was cross-platform interchange between a pair of lines in both directions of travel, with further BR services available 'upstairs'.

Left: **The Underground acquired the intermediate stations alongside the LTS line from Bromley-by-Bow (seen here as rebuilt in 1970) right through to Upminster (exclusive) from BR Eastern Region in 1969. Barking also remained with BR. This photograph was taken in June 2003.** *Author*

Descending steadily now to Seven Sisters, the 3.15km of this stretch became the longest distance underground on the system between adjacent stations. This is the interchange with NR electric services to Enfield Town and Broxbourne. The station has three platforms, the centre one leaving the eastbound line just west of the station and subsequently offering access to Northumberland Park depot. The outer ones are the north and southbound tracks, the latter receiving the exit road from the depot a little to the east of Seven Sisters. The pair of depot tracks swing northward in tunnel for 1.38km, coming to the surface alongside the Network Rail Lea Valley line. The extensive site was built to cater for the complete fleet of 1967 stock trains.

The tube running tunnels continue northeast, descending to Tottenham Hale where Lea Valley rail connections are made for passengers. The line then rises again and swings eastward to continue a mile to Blackhorse Road (interchange with the Tottenham and Hampstead Network Rail line) and to its terminus below the Network Rail Chingford branch station of Walthamstow Central.

Beyond Finsbury Park, the Victoria Line broke virgin territory for the Underground; from Tottenham it followed beneath the old road over the River Lea and then through misty marsh and reservoir country on the route to Epping Forest. The Great Eastern Railway colonised Walthamstow and other parts of northeast London with steam trains from the 1870s on, but the Victoria Line had no such development aspirations. Instead, it aimed to attract traffic from this built-up area and beyond through interchange with the surface railways.

All the running tunnels of the northern end of the line were driven through blue clay, as was part of the southern end, and excavated by shield and rotary cutters. For the larger diameter station tunnels and for a crossover at Walthamstow the tunnel lining is in the form of cast-iron segments, the running tunnels being in concrete segments. Much of the southern end was lined with cast-iron segments, some of the new design similar to those used in the experimental tunnel, but for water-bearing and other difficult ground, conventional bolted cast-iron segments were used.

Furnishing of the line was according to the practice of the time, and used wood sleepers concreted into the road bed to support bull-head rail, long welded into 91.4m lengths at Northumberland Park and fed into the tunnels from there. A narrow concrete shelf was affixed to the tunnel walls at platform height to contain the noise of steel wheel on steel rail. The station decor was plain to today's eyes with grey tiling everywhere (except where it has since fallen off), relieved only by a motif illustrative of each

Below: **Despite being in Underground ownership for over 30 years, Eastern Region blue enamel signs at Plaistow still indicate which side of the staircases are intended for 'up' and 'down' movements. Sometimes the Underground can exhibit remarkable reminders of past events.** *Author*

station. While the maze at Warren Street and the cameo of Queen Victoria were apt and well chosen, the association of seven trees with Seven Sisters was tenuous, while the use of the Doric Arch, then so recently demolished, to denote Euston seemed almost vindictive.

AUTOMATIC TRAIN OPERATION

The opportunity to construct a brand-new line was unique for London Transport, and the decision was made to go for full automation of operation as represented by automatic train operation (ATO). As applied, it reflected the technology of the time, and is described here in some detail.

Under non-automatic conditions, the train driver applies power to the traction motors, cuts it off or applies the brakes as dictated by the track and signalling conditions. With ATO, the human element is almost completely removed, and the train is under a dual system of control. The most important system safeguards the train by employing an inductive pick-up to receive continuous coded signals from the track, with equipment on board the train to interpret and act upon these signals. No code means no movement. This is the safety signalling system. The other, the 'driver command' system, receives impulses at predetermined spots along the track. These cause power to be applied, or cut off for coasting and the brakes to be applied; a series of commands controls the stopping of trains in the station platforms.

In more detail, the safety signalling codes are formed by current from the mains supply. In a relay room this current is interrupted into codes electronically or by the action of pendulums operating electronic switches. One pendulum,

swinging 180 times a minute, produces a '180' impulse code. A faster swinging pendulum produces a '270' impulse code. This coded signal current is fed into the running rails (which are sectionalised by insulated joints), passing along one rail, through the wheels and axles at the front of the train, and then back by the other rail.

Coils mounted on the front of the train are affected by the code in the rails, and a signal is passed to the train equipment, amplified, and recognised by the electrical circuits responding only to an appropriate code frequency. A '180' code indicates that the train is safe to proceed at up to 40km/h provided current is not being fed to the traction motors. It is made to conform to this speed by a mechanical governor, actuated by the train wheels, that ensures that this speed is not exceeded for as long as the '180' code is being transmitted.

A '270' code allows the train to run under power at up to 40km/h; a '420' code indicates that a train may proceed at full speed. While one of these safety signal codes is being received by the train, current from the train battery holds an emergency brake valve in the closed position. If the code should cease to be picked up by the train, the current would be cut off from the brake valve and an emergency application of the brakes would result.

DRIVER COMMAND SYSTEM

The other part of ATO is described as 'automatic driver signal command'. These commands are also derived from current fed into the track, but in this case only in short 3m sections of running

Above: **Bow Road station entrance, serving the District and Hammersmith & City rather than the Metropolitan Line. The station was built by the Whitechapel & Bow Railway and opened in 1902. It is a listed structure.** *Author*

rail. An electronic generator produces current of a special frequency which is obeyed by equipment on the trains. Current at 100Hz equals 1.6km/h permitted to the trains; at 1,000Hz it equals 16km/h, at 3,000Hz 48km/h, and so on. One of the main purposes of the driver command equipment is to apply the brakes to stop the train accurately in the station,

and careful calculations are made to enable command spots to be positioned along the track at the right places. This, incidentally, is one of the major difficulties in applying ATO to lines in the open, since rail conditions and hence braking requirements vary according to the weather.

The command signal frequency, picked up by an inductive coil on the train, is counted by an electronic counter and the frequency compared with that produced by a speedometer generator on the train. Electrical circuits regulate the train's progress to the correct predetermined speed required, by causing brake application or

release. This occurs at station approaches, but there are also command spots along the line where the train has reached sufficient speed to allow it to coast to the next station. The frequency at these spots, 15,000Hz, is outside the speed range of the train, and is recognised by a special circuit which issues a command to cut the motors.

For example, in operation a train may have left one station, but some distance ahead another train is standing in the next station. Between the trains would be a '420' signal-coded section (speed unrestricted), followed by the restrictive '270' and then '180' coded sections. Ahead of that a 'no code' section protects the train in advance. When the advance train clears the station to leave an unimpeded run to the following train, the latter would be able to proceed under '420' code to a 15,000Hz command spot, cutting the flow of current to the motors and causing the train to coast to the first of the command spots at the approach to the station. Here it would pass, successively, command spots at 3,000, 2,500, 2,000, 1,500 and 1,000Hz, each producing an 8km/h speed reduction through to a final halt. This would be at a predetermined platform stop, which the train would approach and stop at in a gradual braking curve, regardless of its load at the time.

All that is left for the driver (or rather 'train operator') to do is to initiate starting the train by depressing simultaneously a pair of buttons on the control desk, and operating the passenger doors. (Manual driving can be performed in the case of ATO failure.) For this he was deemed to need a clear view back along the length of his train, supplemented by closed circuit television cameras to view from the rear. This meant straight, or nearly straight, platforms, a condition which could not be provided on the existing system. The Victoria Line was the first application of OPO on the Underground, which was a welcome gain in productivity. But overall, not using the driver as a skilled man seemed to represent rather a waste of talent.

The Victoria Line is the only line which is ATO operated, the Woodford-Hainault 'guinea pig' service having reverted to normal OPO. The only other installations were experiments on the District Line in the early 1960s, while the rather different 'moving block' installation on the Jubilee Line was abandoned.

On 7 March 1969 HM The Queen became the first reigning monarch to ride in the cab of a tube train when she opened the Victoria Line, travelling between Green Park and Oxford Circus.

Left: **The Central Line updating and resignalling enabled all the previous signalboxes to be closed. This one at Leytonstone sees a 1992-stock train on a Hainault loop service passing in June 2003.** *Author*

Right: **This is Hammersmith depot on the H&C line, as seen from the station in May 1995. It has changed little since it was built, and is very restricted in size. A selection of C-stock trains is seen; Goldhawk Road, the next station, is in view in the distance.** *Author*

SOUTH TO BRIXTON

Work on extending the Victoria Line a further 5km south to Brixton began in 1967, shortly before the main section to the north was opened in sections in 1968 and 1969. Twin tunnels driven south led to Pimlico (built at the behest of the local authority and the only station without interchange to another railway), and on under the Thames. Crossing at its lowest point 7.3m below the river bed, the line reaches Vauxhall, with interchange for National Rail. On 12 July 1968 HRH The Duke of Edinburgh and HRH The Prince of Wales inspected tunnelling work under Vauxhall, on the Brixton extension.

The familiar cross-platform arrangements were provided once again at Stockwell with the Northern Line. Brixton station is the terminus, serving a particularly densely populated area. The finished product, largely completed in July 1971 but with the opening of Pimlico delayed until September 1972, brought Brixton and Walthamstow, 21km apart, within 32 minutes of each other. It was indeed a *tour de force*, and in its time was hailed as the world's most highly automated underground railway.

The Brixton extension was opened on 23 July 1971 by Princess Alexandra.

GREATER LONDON COUNCIL

The 1960s had not been good years for London Transport, which found the Board sinking slowly into deficit despite the demands of the 1962 Act for the undertaking to pay its way. This was compounded by growing staff shortages and industrial relations problems. The Greater London Council had been created in 1963, and was complaining that if it was to be the strategic planning authority for London, it should also have control of London Transport.

In its 1968 'Transport in London' White Paper, the Labour Government agreed, and was determined to hand the undertaking over to the GLC. The hope was expressed that this would offer a comprehensive approach to the efficient planning, provision, operation and financing of transport in London. There would be the 'closest possible harmony' with the wider aspects of land use and development. Significantly, the completeness of the transfer was marked by the abolition of the Transport Tribunal's functions on fares in London, with the structure and general level of fares to be determined by the GLC.

A new London Transport Executive was set up from 1 January 1970 under the control of the GLC (Transport London Act, 1969), 'for the purposes of implementing the policies which it is the duty of the Council to develop'.

The GLC therefore became responsible for appointing the members of the Executive, establishing their general policies and approving their budgets and fares policies. The Government heaved a sigh of relief; it was very much 'over to you'.

GROWTH FALTERS

While the Victoria Line was being built, the question was inevitably 'what next?' Office space in central London was being expanded, and it was thought that further travel demands would arise. By the end of 1965, Parliamentary powers to extend the (then) Aldwych branch of the Piccadilly to Waterloo had been obtained, while proposals for a new 'Fleet Line' saw the light of day. In both cases, what actually happened proved to be somewhat different!

Both in the inter-war period and the 1950s it had seemed as if the growth in demand for travel by the Underground network would go on expanding for ever. Yet the growth was faltering. The Location of Offices Bureau did its best to encourage firms to move out of London, and by the time that the London Rail Study reported in 1974, the extensive plans and optimistic proposals for capacity increases had to be judged against a background of static traffic levels. The growth that there was began to be taken up in the outer suburbs, with centres such as Croydon, Watford and Uxbridge bearing the brunt. And, in these, there was little or no traffic for the Underground.

Above: **The Northern City Line became part of British Rail. Before the transfer took place, it would be found on the route displays in tube cars, as here. This shows trains continuing to Finsbury Park, although the line was cut back to Drayton Park in 1964.** *Author*

GREAT NORTHERN ELECTRICS

One development represented a loss to the Underground network. What had become a detached part of the Northern Line north of Moorgate in the frustrated expansion of the 1930s finally had its fate determined. From autumn 1975, Underground trains were withdrawn from the Moorgate to Finsbury Park (latterly Drayton Park) section, and the line was handed over to British Rail's Great Northern Electrics. It had always been a difficult part of the Underground to work; for instance, to transfer trains to Acton Works, it was latterly necessary to drag them via a spur up to British Rail at Finsbury Park, haul them down to King's Cross and the Widened Lines, and back on to the Underground. Transfer was then via the Circle Line, Earl's Court and Hammersmith.

British Rail's suburban electric services started late in 1976, connecting Moorgate with Welwyn Garden City and Hertford North. The Class 313 trains were dual voltage, using 25kV ac south to Drayton Park where they entered the tunnel section. While the train was standing at the platform, the pantograph was lowered and the current pick-up was made from the 750V dc third rail instead. A dead overhead wire section is installed in the tunnel as far as Highbury in case the pantograph does not lock down!

Great Northern services on the Widened Lines were withdrawn. These tracks were later transferred to British Rail for the use first of 25kV ac Midland Suburban Electrics to Moorgate, and subsequently the Thameslink service through the Snow Hill tunnel via Farringdon, City Thameslink and Blackfriars. This brought the third rail through to Farringdon in 1988, where a similar pantograph ceremony takes place.

JUBILEE LINE STAGE I

The Bakerloo Line south from Baker Street had long been the most overcrowded of the Underground lines in central London, and relief was planned to enhance its capacity by eliminating the junction of the Queen's Park and Stanmore lines at Baker Street. The Stanmore branch would henceforth be connected to a new 'Fleet Line', as follows:

Stage I From Baker Street via Bond Street and Green Park to Charing Cross

Stage II From Charing Cross on to Aldwych, Ludgate Circus, Cannon Street and Fenchurch Street

Stage III From Fenchurch Street to Surrey Docks (now Surrey Quays), New Cross and Lewisham, with a branch from Surrey Docks to New Cross Gate

Or such was the plan, which was amended many times subsequently. Only the first part of Stage I, linking Baker Street to Green Park, survives today in the completed project. In this era, the route through and beyond the City was seen as problematical, while the regeneration of Docklands was not yet being talked about.

The main problem was that traffic on the Underground system was falling, quite fast. The go-ahead for Stage I was obtained in 1971, with work starting the following year. When Stage I was opened well behind time, in 1979 and two years after the Queen's Silver Jubilee, to honour which the line's name was changed, the need for the line to exist at all was being questioned, as were most certainly the extensions. Consequently, the cost of further construction which would largely parallel the District Line was not favoured, while a new concept (named the River Line) arose for the further eastern projection.

The 1974 London Rail Study had pronounced in favour of an Underground link binding together the north and south banks of the Thames, to be tagged on to the Fleet Line by a junction at Fenchurch Street. The line would cross beneath the Thames no less than four

times, with a terminus at Thamesmead. However, without Stage II, discussion of Stage III alternatives foundered; they came to be resurrected in totally different circumstances several years later.

CONSTRUCTION WORKS

Separating the Bakerloo Line branches at Baker Street, deep underground, so that each branch would have its own two platforms but all four interconnecting in the same station, presented problems. Two new step-plate junctions were built, one just to the south of Baker Street and one 300m to the north and about 15m below Marylebone main-line station. Additionally, a new station tunnel and a new running tunnel were driven on the north side of the existing Stanmore platform. The end result is that this latter now became the southbound Jubilee Line platform, and the new station tunnel and platform became the northbound Jubilee tunnel and platform.

To achieve this, the northbound Jubilee Line running tunnel had to be made to roll over the southbound tunnel both north and south of the station, which resulted in the new line's running in the station being the reverse of that of the Bakerloo Line. This is how a simple design concept in terms of passenger convenience was met through an ingenious and complex, but thoroughly elegant, solution.

At depths of between 21m and 42m, the twin tunnels run south and east from Baker Street for 4.68km. At Bond Street, only 2.1m separated the station tunnel from the (now defunct) Post Office Railway's driverless trains above, an indication of how existing services and building foundations can constrain new lines and facilities. Bond Street ticket hall was much enlarged, and as at Oxford Circus some years previously, an umbrella raft was erected over the roadway to allow work to proceed more or less unhindered. The line then veers southeast to Green Park, where it passes beneath both the Piccadilly and Victoria lines to reach the new station platforms, east of and below the latter's station. There is interconnection between all three lines, aided by new passages and escalators, but geography here as elsewhere on the Jubilee Line has imposed limitations on how convenient these interchanges can be made.

Reconstructing the Northern Line station at Strand and the Bakerloo Line station at Trafalgar Square resulted in the disappearance of both those names and the appellation Charing Cross being applied to them as well as the new Jubilee Line terminus. (The then Charing Cross station was renamed Embankment.) During the building work, Strand had to be closed, as a shaft for a bank of three new escalators was to be driven diagonally through the former lift shafts. Here too an umbrella was constructed in the BR station forecourt, after carefully underpinning the 300-tonne Queen Eleanor memorial.

Tunnelling followed established practice, but a laser beam was used to assist in setting out the tunnels and keeping the tunnelling machines on course. A beam from a point in the rear of the workings is directed on to a mark at the face, where it appears as a spot of light and thus acts as a guide for the shield operator. The line's over-run tunnels continued 0.51km beyond the platforms, ending just north of Waterloo Bridge.

The new part of the line was constructed with automatic train operation in mind, but it was driver-only operation which was adopted eventually without the complications of ATO. From its opening, the Jubilee Line was operated by the 1972 Mk II stock, although subsequent reshuffles led to it being equipped with the purpose-built 1983 stock. A consequence of the divorce from the Bakerloo was the depriving of that line of its maintenance depot, and a new facility was built at Stonebridge Park. The connection between the lines at Baker Street remains, although not in normal passenger use.

On 30 April 1979 HRH The Prince of Wales opened the line, travelling from Charing Cross to Stanmore. It is not usual for those performing such ceremonies to take such a long ride, but it is understood that he genuinely wanted to get to Stanmore for another engagement. Perhaps he was following the Underground's advertising of the period, which advised the reader to 'Get out of Charing Cross, fast!' And so the Underground

Below: **Rayners Lane is again one of the impressive station constructions of the inter-war period.** *Author*

did, but not until two decades later. The further development of the Jubilee Line is continued in Chapter 11.

HEATHROW CENTRAL

In 1929 grass runways for test flying were established at a site in west London. During World War 2 the aerodrome was chosen as a base for RAF long-range transport flights, and by 1945 military aircraft were taking off from its sole runway. Civilian airlines arrived in 1946, and LHR or London Heathrow was officially opened in May of that year. At that time, with an annual passenger usage of under two million, it was said that an Underground link would probably be built within six years. However, false prophets in a 1956 study concluded that the expected passenger use would not justify the cost, and that the proposed M4 motorway would suffice.

A skirmish between British Rail and London Transport interests was finally resolved in favour of the latter. With air passenger traffic predicted to reach 20 million a year in 1973 (it is now around 70 million and growing fast), the go-ahead for the Piccadilly Line extension was received in 1971. Few pretended that the Underground was the perfect solution for Heathrow; the Piccadilly is an integral part of the Underground, carrying commuters to and from central London and used for a variety of journey purposes within London. It is thus an ordinary urban railway and accordingly passengers have

to handle their own luggage up and down escalators and in and out of trains. Extra floor space for luggage was provided in the 1973 tube stock with which the Piccadilly Line was re-equipped, but with limited success when it came to avoiding impeding other passengers.

However, there were also advantages. One was that the scheduled service needed to be very frequent to cater for the combined needs of airport users and others; another gain was the multiplicity of destinations available directly or with a single change of train. King's Cross proved to be the single most popular destination.

The Piccadilly Line runs in the open between Barons Court and Hounslow West, from which point it was extended mainly in 'cut and cover' tunnel 2.91km to Hatton Cross (save only to emerge into the open for a short distance to cross the River Crane). From here it is in deep-level tube tunnels under the runways for the 2.09km to Heathrow Terminals 1, 2, 3. That station is built in a reinforced box 120m long and 23m wide, right in the centre of the airport. Escalators join the platforms 13.4m below ground to a sub-surface concourse, from which there is direct access via subways built by the British Airports Authority (BAA) to the three terminals. A further exit is to the bus station immediately above. HM The Queen formally opened the Heathrow extension on 16 December 1977, riding from Hatton Cross to Heathrow Central in the process.

The LONDON CONNECTION

Rail, Underground and Bus travel in and around London

EAST LONDON

A modernisation scheme for the East London Line, which sorely needed it, was started in 1979. In the pre-Docklands-boom days, traffic levels were low and declining, but the condition of the stations was deplorable. Refurbishment was later to become a major programme on the principal Underground stations; that on the East London was confined mostly to installation of fluorescent lighting, platform resurfacing, repainting and minor works, together with the plastic-faced panels to cover up the grimy platform walls. At Wapping, the panels tell the story of the Thames Tunnel. Shadwell was provided with lifts to replace stairs, as well as a new surface building. Wapping received new lifts, Rotherhithe's rebuilding featured a pair of escalators, and Surrey Docks had a complete new surface station. At Whitechapel, the ticket hall was renewed.

LONDON'S TRANSPORT MUSEUM

The London Transport Museum was opened in the former Covent Garden flower market building in 1980, replacing the earlier display at Syon Park, and at Clapham before that. Major as well as minor exhibits, many of which are mentioned in this book, are displayed here permanently.

BEYOND THE FRINGE

Travelling beyond Northwood on the Metropolitan or on the far side of Woodford on the Central, a curious but imperceptible change took place. For this was territory outside Greater London and hence beyond the writ of the Greater London Council.

It cannot be said that the 1969 Act ignored this spread of the Underground beyond the GLC boundaries, since that authority had to approve the fares charged, but the financial consequences were not perhaps appreciated. This was peripheral territory, of marginal profitability at the best of times, with both the Watford and Ongar branches having been less than successful financial ventures. 'The Counties shall pay for these services if they want them,' said the GLC. It turned out that the Counties did want them, but politely declined to contribute, arguing quite reasonably that it was a mere historical quirk that such services were operated as part of the Underground rather than British Rail. Faced with this, London Transport was instructed to raise fares to a quite ridiculous extent (Ongar to Debden, 15.74km, £1.55 single at 1980 prices).

In an effort to save costs, the Epping–Ongar line was staked out as a closure proposal; the usage of this rural branch, which had already been reduced to operation by one train, was less than 1,000 passenger journeys a day. The

Left: **The bringing-together of the various providers of public transport in London began to move forward again during this period, with the publication of this rail/bus/Underground combined leaflet in 1982.** *Author's collection*

Minister refused outright closure, but Blake Hall station in its remote glory was having difficulty in generating even double figures of passengers on a good day and was closed in 1981, by which time it was claimed to have the lowest patronage of any underground-line station in the world. The rest of the service was reduced to run in rush hours only, which were generously interpreted in the 1982 timetable revisions. Unexpectedly, a local management decision, albeit short-lived, was to restore the all-day service in 1989.

BAKERLOO LINE TO HARROW

When London Underground wanted to build the new depot at Stonebridge Park as the only possible location for the separated Bakerloo Line operation (following inauguration of the Jubilee Line in 1979), the British Railways Board decided to make what amounted to punitive access charges. However, there was no alternative for the Underground.

Bakerloo services were withdrawn between Stonebridge Park and Watford Junction on 24 September 1982. They were restored, to Harrow & Wealdstone only, on 4 June 1984. There was thus a period of a little under two years when the stations of Wembley Central, North Wembley, South Kenton, Kenton and Harrow & Wealdstone had no Underground service.

Service restoration was achieved on a *quid pro quo* basis. What are now the Silverlink Watford dc services were having capacity problems, which would be expensive to rectify, while LU could offer the necessary capacity at small cost. A deal was done on the basis that each operator would bear its own operating costs and that no additional charges would be made by BR for LU operation to Harrow & Wealdstone. The service continues today.

FARES WITH THE GLC

Fares provided the graphic example of shifting priorities. At first, London Transport was expected to break even after depreciation expenses, to provide for any surplus which the GLC might determine, and to set aside a general reserve. The incoming GLC administration of 1973 decided to implement a fares standstill until 1975, when spiralling inflation led to a policy reversal. The original wholly unrealistic remit was thus turned into a fares relief grant, first made in 1974. The cost escalated alarmingly, and fares were doubled in 18 months during 1975/6 to restore the position.

After that, fare levels continued to climb slowly in real terms, reaching a historically high level in 1981. 'Fares Fair' then intervened. This was a GLC attempt to put fares back to their 1969 levels in real terms. But such had been the growth of inefficiency in London Transport with staff levels up, traffic levels down, a falling London population and a miserable operating performance, that the cost was too much for some to swallow.

Prime critic was the London Borough of Bromley, whose High Court action succeeded in having the policy declared unlawful on appeal. Consequently, fares were increased by 96% in March 1982, with the result that patronage, which had been rising, took a nosedive again. Services were reduced to match the new traffic levels in December of that year.

In many ways, this was the Underground's darkest hour; from such a position, matters could only improve. Fewer than 500 million passenger journeys were recorded in 1982 – the lowest since 1943, when the network was much smaller and circumstances wholly different. Yet in the turmoil of the Greater London Council's fares policies for London Transport had been the introduction in 1983 of zonal pricing on the Underground – a necessary precondition for what was to follow in the best-selling product of the Travelcard.

The essentials of today's London Travelcard scheme, which is a season ticket offering travel to the holder within a specified geographical area, are:

- definition of six concentric zones around central London, Zone 1 encompassing the Circle Line and a little more, Zone 6 coinciding more or less with the Greater London boundary
- ticket availability and pricing for the number of zones required
- validity for unlimited travel on London Underground, London bus services, Croydon Tramlink, Docklands Light Railway, and National Rail services within the zone(s) selected
- issue for one week or for any period between one month and one year

A further one-day ticket gives similar benefits, but this was not available before 09.30, Mondays to Fridays. The peak facility only became available, at a higher price, in 2003. Underground single-journey fares were also converted to a zonal basis.

The original Travelcard scheme was launched in May 1983. This date marked the introduction of the GLC's 'Balanced Plan' for transport, whereby a strategy for transport as a whole in the capital was unveiled. For London Transport this meant an overall fares reduction of 25%, the legality having first been verified by a 'friendly' High Court action between LT and the Council. The result was a restoration of the real fares level to a position midway between that before and after 'Fares Fair'. By the end of that year there were 600,000 holders of Travelcards, and passenger km travelled on the Underground rose by no less than a fifth. The number of passenger journeys made over the early 1980s reflected the fares structures; for the years 1981, 1982, 1983 and 1984/5 these were, in millions, 541, 498, 563 and 659 respectively.

HEATHROW TERMINAL 4 LOOP

Before leaving the GLC period, it is perhaps timely to consider the major project of the Heathrow Terminal 4 loop at the western end of the Piccadilly Line, completed under LRT auspices. Underground traffic at Heathrow had built up very satisfactorily but, unfortunately, the planners had anticipated that, if a fourth terminal were built, this would be on the Perry Oaks site further west. (This, it later turned out, was to be the fifth terminal.)

The station, originally Heathrow Central, was thus aligned on a northwest-southeast axis, which posed something of a problem when the decision was reached to construct Terminal 4 a couple of kilometres or so away on the southern perimeter. After desultory talk of a travelator link to Hatton Cross, the decision was reached to

Below: **A historic piece of infrastructure, and it works, although it doesn't tell you how long you are likely to wait. These indicators are at Earl's Court, on both District Line platforms.**
Author

Above: **Earl's Court station, as seen from the Exhibition Centre with a D-stock train departing.** *Author*

build instead a terminal loop for the Underground, starting at Hatton Cross. Trains would proceed only in a clockwise direction around this loop, calling successively at Heathrow Terminal 4, Heathrow Terminals 1, 2, 3 and Hatton Cross again. This meant the effective abandonment of one of the two existing running tracks west of Hatton Cross, constructed only a decade previously.

The building of the loop led to some novel problems. Excavation just west of Hatton Cross station had to take place almost directly under the flight path of aircraft. No component part such as lifting gear and stacked material could be allowed to rise above a level which would have created radar interference and thus affect aircraft in flight. So the large working area had first to be turned into a kind of shallow pit, and in a deep trench below that a new rail junction plus a 400m section of tunnel had to be built and then covered in.

The new junction was built within a concrete sub-surface formation, necessitating careful demolition of the original 'box. Then followed an ascending section of tunnel with cast-iron lining, built in trench and backfilled. Tunnelling shields were used from all three working sites to drive the running tunnels through the London clay, thrust forward by hydraulic rams. Face cutting was by boom cutters, and the spoil was removed rearwards by conveyors. Eventually this reached the surface up inclined drift tunnels. Most of the running tunnel was lined with pre-cast concrete rings.

Where the new single-track tunnel divided to link with the two original over-run tunnels, a step-plate junction was constructed. Flat-bottom welded rail on pre-stressed concrete sleepers made its first appearance on the tube system here. In an effort to reduce noise, sleepers on part of the new track rest on rubber fittings. Finally, two ventilation shafts were constructed. It was a shame that delays in deciding how the new terminal should be served resulted in the station at T4 not being ideally sited, with rather a long walk from the vast terminal proper. On 1 April 1986, the station and loop were opened, together with the whole of Terminal 4, by the Prince and Princess of Wales.

END OF MUNICIPALISATION?

The introduction of the Travelcard was, however, too late to save the GLC, and the Government abruptly wrenched London Transport away from the Council's control with its London Regional Transport Act on 29 June 1984.

Although the GLC years produced some tangible results in terms of new trains and some line extensions, the whole period was characterised by the warring which took place with central government, to which the Council was often politically opposed. The Jubilee Line was a case in point. Denied a capital grant from the (Labour) Government to continue east from Charing Cross, the (Conservative) leader of the GLC said that 'the line would be built whether the Government agrees and helps or not ... if we cannot borrow the money we will raise it from the rates and damn the government'. The extensions were not built.

GLC influence was far from consistent over the years, as administrations oscillated from one party to the other. Policy shifts are all very well, but when capital investment can last for a century or more for infrastructure and 30-40 years for rolling stock, a degree of continuity and freedom from political meddling is called for.

CHAPTER ELEVEN

London Underground Ltd

The creation of London Regional Transport in June 1984 and the subsequent formation of London Underground Ltd (LUL) in 1985 as a wholly owned subsidiary represented a complete change of direction. Originally, LRT had three main tasks:

- an overall responsibility for the planning of public transport services in London
- securing the provision of those services
- the effective running of a series of businesses related to bus and Underground operation

THE SUBSIDIARIES

LRT was created as the strategic planning and management body, while London Underground Ltd, London Buses Ltd and Docklands Light Railway were its three transport operations. They were separate subsidiary companies operating independently, but co-ordinated by LRT. Just to confuse matters, 'London Transport' was the collective name used latterly for London Regional Transport itself. London Transport also included the bus services provided by outside contractors as an integral part of the network, and the common activities such as ticketing, marketing and service information. The collective name was also applied to the activities of London Transport Advertising, London Transport International (the consultancy), London Transport Lost Property and London's Transport Museum.

Times change, however. The loss of the Docklands Light Railway to the London Docklands Development Corporation, the privatisation of the London Buses subsidiaries during 1994 and the sale of other businesses left London Underground as LRT's only directly controlled transport operation.

In discharging its principal job of determining what services should be provided or secured for Greater London, LRT had to have regard for London's transport needs, and to satisfy the financial objectives laid down by the Secretary of State for Transport. This meant that it needed to break even after grants.

The initial emphasis of London Regional Transport was on cost reduction and consolidation after the turbulent years of the previous decade. But other forces were also at work, and one of the main factors causing the strategy to be rethought was the upsurge in

Right: **An early try at corporate rebranding produced this C-stock train in the same range of corporate colours as adopted, but the final result was a blue band along the bottom of the body sides, grey above, with red doors.** *IAL*

> 'The system carries more passengers than the national railway network and usage (832m journeys) is at the highest level on record.'
>
> *Annual Report, 1997/8*

passenger usage, fuelled by a growing economy and the runaway success of the Travelcard.

FARES POLICIES

The first moves away from the traditional charging methods based on distance travelled were made in 1981 with 'Fares Fair', which established a system of zonal charging on buses throughout Greater London and on the Underground in the central area. It was not until the May 1983 fares revision, though, that zoning was fully established. Beyond the central zone, an inner zone equivalent to its bus counterpart was formed, to be followed by three concentric ring zones roughly three miles apart, covering broadly the same area as the bus outer zone. The most significant change, however, was the replacement of Underground season tickets and bus passes with Travelcards. These gave their holders freedom to interchange without penalty, and to make additional journeys at no additional cost. Indeed, the greater the use made

of the Travelcard, the better value the user obtained from buying it – irrespective of whether the fare level was low or high. Usage shot upwards. This was, of course, still under the GLC regime. Progressive improvements subsequently added in British Rail services in 1985, initially at a premium, and one-day tickets available outside the morning peak. In 1991/92, Travelcard sales accounted for 62% of all London Underground revenue.

There were two basic thrusts to the fares policy. Simplification asked whether the complexity of graduated fares was really necessary, and found that it was not. Integration was a more positive and creative approach, which attempted to develop new and attractive ticketing products for passengers. It was hoped that this would in turn result in a fundamental shift in the market for travel, thus enlarging the core of intensive users whose patronage is critical in sustaining the system, and abating the drift towards the use of the private car. After all,

Travelcard and the car have similar economics for their users. Following the initial outlay, the marginal cost of use of Travelcard is zero; what is more, its user doesn't have to park the vehicle!

The fares policies were certainly successful. Starting from such a low base, the system at first had ample capacity to absorb traffic growth. But traffic grew and kept on growing, and in time coping with the effects became a major preoccupation. Overcrowding and congestion thus once again became part of the vocabulary of public transport operators in London, matters which had been of limited importance, other than in respect of road traffic generally, for a long time. Demand was racing ahead, stimulated also by economic growth. Such was the turnaround that the 498 million passenger journeys of 1982 – the low point – reached 815 million in 1988/89, an increase of over 60%.

MANAGING THE UNDERGROUND

The studies of and possibilities for new rail services are discussed later. Meanwhile, how was the Underground being managed? In the real world, productivity measures were being pursued, as exemplified by the Underground Ticketing System and DOO trains, as already described; in the five years from 1983, unit costs were cut by 15%. Infrastructure investment has been more than doubled, both to secure reductions in future running costs and to modernise and improve the amenity value of the system. After years of underfunding, much of the Underground was still undeniably squalid, and perceptions of the quality of service offered were correspondingly low. 'Tubular Hell' was one newspaper's way of describing it, while an (often exaggerated) view of crime in the Underground caught the public attention.

Neither public nor staff confidence had been improved by the major fire at King's Cross in November 1987 in which 31 persons died, and the sad tale of shortcomings unravelled by the public inquiry was followed by the deafening sound of stable doors being very expensively bolted. The railway was not being run professionally, and it ran out of luck. The most lasting result to come out of this incident was a realisation that safety has to be managed positively: hazards must be identified and rated according to their potential impact and likelihood of happening – and of the cost of remedial measures. This includes not only standards, materials, communications and emergency arrangements, but also the need for crowd control plans at major stations and thus the means of providing for the growing problem of congestion relief.

Another result was a complete change of top management.

TRAVEL VOLUMES INCREASE

If poor quality in a world of rising expectations was one problem, the other conundrum was growth. The level and pattern of demand for Underground travel is a resultant of multiple factors, many of which are way outside the

Above: **The pre-1938 stock on the Isle of Wight was retired and replaced by the venerable 1938 stock. This time two-car units took the place of three- or four-car formations, and the few that remain often run singly. No 483005 approaches Brading from the north on 17 June 1992, the piece of rail in the 'four foot' giving a good impression of fourth-rail electrification, which it is not.** *Author*

control of any transport undertaking. Population, employment, personal incomes, car ownership, road conditions and tourism are among those factors. As with personal investment warnings, 'passenger volumes may go down as well as up'. And down by 10% they have gone since the heady days of 1988/9 when 815 million journeys on London Underground were recorded, to reach a low of 728 million journeys in 1992/3. But by 1994/5 volumes had recovered to 764 million. What next?

To start with, sustained growth when it comes may not be uniform. If, for example, future employment is associated with major developments in Docklands, the City, King's Cross and Heathrow, the loads imposed on the Underground network will be very uneven. Also, the spread of traffic throughout the day and between days of the week may change; thus there is some recent evidence of people starting work earlier.

It all boiled down to a conclusion that without action being taken, probably irrespective of any fares levels which might be considered reasonable, system capacity would become totally inadequate.

STRATEGIC ISSUES

There were five strategic issues facing London Underground Ltd in the late 1980s:
- The network capacity was constrained at the peak.

- There were service quality as well as safety problems as a result.
- The anticipated growth of demand would be a further 20% at peak and 30% at off-peak by 1997/8.
- Major additions to capacity needed large investments and long lead times.
- LUL had neither the cash nor the borrowing powers to fund extensive new investment in either the short or medium term.

What, then, would be the likely effects of taking various broad courses of action? Four scenarios were painted:
- Commercial network. This would make money, and be cash rich within a decade through high fares and the lopping off of the extremities, such as everything north and west of Harrow-on-the-Hill. Lines such as the Bakerloo which are paralleled (in this case mostly by the Jubilee Line or BR's Watford local services) would close completely. Overall, the network would shrink to about half its present size.
- Quality network. The quality of provision would be brought up to predetermined levels, but essentially the system would remain within the limits of the existing infrastructure.
- Expanded network. As quality network, but providing additional works to relieve congestion and serving new areas of London as could be justified.
- London showpiece network. This would be an attempt to make London resemble Paris, but at a capital cost of £10 billion which could come only from outside sources.

What would the pursuit of a commercial network mean for London? High fares would certainly reduce passenger congestion on the Underground and would enable service quality

Above: **A train of unrefurbished A stock arrives at the new Hillingdon station, opened in 1992 as a result of the A40(M) road construction.** *Author*

to be improved significantly; the revenues could be used to fund investment. However, higher fares would also reduce demand and encourage relocation away from London. Was that what London Underground (and its LRT parent body) were there to do? A reading of the 1984 London Regional Transport Act confirms that LRT is there 'to have due regard to the transport needs for the time being of Greater London'.

If, however, unchecked demand-led growth were to resume, perpetuation of the present financial regime would result in service volume,

Below: **The Metropolitan's No 12** *Sarah Siddons* **is seen here on display at Eastleigh amid some rolling stock of obviously BR origin. It claims to be the 'Director of Mechanical Engineering's Brake Block Test Locomotive'. What it is to have a research budget which is sufficiently generous to let one maintain a venerable piece of equipment like this!** *Author*

quality and safety all suffering. The problems of inadequate capacity have to be addressed; unfortunately, the levels of investment needed are not related to the volume of business, nor to the fares levels charged, nor even the latent demand for services. It is simply not tenable to allow more and more passengers to crowd into the system unless it is expanded to cope. The safety of passengers in overcrowded conditions is at risk, and the congestion factor as on the roads would result in the overall throughput diminishing as trains were forced to spend longer at station platforms.

This raised the spectacle of some central-London stations having to be closed for the

duration of the peak. This situation was nearer than it might have seemed, with for example Chancery Lane being available for exit only during the morning rush hour, while King's Cross adopted an elaborate one-way system to keep the two flows of passengers apart.

PERFORMANCE MEASURES

Financial performance of the business cannot be separated from the above, and it is just not possible to have everything. An equation has to be found which balanced the following factors:

● financial performance
● adequate service quality
● volume of service provision
● safety

What the customers of London Underground merited was a policy which allowed government funding for major investment in expanding service provision, offset against internal efficiency improvements and restructuring of the business to improve its management, and the results showing within a five-year timescale. There needs to be a co-ordinated framework.

During this period, the standards of customer service and company performance must improve steadily, the gains must be consolidated with past standards restored, and the strength of the improved position used as a justification for further expansion. While the first stages were a matter for Underground management, the latter could only be accelerated or even achieved at all with the financial help of the Government and/or the private sector. Realistically, the returns for private investment in rapid transit are just not there, with the result that public cash is needed in the vast majority of cases. With LUL at present, a substantial proportion of investment comes from operating profits, and the rest from external sources.

MAKING IT HAPPEN

If that is the strategy, how could it be made to happen? The management organisation was reduced to a small executive Board, with four non-executive positions. Each Underground line was made into a profit centre and given its own general manager. These managers were also responsible for costs, revenues, the performance of the physical assets, and of that all-important asset – people. Everything else was a support function. Staff were responsible to one named manager.

What was the then state of London Underground? Customer perception was decidedly poor, rating the Underground's value for money as inadequate. Both the capacity of the system and the conditions in which people had to travel were found wanting. Staff were perceived as unhelpful, restrictive practices abounded, and their efficiency was poor. There had been many improvement measures, but overall they had not been focused sufficiently; frustratingly, in spite of all the efforts made, the results did not show and were neither recognised nor appreciated.

It was not just the politicians who had been at fault, as the Underground's 1988 'Plan for Action' frankly admitted:

'Though this thoroughly unsatisfactory situation derived in large part from the political and national economic context of the business, there were also major weaknesses in the organisational structure and performance of management in the Underground.'

From such a base line, the only way to go is up. The company set out a long-term objective that the total service would be of the same standard which is implied by new trains, updated control systems and signalling, well-maintained track and modernised stations. The financial performance needed to be maximised within the constraints of volume and the extension of quality and safety of service. Market potential was to be optimised, and it was essential that long term total costs were brought down to the lowest possible level.

CENTRAL LINE

The immediate response provided for a number of major upgrading proposals, of which the Central Line was by far the most extensive and offered complete re-equipment. The 85 new trains of 1992 stock and their derivation from the 1986 stock have already been discussed. Line refurbishment included the installation of new fixed block signalling and centralised control. The power supply system was to be replaced and uprated to allow trains to run faster and thus reduce journey times by 12%. There were also minor track realignments to raise speed limits.

The new signalling aimed to increase the previous 30 trains per hour throughput to 33/34tph. Restrictions, such as speeds over the tortuous curves at Bank and the time taken to discharge passengers at Liverpool Street and other busy stations, were as much constraints as was the signalling when it came to increasing service frequency. Speed control signalling, a feature of inter-war installations, had been removed in the declining traffic years of the 1960s and the 1970s. The new signalling offered the opportunity to get back to frequencies achieved in the past. While a transmission-based signalling system based on a moving block section and offering a potential 38 or even 39tph was available, it was not judged sufficiently developed or cost-effective for Central Line use. The whole project was aimed at increasing the total line carrying capacity by about 16%.

In the event, Automatic Train Protection (ATP), which ensures that all traffic moves at a safe speed, was introduced progressively to the Central Line between 1995 and 1997. This was followed by Automatic Train Operation (ATO). This drives trains automatically, and aims to achieve the optimum operational performance in terms of journey time, headway and energy consumption. It was installed between 1999 and 2001. With ATO, centralised control from the new West London Control Centre enabled the remaining signalboxes along the line to be progressively taken out of use.

NORTHERN LINE

The Northern Line is the second-busiest, with around 700,000 passengers a day. Large-scale investment was needed, and one of the major schemes was Angel station. New office building at Angel had seen traffic rise by 123% in six years, with more to come from redevelopment. The station had been provided only with lifts, but under a £70 million scheme, a new entrance and ticket hall were built to lead to the longest escalator shafts on the Underground. From there, a second short escalator flight descends to a circulating area to the west of the previous island platform. The northbound track of this was filled in as was done at Euston (old Northern City Line northbound platform) when the Victoria Line was built, and a direct passageway made to the new circulating area. A totally new northbound platform was constructed in a new station tunnel, and the line diverted into it. Work was completed in 1992.

A number of shorter-term improvements were also undertaken. Transfer of additional trains from the Bakerloo as part of the repercussions of the delivery of the 1983 tube stock boosted the number in service. Highgate depot was reopened and modernised, while 11 stations at the southern end of the line were refurbished – with special attention paid to anti-graffiti measures. The dot-matrix information displays were upgraded at all 49 stations, with more passenger security measures at the southern end. This had seen some growth of late evening traffic in response. Dot matrix indicators were provided in some ticket halls so that passengers need to descend to platform level only when their train's arrival is imminent. Aerials were installed in the ceilings of underground passages so that staff can remain in contact by personal radio.

ROLLING STOCK

In the early 1990s the Northern was operated by a mixture of 1959-62 and 1972 Mk I stock - very much the bits and pieces left over from other lines - and this needed replacement. The Northern has long continuous tunnel gradients to the north, and a high proportion is in tunnel. Station platforms are also relatively restricted in length, and operationally it would be desirable to get away from an inflexible seven-car formation.

Below: **A train of 1972 Mk II stock in LUL corporate livery arrives at Kensal Green with a southbound working to Elephant & Castle. As can be seen from the tunnels, rolling stock of a much larger size can be accommodated; the rest of the service is maintained by Class 313 units operated by Silverlink.** *Author*

It was announced late in 1994 that a new fleet of 106 trains was to be built by Metro-Cammell (later part of GEC-Alsthom) in an entirely new form of contract.

Meanwhile, refurbishment was carried out on three trains of 1972 stock as the remainder were too old to justify it. The new décor was designed to offer a brash exterior and a homely interior. Lighting was softened to reduce glare, while providing the popular end-bulkhead lights to brighten up the gloomy corners. Repositioned grab rails encouraged standing passengers to move away from the door area. Panels and fittings assessed as potential fire hazards were replaced, and public address fitted. Comparable work was carried out on the similar Victoria Line (1967) and Bakerloo Line (1972 Mk II) stock.

The new 1995 stock was a scheme under the Private Finance Initiative (PFI), and the manufacturer Alstom retained ownership of the trains. This included responsibility for their maintenance over a 20-year period, and there are opportunities to extend the contract to a total of 36 years. The contract is performance related and the reliability target includes a failure rate of 1 in 30,500km; this compares with 1 in 4,000km for the fleet being succeeded. There is also a 'small payment' related to the number of passengers carried on the Northern Line. The rental payment to LUL is expected to amount to between £40 million and £45 million a year.

Thus LUL has entered into a 'power by the hour' usage contract, with a substantial element of risk transferred to the private sector. Each day,

Alstom as the service provider, must deliver a fleet of reliable, clean trains which are returned to it at night. Non-availability or performance shortfalls are reflected in the usage payments.

Unfortunately, past investment cutbacks mean that London Underground has had difficulty in making as much use of the enlarged Northern Line fleet as had been intended. Strengthening of power supplies and the renewal of signalling are both needed. In prospect are a reduction of journey times, for

which the permanent way needs to be brought up to scratch, coupled with increased service frequencies. Flat-bottomed long-welded rail will become standard equipment.

SIGNALLING

The Northern Line's capacity had been reduced in the years of passenger losses by signalling-simplification schemes, which are now much regretted. The practical maximum on each of the Charing Cross and City branches is presently 25tph, although theory says that more ought to be possible. Transmission-based signalling is the favoured means to overcome the problem; through the use of this, the train service might be increased to 32tph. Journey times via the City are 4min longer than via Charing Cross. This tends to lead to movements at junctions which conflict with each other at either Camden Town or Kennington.

The 106-train fleet would signal its position and its speed via the track to a central computer,

Left: **Signalling is a Northern Line priority; this installation at Borough does not exactly impress. This is only a repeater signal for the benefit of guards, of which there are nowadays none, but does it give an indication of the state of the rest of the installation?** *Author*

Below: **Morden station at the southern end of the Northern Line has three lines but five platforms, since it was deemed a good idea to be able to separate incoming and outgoing passengers. 1959 stock is fully occupying the premises in this view of 31 May 1990.** *Author*

which would then analyse the information every 0.5sec and 'instruct' the train accordingly. Such measures are now favoured over earlier ideas such as splitting the line into High Barnet/Mill Hill East to Morden via the City, and Edgware to Kennington via Charing Cross. Difficulties with this option include the vast numbers of passengers who would have to change (especially at Camden Town) and the implication for station dwell times, and the likely imbalances of peak and off-peak traffic requirements on the two routes. A further complication is the imbalance of depot engineering facilities. Spending £75 million or so to rebuild Camden Town seems a lot merely to inconvenience passengers.

The trains are being maintained at Golders Green and Morden as previously; both depots are now under Alstom, which employs the former depot staff. The 1995 stock began to enter passenger service in 1998. The trains themselves consist of two sets of three-car units, each made up DM+T+UNDM. All seating is longitudinal, but unlike the (earlier) 1996 Jubilee Line stock to which it is closely related, there are tip-up seats which, in theory anyway, fold themselves up to a vertical position when vacated. They are in the area intended nominally for wheelchairs.

In the cabs, the driver's seat has a control built into the armrest. A pair of small CCTV screens are built into the driver's panel, with the door controls to either side. There are steps built into the end door to allow passengers to be detrained if required rather more expeditiously than hitherto.

STATION MODERNISATION

Throughout the system, station modernisation has absorbed large chunks of funds. The work is difficult, as it cannot be carried out when trains are still running and the station is in use. Consequently, much of the re-tiling and platform resurfacing can be done only at night or during periods of extended line closure. There were also unforeseen hazards: it was a materials store being used by a contractor during station

modernisation at Oxford Circus in 1984 which caught fire and wrecked the northbound Victoria Line platform.

A wide variety of schemes has been tried; one of the most successful was that at Baker Street on the original 1863 Metropolitan and Circle platforms. The original station was lit by gas at night, but by day natural daylight came from the shafts above the platforms which had been installed to allow the escape of smoke from the locomotives. Later, accumulated grime, advertising hoardings and fluorescent lighting made it a dismal place indeed. The refurbishment involved stone cleaning, the introduction of artificial daylight through sodium lights in the old shafts, and new seats and fittings.

Other notable past refurbishments have been David Gentleman's mural of the mediæval craftsmen building the original Eleanor Cross above at Charing Cross (Northern Line), and a complementary portrayal of some of the treasures of the National Gallery and the National Portrait Gallery on the Bakerloo Line platforms. Eduardo Paolozzi's unique hi-fi-inspired mosaics at Tottenham Court Road, the British Museum theme at Holborn, and the Brunel tunnelling shields at Paddington are others which catch the eye. Throughout, fittings such as cable ducts and seats are in the line colour, and standard roundel-style station names are used. Various experiments have taken place with signing.

STATION CONGESTION

The relief of station congestion has produced a list which included Monument (District Line) and Bank (Northern Line), both as a result of the DLR extension, and Goodge Street as a result of the Underground ticketing system (UTS). The problems vary between locations; lift or

Below: **Baker Street Metropolitan Line platforms are adequate, but they show their age as does much of the system. There is huge scope for updating. This view was recorded on 10 April 1998.** *Author*

escalator capacity (*eg* Russell Square), the ticket barrier or ticket hall capacity (*eg* Bayswater, High Street Kensington), platform capacity (*eg* Liverpool Street, Central Line and Victoria, Victoria Line). At Euston Square, consideration was being given to 'double-ending' the station by providing a ticket hall at each end of the platforms; here that would have the additional advantage of improving the access to Euston Network Rail station.

At Tottenham Court Road, better street access was needed, as was a new escalator shaft. In all, 24 or 25 stations have a measurable present problem, while an eye to future expansion as a result of new lines is also important. Thus a rebuilt Tottenham Court Road would include embryonic provision for both Crossrail and the Chelsea-Hackney lines. But will either ever be built?

The difficulties at Victoria were complex. The Victoria Line ticket hall needed enlargement, with augmentation to the escalators and the lower concourse. Restricted platform widths increased station stop times, which had serious implications for the train service which could be operated. If trains are halted by up to a minute to allow passengers to alight and board (preferably in that order!), this constrained the number of trains per hour which could be run on the whole line. The possible solutions, all of which were exceedingly costly, included widened station platforms, additional platforms, and 'double-ending' the station.

In such cases – and Liverpool Street Central Line was as bad – the aim must be to control stop times, and, if this needed new track layouts, rolling stock modifications, staff training or signalling changes, these had to be built into the plans.

LINE CAPACITY

The capacity of lines is governed primarily by train lengths and service frequencies. More trains and longer trains were among the options being pursued by British Rail, but on the existing Underground, with traditional signalling, it is considered that something like 30 trains per hour is the realistic maximum. This is despite schedules in the past on the Bakerloo and District lines offering a (perhaps theoretical) 34 or 36tph. Train capacities vary, but, using the Underground's formal loading standards, a formation of 8 x A stock will carry 680, while both 6 x C stock and most tube-stock trains will carry 550. More passengers can, of course, squeeze themselves on.

NEW OBJECTIVES

In the spring of 1989, London Regional Transport was set new objectives for its rail services by the Government. These were as follows:
- to carry through the recommendations arising from the King's Cross fire
- to provide for the continuing increase in traffic on the Underground, and for growing needs in Docklands
- to improve the quality of services and security for the traveller

Above: **A 1992-stock train disappears eastwards from East Acton Central Line station.** *Author*

POWER ELECTRONICS

Power electronics for rolling stock offer tremendous potential. The positive effects include energy saving, regenerative braking, jerk-free operation, wheelslip control, elimination of fire hazards through doing away with dc starting resistances, response to supply variations, and no contactor maintenance. Conversely, they add weight, interact with signalling and power supply, and need a greater engineering input.

Similarly, there are huge gains to be made in the interrelated fields of signalling, traffic control, communications and passenger information. What could be more antiquated in concept than traditional block signalling when track capacity is the most precious asset? Computer-aided engineering enables calculations on matters such as safety and immunisation to be made more accurately. This therefore reduces the likelihood of wasteful over-engineering. Simulation for site specific designs can be carried out, and the testing of trade-offs. The need to build prototypes for engineering reasons has now largely passed.

Another fast developing field includes management information systems; the instant calculating ability of computer systems vastly enhances the capability of flexible systems scheduling. The concomitant need is for wholly satisfactory agreements to be reached with the staff.

The conclusion is that the sheer scale of potential technology impacts must be managed, with London Underground determining where it is going and organising itself accordingly. Engineers determine standards. Equipment

With the scene having changed significantly, formal targets were set for service quality. Among these was the performance of lifts and escalators. Only 75% were in working order in 1989, which was freely admitted to be unacceptable. Those on the Victoria Line, which were only 20 years old, were failing. Underground escalators may now be the cleanest in the world in the aftermath of King's Cross, but the incapacity of the industry and the high loads being carried for hours at a time have played havoc with performance. New escalators are being installed at 12 a year for the foreseeable future.

In escalators, as in so much else, the largely unsung role of the engineer is crucial. Here too there are changes. Technology offers the ability to squeeze more out of existing infrastructure, to increase construction benefits and to reduce operating costs. But new technology is demanding. New skills are needed, a control over specifications is essential, while there is a need to learn from those outside. It is much more cost-effective to learn from the mistakes of others!

Above: **The Bank/Monument complex is the largest on the Underground, catering for five Underground lines plus the Docklands Light Railway. It is possible to move between all parts of the stations without going through a ticket barrier.**

procurers (not all of them engineers) draw up specifications. Contractual obligations ensure (one hopes) reliability. However, while procurement by the output required rather than a technical specification might encourage the supplier to innovate, it has to be seen in the context of managerial responsibilities. What is the best value for the business?

FARES REVENUE

The Underground needs more revenue. By the end of the 1980s, it was noticeable that official noises were beginning to be made about fares levels; a slow real increase in fares since LRT took over in 1984 was approaching a cumulative 20% five years later. The harder line asserted that fares had not grown faster than earnings, and that fares levels still offered good value for money. Indeed, the average fare per passenger journey in 1993/94 was 87p, compared with the then minimum fare of 90p applicable in the Central Zone 1. The users of the system are predominantly under 35 years old, while 70% are in the ABC1 social groups and relatively well off. With a Government view that passengers must pay for the benefits they receive, further real fares increases with alterations to the Travelcard zonal system in order to finance investment, at least for renewals, seemed inevitable. However, pricing limitations by the Rail Regulator on National Rail's fares also affect London Underground pricing.

Such, at any rate, was the view of the Monopolies & Mergers Commission in its 1991 report. With economic recession biting into traffic levels, and following some financial misjudgements, the company had to make economies. The MMC was critical of the physically decayed state of much of the infrastructure. 'The public's perception of an erratic, overcrowded and poorly maintained service in many areas is broadly correct,' it said, albeit acknowledging that the overall picture was more favourable. It too concluded that higher fares would be needed in order to finance investment and renewals, endorsing as it did the need to inject £0.75 million a year for the foreseeable future.

Meanwhile, the public were invited to see how perceptions matched up with reality through the Customer Charter.

There was – and remains – a key need to catch up on the investment and renewals expenditure which was denied in the mid-1980s. Otherwise, insufficient investment leads to higher asset age and failure rate, to higher maintenance costs and the costs of inspections and repairs. This results in a reduction of funds available for investment and thus to even higher asset age and failure rates…and so on.

INVESTMENT PROGRAMME, OR NOT?

The recommended investment was not to be, for in its Autumn 1992 statement the Government cut the promised 1993/4 programme by a third, with similar reductions in subsequent years. The result was a drastic slowing-down or cancellation of projects, with station refurbishment being the worst hit area. Station modernisations, like those carried out successfully at Edgware Road (Bakerloo),

Gloucester Road, Hammersmith (District and Piccadilly), and Hillingdon were among the schemes most easily dispensed with. Track reconditioning plus attention to tunnels, earthworks, bridges, power supplies, pumps, drainage and ventilation, lifts and escalators, and lighting are, perhaps regrettably but certainly realistically, far more important.

London Underground returned to the fray in 1993, when the 'Decently Modern Metro' was launched. Its aim is to provide up-to-date infrastructure supporting a railway which is safe, quick, reliable, clean, comfortable and efficient, and which gives good value for money. As Denis Tunnicliffe, LUL Managing Director, suggested to the Chartered Institute of Transport: 'This is not too much for Londoners to expect of their Underground system.'

With a total spend of about £7.5 billion over a decade, the main components of the 'Decently Modern Metro' were:

- Trains, including signalling, power supplies and depots   £1.2 billion
- Stations   £1.1 billion
- Infrastructure   £2.0 billion
- Line developments (eg Central and Northern lines)   £1.6 billion
- Other expenditure (eg new line development)   <u>£1.6 billion</u>

- Total   £7.5 billion

Of this, London Underground itself might fund a quarter out of revenue gains and cost reduction; the remainder has to come from Government, at a rather higher rate than it was intending to

Left: **A 1960 Cravens unit has been preserved by Cravens Heritage Trains. It is seen here on 30 April 2000, leaving Kensington Olympia. The separation of LUL from National Rail can be seen.** *R. L. Sewell*

spend! Nevertheless, London Underground was setting itself a goal to become financially self-sufficient by the year 2004/5, once the investment backlog was cleared.

RAILWAYS ACT 1993

One indirect consequence of the Railways Act 1993 was the transfer of three parts of the railway system in the London area to the Underground. This took place on 1 April 1994, when London Underground became the owner and operator of the Waterloo & City, the Wimbledon branch of the District Line beyond Putney Bridge station, albeit excluding Wimbledon station itself, and the Kensington (Olympia) stub end.

The Underground-owned network increased in length by about 8km. Acquisition included the liabilities as well as the benefits; for example, Fulham Bridge (the railway bridge over the Thames at Putney) needed £7 million worth of repairs after being struck by a barge in 1991. Power supplies and signalling remained with what is now Network Rail. Also new to the Underground was the inheritance of the two Travelators installed at Bank W&C station.

Perhaps a more far-reaching change was the need for the Underground to develop a safety case under the Railway (Safety Case) Regulations, 1994. This demonstrates the organisation's ability to conduct its operations safely, with the principle that the Railway Infrastructure Controller has overall responsibility for safe railway operation over that infrastructure. In the case of London Underground, this needed to cover the three aspects of stations, trains and infrastructure. LUL had to satisfy HM Railway Inspectorate on this but also, as an operator, had to have its own case accepted by Railtrack where it ran trains over its lines to Harrow & Wealdstone and Richmond. It also had to accept cases from other operators running on LUL lines, notably between Harrow-on-the-Hill and Amersham, and this included freight operations.

ALDWYCH AND ONGAR

Although there are many possibilities for system expansion, times change, and there are also those parts which have perhaps outlived their usefulness. An Underground line closure is a rare event, yet on 30 September 1994 both the Aldwych branch and the Epping–Ongar line saw their last trains. At Aldwych the *coup de grâce* was the need for replacement of the 1906 lifts; daily usage by 450 passengers was judged inadequate to justify around £3 million in engineering capital expense.

For Ongar and the one remaining inter-mediate branch station of North Weald, a residual traffic of 80 people per day over a 9.85km single line with deteriorating track was

clearly insufficient. This third attempt at line closure succeeded, the last having been over a decade earlier.

Railways thrive on volume; urban systems are in their element when moving perhaps 20,000 passengers per hour, per direction. If, however, there are no more passengers than a few buses can carry, it is difficult to defend the incurring of operating costs, let alone spending on maintenance and renewals for a specialised right of way with no alternative uses.

JUBILEE LINE EXTENSION

To the surprise of many, it was the 16km Jubilee Line Extension (JLE) to Stratford, for which a Parliamentary Bill was deposited in 1989. This followed pledges of financial support from private sector developers in Docklands. However, even after interminable wrangles, these turned out to be only 15% or so of the then anticipated capital costs. The Jubilee Line, on the chosen alignment, did not even appear on the list of options in the Central London Rail Study, but was the subject of the later East London Rail Study.

The expectations for the Jubilee Line Extension were set out in detail when the authorising Bill was before Parliament. Passenger flows were predicted for the period 10 years after the proposed opening, or in 2005.

The importance and indeed dominance of Canary Wharf as a destination was clear from the projected busiest morning peak hour eastbound flows. From a flow of 20,500 passengers per hour on leaving Baker Street, they fell to a low of 14,400 from Westminster to Waterloo, on leaving which they rose to 17,000, and again to 18,400 on leaving London Bridge. This reflected the influx of between four and five thousand

commuters from the main-line railways at each of these stations. However, numbers fell abruptly with 14,700 alighting at Canary Wharf, with only 3,500 on trains leaving that point, and remaining at broadly that level through to the new Jubilee Line terminus at Stratford.

Similar effects were noticeable in the westbound direction, with 6,000 or so passengers joining at both Stratford and West Ham. Only 7,200 of the 17,600 predicted then to be on board alighted at Canary Wharf. Others travelled on, mostly to the West End, and were joined by more commuters from the main lines at London Bridge, Southwark (for Waterloo East) and Waterloo.

ROUTEING OPTIONS?

The route east of Green Park was also open to discussion, with the sticking point being the need for a station at Waterloo. With a station at Charing Cross already in existence, and over-run tunnels constructed as far east as the north end of Waterloo bridge, could it not be routed that way? This would also protect those Jubilee Line passengers presently using Charing Cross. The diagram below shows the problems associated with this, as well as the severe curvature which would have resulted from this option or, indeed,

Below: **The Jubilee Line Extension beyond Green Park had the problem of what to do about Charing Cross, where the over-run line finished in the vicinity of the north end of Waterloo Bridge. Could this be used as the starting point, with the line still running via Waterloo? That way, Charing Cross Jubilee Line platforms could remain open. London Underground produced this scale plan showing the various alternatives; the House agreed that the route via Westminster as proposed had much to commend it.**

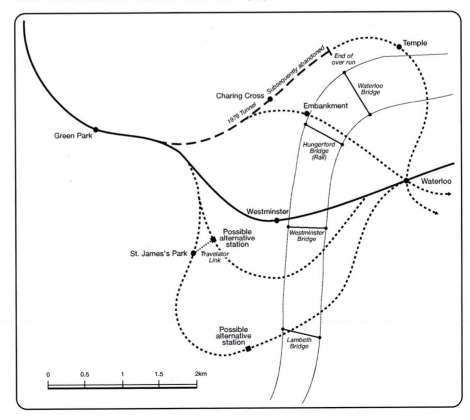

Right: **Westminster, Jubilee Line, has a number of escalators, whose overall effect is most impressive. The feeling is of space – not something one has been conditioned to expect underground.** *Author*

other options routeing the extension further south. It is perhaps as well that the preferred route via Westminster was adopted.

The scheme was authorised on 29 October 1993 by the Secretary of State for Transport and the then LRT Chairman Sir Wilfred Newton, who promised completion by 29 March 1998 and to budget. Both were sadly astray; opening of the whole line, in stages, was just achieved by the end of 1999, while the final cost was twice the £1.9 billion anticipated.

CONSTRUCTION CONTRACTS

The major construction contracts and their value were as follows. These details are provided to enable readers to assess the scale of such an undertaking. They also give some indication of the range of skills required. Civil works covering the tunnels and station construction were divided unto 12 geographically based contracts. The largest of these was contract No 102 awarded to Balfour Beatty-AMEC; this covered construction of the tunnels from Green Park to Waterloo, plus Westminster and Waterloo stations. This section included the first of the four crossings of the Thames on the new line.

To these may be added separate contracts for trackwork procurement (£20 million), the rolling stock depot (£18 million), and the service control centre at Neasden (£4 million). Electrical and mechanical design-and-construct contracts covered the following:

- provision of station and tunnel ventilation   £34 million
- station and tunnel services   £40 million
- works locomotives   £6 million
- works wagons   £2 million
- power cables and conductor rails £53 million
- power intake at West Ham substation   £4 million
- depot equipment   £10 million
- communications   £61 million
- signalling systems   £61 million
- signal control   £10 million
- lifts and escalators   £52 million
- passenger rolling stock (Alstom) £249 million
- platform edge doors for the underground section   £9 million
- Underground ticketing system   £11 million

Upgrades to the North London line for items such as cable routes and resignalling where it runs adjacent to the JLE are omitted.

For underground construction south of the Thames, the entirely suitable London clay gives way to the less acceptable sands and gravels. The problems arise from the frequently waterlogged nature of the latter, with the result that earth pressure balance machines need to be used for tunnelling. The work was carried out under compressed-air conditions. This literally forces back water into the excavated

ground while the concrete lining rings are put in place.

East of London Bridge, the line entered areas of Woolwich and Reading beds, and remained in them or the lower Thanet sands until North Greenwich. From here, the tunnels returned to London clay.

There are 11 station on the extension, and every effort has been made to provide interchange with other lines. The result is that every other Underground station can be reached with one change of train only. Strictly, the only exception, Kensington Olympia, is a Network Rail station. However, passengers for Chesham would normally be well advised to change at Chalfont & Latimer for the branch shuttle, while a number of other journeys might be rather quicker with a second change. The line control centre is at Neasden.

The principal features of the JLE are outlined in the table on the opposite page.

The range of opportunities for making further journeys continues the long tradition of inter-linking Underground services with others; bus services are not considered here. The extension is entirely underground for the first 12.4km of construction, rising to ground level just south of Canning Town, from where it is a further 3.6km to the Stratford terminus.

NEW STANDARDS

The extension was built to rather higher standards than those used hitherto; on the underground section, the new running tunnels were bored to 4.35m diameter, to allow for the installation of a side walkway. This aids maintenance and considerably eases the detraining of passengers should this be necessary. It does not, however, allow for larger diameter rolling stock, since the existing tunnels north from Green Park were constructed to 3.7m diameter as was previous practice. The platform tunnel diameters are 7.7m with a platform length of 130m.

A typical station layout underground includes a ventilation shaft at each end, emergency stairs

and a lift for disabled passengers. The lifts can also be used by those accompanied by children or with luggage. Escalators are in groups of three or four, with either one or two banks needed to cover the vertical distances. Thus, a remarkable total of 115 escalators has been provided on the extension as a whole, representing very nearly half as many again as existed previously on the whole of London Underground.

On the edges of the platforms, automatic platform doors are installed for the first time in Britain on a commercial railway, as opposed to people-mover installations as may be found at Gatwick Airport.

PLATFORM SCREEN DOORS

The electrically operated platform doors separate the passenger from the train, and double or single doors are installed to coincide with the position of those on the train. As it arrives, the accurate positioning of the train by the driver is critical to the success of the doors; too far away, and neither the train doors nor the platform doors will open. The two are synchronised to work together. Potentially, there can be severe effects on station dwell time; besides the lengthening of train journey times, this is also a major determinant of line capacity.

The installation of platform doors affects the functioning of the whole ventilation system, controlling wind direction, velocity and hence platform draughts caused by the movement of the trains. They also reduce the circulation of accumulated dirt. Doors prevent trespass, suicide or accidental falls, and the throwing of rubbish onto the track.

On the debit side, each door needs its own operating system, with sensors to detect any obstruction from a passenger to the handle of a bag. The net result is a doubling up of the train door mechanisms and safety devices, so there are roundly twice as many things to go wrong.

While the installation of platform doors is achievable with new construction, it is much more difficult to retro-fit them to existing lines,

Jubilee Line Features

Green Park (north bank)	Step-plate junctions, where the diameter of the tunnel is increased in diameter until it is sufficient to accommodate a diverging junction were constructed south of station for the new line to leave the 1979 alignment to Charing Cross (and now closed).
Westminster (north bank)	New deep-level platforms, eastbound above westbound due to site constrictions such as the avoidance of disturbance to Big Ben clock tower. Interchange with District/Circle lines, whose own tracks and platforms had to be lowered. New ticket office.
Waterloo (south bank)	Conventional island platform arrangement, but well separated with lower escalator landing in between. Deep, at 35m below ground level. Interchange with three other tube lines (via new Travelator to Bakerloo and Northern), National Rail and Eurostar. New ticket hall fronting onto Waterloo Road.
Southwark (south bank)	Similar island platform arrangement as at Waterloo, shared also by subsequent below ground stations. Direct interchange with Waterloo East National Rail station platforms, but otherwise completely new construction.
London Bridge (south bank)	Below Network Rail concourse; total reconstruction of south bank station entrances. Interchange with Northern Line below ground and National Rail above.
Bermondsey (south bank)	Completely new station with rails only 20m below concourse level. Designed within an open well, which allows daylight to reach platform level.
Canada Water (south bank)	Another completely new station below new platforms provided for East London Line at right angles, which offers interchange. This is a cut-and-cover box construction.
Canary Wharf (north bank)	Huge underground station with a total of 20 escalators and two ticket offices, built in the bed of a reclaimed dock. There are 37 UTS gates. Access is through three glass domes, rising out of a newly created park. One entrance is yet to open. Interchange to Docklands Light Railway Heron Quays station.
North Greenwich (south bank)	Completely new station of vast cofferdam construction (400m long x 30m wide x 20m deep), which has an additional turnback platform for trains from either the Stratford or Stanmore directions; built primarily to serve the Millennium Dome. Could be adapted to allow construction of a diverging branch towards North Woolwich and then Thamesmead at some future date.
Canning Town (north bank)	First above-ground station, again island construction, with Docklands Light Railway above. Completely new construction. Interchange with National Rail, North London Line. From here, the Jubilee Line makes use of formation formerly occupied by two tracks of the four-track Great Eastern branch to Stratford.
West Ham (north bank)	Above-ground station, again new construction, with interchange to North London and c2c lines, also District / Hammersmith & City, after a rather long walk.
Stratford Market (north bank)	Line rolling-stock depot on west side of formation.
Stratford (north bank)	Three-platform traditional island platform layout, at right angles to Great Eastern main line. Interchange also to Central and North London lines, and Docklands Light Railway.

or at stations from Green Park northwards on the Jubilee. Effectively, they take up part of the platform depth as measured from the back wall, and this is already less than desirable in many cases. More perplexing is the problem of severely curved platforms; while straight platforms have always been desirable to minimise the train to platform gap at all points, and to offer a clear view for staff (or cameras) along the length of the train, there are many places featuring curves, or even reverse curves, for a number of historical reasons. Both problems could be addressed, but they do imply major disruption and expense in order to achieve universal provision at below-ground stations.

Installation at above-ground locations would have to take into account the effects of exposure of the doors and their mechanisms to high winds, hot sunshine, rain and snow, unless the station itself were largely covered over. Although platform doors are installed at all the below-ground sections of the Jubilee Line Extension, there are none on the new East London Line platforms at Canada Water. This

Right: **Platform doors are in operation here at Canada Water Jubilee Line, giving an altogether different 'feel' to the station.** *Author*

Above: **Stratford Jubilee Line platforms see a train of 1996 stock arriving in June 2003. The zeal with which London Underground now prevents access of any sort to its property by unauthorised means may be seen by examination of the footbridge spanning the railway.** *Author*

location offers an interesting contrast of what is essentially the same architectural treatment with and without this feature.

ROLLING STOCK

New trains were required also for the Jubilee, and the decision was made to replace the 1983 stock trains (of which there were only $31\frac{1}{2}$ anyway, divided into two batches) and build afresh. This avoided all the compatibility problems and mixtures of stock.

The 59 trains which emerged as the 1996 stock were assembled by Alstom at Washwood Heath in Birmingham (the former Metro-Cammell works), with components sourced from Spain, Canada and France. They are outwardly similar to those on the Northern Line. From the passenger's viewpoint, the main difference is in the seating, as the Jubilee units have merely a place to rest one's bottom at the outer ends of the centre section of each car, as opposed to the tip-up seats on the Northern.

KEY ASPECTS OF THE EXTENSION

Some of the findings have been as follows:
- Westminster station is almost as important as Bank for connections.
- Southwark has low population density but had special justification as an area which needed stimulus. It also offered an interchange alternative for National Rail passengers using Charing Cross.
- London Bridge is important for West End and central-area distribution, and also the Tate Modern.
- Bermondsey is a high-density area with social problems, and the Underground provides access to jobs.
- Canada Water interchange takes 20sec.

- Canary Wharf station is not as well sited as the DLR, as there was too much development already in place. It would be better under the tower, but instead there is a wet and windy walk. Further developments are in prospect.
- At Stratford there is one ticket window for Great Eastern and other National Rail tickets, but 70% of ticket issues are for Underground destinations. The walking distance from the barriers to the trains is too high.

MILLENNIUM CELEBRATIONS

While the Jubilee Line Extension opened in time – just – this was only incidental to the celebrations to mark the end of 1,000 years (or 999 years, as some preferred) of the second millennium. On offer was all-night activity in central London, with firework displays and what were confidently predicted to be huge crowds of people.

The result was a decision to run Underground services all night long in the 42-hour period from the start of traffic on Friday 31 December 1999 to last trains on Saturday 1 January 2000. This had been attempted on only one previous occasion – 11/12 May 1937, for the Coronation of King George VI. Services approaching an all-night operation had been run before, but the Railway Inspectorate imposed a limitation. As early as 1901 the Chief Inspector said that the line should be patrolled and examined every night so that necessary repairs could be carried out, and his view was respected.

It was anticipated that in 1999/2000 $2\frac{1}{2}$ million passengers would be carried over this extended opening period.

What would be the impact of the Millennium celebrations? There was a large element of conjecture, but the key points were as follows.

First, the people. There would be more visitors to London than normal, and hence more passengers unfamiliar with the network; there was also expected to be a larger proportion of family groups than usual. Demand was likely to be continuous and heavy. Many passengers were likely to be intoxicated and/or in high spirits, while there might well be more litter dropped.

Operationally, crowd control requirements were likely to mean the selective non-stopping of trains for short periods, and station dwell times would need to be managed actively to maintain an even service frequency. Station staff were asked to keep an eye on numbers building up, and to take action to avoid overcrowding on platforms, stairs or escalators. Some passengers might need to be advised that it would be quicker to walk, rather than undertake short journeys, or those requiring interchange.

The closure of some stations would require public address announcements on trains by the train operators, and detailed scripts were provided for advising passengers. This also affected the response to the operation of the passenger emergency alarms, and there were scripts for this eventuality too. However, the stations would remain staffed and available for use in such circumstances.

All scheduled engineering maintenance was suspended, but engineering support was to be at full strength. Any rectification of defects would have to be carried out without the benefit of night-time engineering hours.

Finally, staff use of the communications system was to be limited to essential calls only, to minimise the risk of its being overloaded. In particular, staff were beseeched not to use the telephone to check what had happened during the Millennium date change, which was anticipated in many quarters to cause major computer problems. The staff were also reminded that they would need their passes to enter police-cordoned security areas.

STREET TRAFFIC

In the streets outside, a Traffic Limitation Zone was established, in which no traffic would be allowed after 17.00 on New Year's Eve. Exclusions also kept buses out, in most cases. The boundaries were similar to those used for the Congestion Charging Zone three years later.

Selective closure of Underground stations was

Left: **The driver's cab interior on the 1983 Jubilee Line stock, which was to have a relatively short life by Underground standards, although 15 years for a piece of industrial equipment is hardly bad.** *Author*

made. Underground service provision offered the following:

● Sunday service on all lines on New Year's Eve until 23.50
● From 23.50 to 04.00 on New Year's Day, one train every 3-6min in central London, declining to every 10-20min on branches
● From 04.00 to 12.00 on New Year's Day, one train every 15min in central London, with normal Sunday frequencies restored subsequently

On National Rail, the last trains into central London arrived by about 22.00 on New Year's Eve, with services suspended until 01.00. Services from central London were resumed from 01.00 to 04.00 on New Year's Day, then suspended again until 11.00, when a normal Sunday service was offered.

Travel on the Underground (but not National Rail) was free between 23.50 on 31 December and 09.00 on 1 January.

The entire operation was completed with no incidents of any significance, to the great credit of London Underground management and staff alike. A similar exercise was mounted for the Queen's Golden Jubilee on the night of 3/4 June 2002.

LONDON REGIONAL PASSENGERS' COMMITTEE

When the 1984 Act took effect, consumer representation on matters to do with London Underground became the responsibility of the London Regional Passengers' Committee (LRPC). The Committee was the official but independent voice of the public transport users, and acted as a focus for passengers' views. In law, the LRPC had certain duties, a few rights, but no powers. Duties included the consideration of objectives as to an Underground closure proposal and reporting thereon. The Committee had the right to be consulted about LRT's three-year statement of policy, and to be informed about current plans for service levels, fares and facilities. It was also required to consider representations from users and to make representations accordingly.

Above: Part of the large order for new Northern Line stock, under construction at GEC-Alsthom (Metro-Cammell). *Author's collection*

Bottom: The interior of Jubilee Line 1996 stock, showing the all-longitudinal seating and the 'bottom rests' provided instead of seats inside the doors. *Author*

The LRPC's aims included the promotion and development of an integrated public transport network, and to represent the interests of all passengers to operators and any other parties involved.

Penalty fares were introduced by London Underground in 1994, backed up by an unambiguous policy. Most stations are now gated, with only the most difficult outstanding, or in a couple of cases where usage is very low. Gating is supported by an excess fares window and visible compulsory ticket area signs. If you haven't got a valid ticket, then you will receive a penalty fare. In other words, you must pay in advance of travel. The system is managed centrally by two revenue-protection managers.

From the point of view of LRPC, this measure, however justified, was largely responsible for a huge increase in consumer complaints.

LATE-NIGHT OPERATION

In 2000 the LRPC undertook research into the services provided by the Underground and also the main-line railways late at night.

The Underground generally closes down some time after midnight, but what level of use is made of it after, say, 22.00? The numbers entering Zone 1 stations to begin their journeys have grown substantially in recent years, and the 1998 census showed a total of 105,000 passengers at the 62 Underground stations in

this group. This was largely a West End phenomenon, with Leicester Square responsible for 12.7% of the total. The growth, compared with 1995, was more pronounced the later it got – though in actual as opposed to percentage terms the numbers were relatively small.

Other very busy stations were, in descending order, Piccadilly Circus, King's Cross St Pancras, Tottenham Court Road, Oxford Circus, Victoria, Covent Garden, Charing Cross, Embankment, Waterloo and Liverpool Street. Collectively, these 11 stations catered for 60% of the total passenger numbers. The inclusion of King's Cross St Pancras so high in the list may be as a result of double counting some interchange passengers, discussed elsewhere, but the general focus is clear.

Amongst the questions raised were:

● What is the cause of late-night travel growth, and is the trend likely to continue?
● At what time should it be possible to leave central London by train and still get home?
● Is there a case for running trains much later (or even all night), as practised in some cities in other countries but not in Britain?

The extension of the times of operation has an equal and opposite effect on the time available to carry out engineering inspections and maintenance work, which is short enough already. Other compensations in operating hours might have to be made as a result. It is however a fair point, which centres on what Londoners can reasonably expect from their public transport system.

The LRPC's remit under Transport *for* London has changed, and it is now the London Transport Users' Committee (LTUC).

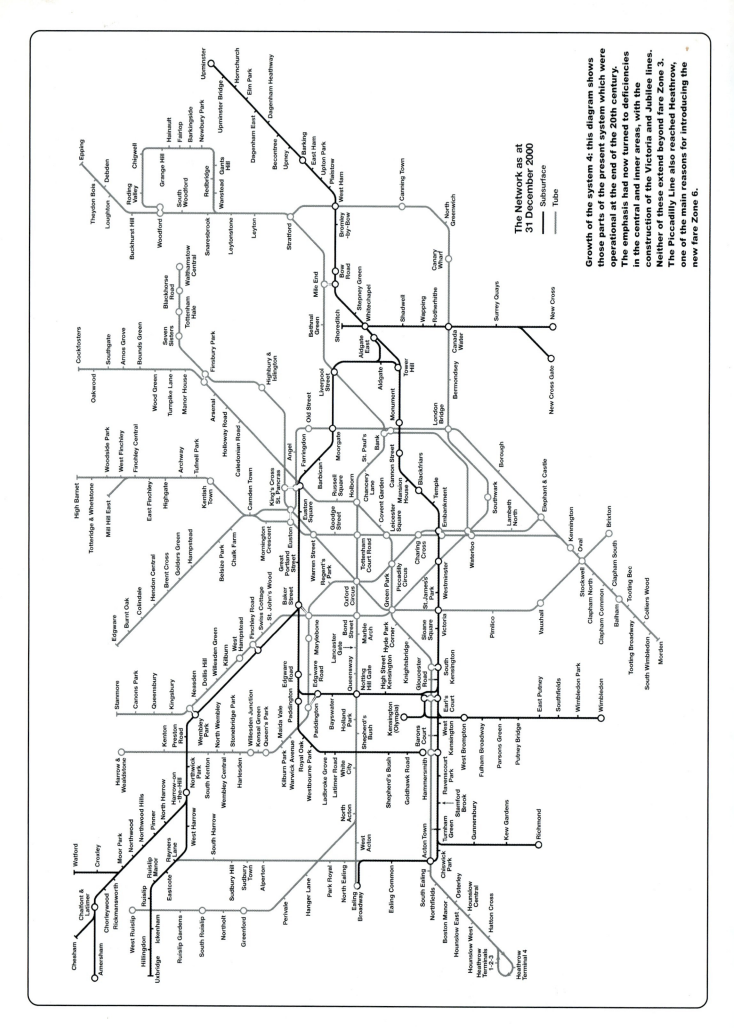

The Network as at
31 December 2000

— Subsurface
— Tube

Growth of the system 4: this diagram shows those parts of the present system which were operational at the end of the 20th century. The emphasis had now turned to deficiencies in the central and inner areas, with the construction of the Victoria and Jubilee lines. Neither of these extend beyond fare Zone 3. The Piccadilly Line also reached Heathrow, one of the main reasons for introducing the new fare Zone 6.

CHAPTER TWELVE

Transport *for* London

'If you, London Underground, are successful, we will see public transport becoming people's first choice. That is our vision.'

Prime Minister Tony Blair, 27 July 1999

Following the abolition of the Greater London Council in 1986, there was no democratically elected, city-wide body for London until the creation of the Greater London Authority (GLA), to which a Mayor and Assembly would be directly elected. The GLA was to have strategic functions, one of which was transport, and the 1997 consultation paper proposed a new body to assume the functions of London Transport and much else besides. This was in fulfilment of the Government's election manifesto.

GREATER LONDON AUTHORITY ACT 1999

The Greater London Authority Act 1999 was the means of returning public transport in London to municipal control. Under it, the Mayor of London, acting on behalf of the Authority, develops and implements policies for the promotion and encouragement of safe, integrated, efficient and economic transport services to, from and within Greater London. The Authority sets fares and service levels for all services provided by its executive body - Transport *for* London (T*f*L) - and may give instructions and guidance to the Strategic Rail Authority (SRA) in relation to the provision of rail services in Greater London (with some limitations).

The Mayor has to produce an Integrated Transport Strategy, which must be consistent with the Government's national transport policies. This strategy forms the framework for projects that will be promoted by the Authority.

The Mayoral election was on 4 May 2000, and the Mayor (Ken Livingstone) took office and Transport *for* London was established on 3 July 2000. T*f*L is responsible specifically for public transport, the network of roads, working with Boroughs, and planning across all modes. On the public transport side, T*f*L was structured into five divisions representing buses, Underground, Victoria Coach Station, Docklands Light Railway and London River Services. The Secretary of State was given powers to dissolve London Regional Transport once all its property, rights and liabilities had been transferred to T*f*L.

UNDERGROUND INVESTMENT

One of the largest problems facing the Underground has been obtaining the funds needed to maintain and update the infrastructure. As this book has demonstrated, the Underground is old, diverse and difficult to manage. The assets need getting into order, with safety requirements met. Care of the infrastructure had not ranked highly in political

Above: **A really busy scene on the northern approach to Leytonstone, Central Line, in June 2003 as three trains of 1992 stock, all on the move, depart for Woodford via Hainault (left) and approach from Epping (centre) and Hainault (right).** *Author*

priorities over the years; as long as nothing falls apart, there is little incentive to spend money on largely unseen assets. Votes are not won by cleaning out drainage systems and providing new pumps to empty them. However, what you do get is declining service levels, while operating costs rise.

Yet some quite major things were going wrong, and the partial failure of power supplies on a number of occasions had led to prolonged stoppages of trains. Eventually, this was dealt with under a Private Finance Initiative scheme, and the power for traction is now completely outsourced. There are a number of other examples, too. Private funds provide the investment needed and deliver the goods, with the company paying a usage charge.

Apart from government funding usually being too low to achieve what was needed, there were other problems. In recent times, the Central Line had starved the rest of network of investment, with the result that LU lost

confidence. (The Jubilee line extension project was ring-fenced). Another was the annuality of the process; this year may be all right, but how much do we get *next* year? Money on infrastructure work can't be spent at short notice, and Underground funding was always in competition with other deserving causes such as the National Health Service.

PPP POSSIBILITIES

The Public-Private Partnership (PPP) concept is based on the public sector working in partnership with the private sector to improve quality and effectiveness of public services. This is done through the provision of capital assets

Above: **The Northern Line will be upgraded; at present it has the new 1995 stock but not much else. A High Barnet train arrives at Finchley Central. The track on the right is for Mill Hill East or terminating trains.** *Author*

and output-based services, which seek to provide better value than the traditional method of asset acquisition. It encourages:

- a long-term partnership between LUL and private-sector companies
- the intensive programming of work on a scale never previously undertaken on London Underground
- the delivery of new projects in the order that gives the greatest benefit to costs and long-term whole-life benefits.

The PPP is about enabling LUL to deliver a series of objectives. The key challenges were identified as asset health, which is in long term decline and needs a sizeable injection of funds, and service performance. In the long term this was to meet growing passenger demand. but short term performance was not good enough and needed to improve. Value for money was always an important criterion; this would depend not only on the risks incurred and who shouldered them but also on the flexibility and enforceability of the 30-year contracts. There was also the safety risk, which must be as low as reasonably practicable (ALARP).

Fundamental aspects of the PPP are:

- financial risk is transferred from the public to the private sector
- the public sector specifies the output required but not how it is to be done
- it creates incentives for the private sector to keep costs down
- delivery within the specified parameters and quality standards is the responsibility of the private sector
- the private sector is remunerated by performance-related charges made for the use of those assets

Could the PPP approach be used for the much larger and more diverse areas of the infrastructure generally – and the trains? The Government thought so, but the Mayor disagreed. The upshot was that, as set up, Transport *for* London was not given responsibility for London Underground. LUL remained a limited company with its headquarters in 55 Broadway, whereas T*f*L was located in Victoria Street. The Government decided that London Underground would only be transferred to the control of the Mayor when the PPP deals for the maintenance of the infrastructure had been completed.

This proved to be a much longer task than expected. The prolonged and at times acrimonious wrangling between the Mayor and the Government meant that years, rather than months, passed with the matter unresolved.

The size of the Underground and hence the tasks must not be underestimated. There is now a total of 458km of route with 275 stations, on which 513 peak hour trains run and $3\frac{1}{2}$ million passenger journeys a day are made. It is a huge enterprise, and London is very dependent upon it.

In retrospect, it was perhaps unfortunate that the alternatives considered in 1996 were not discussed openly. These were:

- no change, whatever the present faults
- selling off the Underground as a single unit, with a share or bond issue
- a horizontal split, as in the National Railways privatisation
- a vertically integrated structure, with groups of lines each sold off separately

The PPP method adopted means that London Underground remains in the public sector,

although it is fair to ask whether it really matters as to who owns the organisation.

IMPLEMENTATION

Three infrastructure companies (Infracos) were formed within London Underground; shadow running started in September 1999, and they became wholly owned subsidiary companies in April 2000.

The companies were formed as follows:

- Infraco BCV   Bakerloo, Central, Victoria lines
- Infraco JNP   Jubilee, Northern, Piccadilly lines
- Infraco SSL   all sub-surface lines

It will be noted that Infraco BCV was made up of the three lines that serve Oxford Circus, while the apparent omission of the Waterloo & City line is covered by the remark that 'when you shake the Central Line packet, you get the Waterloo & City as a free gift'. What it is to be a London Underground spokesman!

While all Infracos incorporate a range of skills and consultancy services, physical assets are not split so easily. As set up, BCV included the Train Modification Unit (refurbishment, repair), TrackForce (specialised maintenance, renewal and reconditioning) and Track Workshops (long welded rail, points and crossings). Infraco JNP included the specialist activities of Transplant (railway engineering support vehicles and equipment), Distribution Services (specialised road vehicles and those customised for railway usage, haulage and waste management services), and the Emergency Response Unit. Infraco SSL had Railway Engineering Workshops (overhauls of anything from traction motors to signals to clocks). These are activities which were carried out on behalf of all Infracos.

Implementation came as follows. First off the mark was Infraco JNP, the final contracts for which were signed by Tube Lines on 31 December 2002. Tube Lines is a consortium of Bechtel, Amey and Jarvis. Both Infraco BCV and SSL went to Metronet in May 2003. Metronet's stakeholders are Bombardier Transportation, SEEBOARD group, Balfour Beatty, WS Atkins and Thames Water.

The PPP contracts are all for 30 years, with three renewal points at $7\frac{1}{2}$ years, 15 years and $22\frac{1}{2}$ years. At the end of the contract, the assets must be returned in a satisfactory state of health.

The infrastructure companies provide the necessary 'capability'; London Underground provides predetermined levels of access to the track for maintenance and renewals, eg the times at which the current will be switched off and then back on again. Longer periods of work are dealt with as 'minor closures'. Infracos have 'points' to spend on these, while there is some flexibility for London Underground.

Penalties for poor or non-performance are based on the impact on customers. For instance, a signal failure at Sloane Square will result in lost time by customers, measured in hours. These will accumulate, and if this results in the cancellation of 16 trains, a fine of £90k will result. A similar approach is taken to the non-availability of escalators, and so on.

The programme sees £10.5bn invested in the system over the next 15 years, with a further £6.5bn on maintenance. How it is to be spent will become clearer over time; the concentration on results means that a

Below: **Some tube stations remain today much as when opened, although the lighting has been much improved, as have communications of all types. This is one of the platforms at Regent's Park.** *Author*

requirement to raise capacity, as on the Victoria Line, means a step up in capability. Such a requirement does not, in itself, require a fleet of new trains – though this is anticipated. New trains are always the most expensive part of a line upgrade. Renewal of the signalling is equally important, as well as track condition etc, etc.

Not all work forms part of the PPP contract. Thus London Underground remains in the lead with the securing of powers under the Transport & Works Act procedures, and also with line extensions. This is also the case with major station capacity works, plus legislative and other mandatory changes such as safety. On these issues, risk transfer is not practicable.

THE MAYOR'S VIEW

One of the most dispiriting aspects of the relationship between the Mayor and London Underground has been the often vitriolic nature of the exchanges.

In the wake of the Chancery Lane derailment, Ken Livingstone claimed that passengers took a risk every time they got on London Underground trains. 'Every day there isn't a fatal accident is another day when we're lucky,' the Mayor said. In response, London Underground dismissed his remarks as being 'a fairly typical barrage of abuse'.

On 7 March 2002 T/L took a full-page advertisement in *Metro*, the free London newspaper, the contents of which are shown in the box. Readers are invited to draw their own conclusions.

A railway like the Underground is a large-scale and complex organisation, and it isn't going to run itself. The management need support from the politicians with whom they have to work. This remains true, even if the ambitions of the latter to have the control that they want over the Underground are thwarted by government.

We need the Underground to work – we all do.

Have Your Say on the Future of London Underground

The Government has proceeded in principle to proceed with an experimental Public Private Partnership (PPP) for the Tube and is now consulting on its proposals.

PPP would break the Tube into four different parts:
- The Public Sector under T/L will drive the trains and staff the stations
- Three separate private sector companies will own the trains, tracks, signals and stations for the next 30 years

T/L's plan for London Underground is faster, safer and cheaper than PPP.

Under PPP:
- Only 12 new trains on entire Tube by 2008
- Splits train operation from track maintenance – think Railtrack
- Payments to private sector – money borrowed at high rates with shareholders to satisfy, no cap on profits and no requirement for 'pounds in the ground' in the contracts.

With T/L's plan:
- Nearly all Tube trains new or completely refurbished within seven years
- Single, unified system – safety is paramount
- Public sector investment – money raised at cheaper rates – public in charge of when, where and how cash is invested.

You can find out more about the Government's or T/L's plans for the Tube (and vote 'YES' or 'NO' to the PPP) by visiting our website…

We promise to pass on your views to the Secretary of State for Transport.

This could be the last chance for Londoners to say NO to the PPP.

OTHER SYSTEMS

The more familiar one is with London Underground, the easier it is to forget that other cities have Metro systems too, and that they may have solved essentially similar problems in a different way. A brief examination of the system in Rome, which has two lines, elicited the following thoughts:
- On Metro Line A, the line diagrams in the cars show which side the platforms will be, station by station, and arrows indicate direction of travel.
- On Line B, the car diagrams show which sections of line are in the open air as opposed to being in tunnel (or cut-and-cover construction).
  (Both of these features are helpful to strangers to the system, and reduce uncertainty as to location.)
- The platforms are about 5m in depth, which was enough space for a passenger to lie full length, with head towards the track, and take a photograph of his friends sitting on a seat against the platform wall. While such

behaviour can hardly be recommended, it did demonstrate how constricted most platforms in London are, especially when large numbers are using the station. The platform was also clean enough for his clothes not to be soiled.

- Plans of fire escape routes are displayed on Underground platforms, complete with a 'You are here' indication and showing emergency exits. Separate platform maps show how the station entrance relates to bus stop locations and routes to various places, *eg* historic sites. This display includes information on conditions of travel.

(This shows a commendable interest in fire safety, while the studying of bus routes was something a passenger could usefully do when awaiting a train.)

- On arriving at the terminal point, train drivers put the train lighting onto half power, which is an effective (and silent) way of indicating to passengers that they have to alight.

(This seemed to result in a rather quicker response than one often sees in London, and for non-Italian speakers does not depend on understanding any verbal messages.)

The days when the LT culture suggested that there were two methods of doing things – the London Transport way or the wrong way – are hopefully now well behind us. London needs to keep up with the best, and there is no shame in borrowing ideas from each other.

KING'S CROSS ST PANCRAS

King's Cross St Pancras is the best-connected station on London Underground, to the extent that it is served by six Underground lines and two major National Railways termini, as well as the Thameslink line to Kentish Town, Moorgate and Blackfriars. Presently under construction is the Channel Tunnel Rail Link (CTRL) which will use a much enlarged St Pancras, while the

upgrading of Thameslink with a new station in tunnel on the west side of and below St Pancras will much enhance the line's capacity.

The tube ticket hall has inadequate capacity, while the steps to the ticket hall for the sub-surface lines and the general layout are far from ideal. The Underground station suffers also in that it is not possible to move between the two ticket halls without exiting and re-entering the system through the automatic ticket gates. The intervening area forms part of a subway used by the public to cross the Euston Road. There are at present around 55,000 users of King's Cross St Pancras in the morning peak, and numbers are expected to rise by 50% when the CTRL is operational in 2007.

Comprehensive updating and extension was the only answer, and this is being tackled as follows:

- enlargement of existing tube ticket hall
- new ticket hall, in part below St Pancras forecourt and in part below Euston Road
- new ticket hall on suburban side of King's Cross, north of Great Northern Hotel
- new access routes to all lines, including new escalators
- new lifts to ease mobility access
- new public subway under Euston Road
- new links from Underground to all main-line stations
- new Station Operations Room

This massive scheme involves partial closures to many roads, including the repositioning of King's Cross taxi rank, and the cordoning off of many areas to create temporary construction and work sites. Train services also have to be interrupted

Below: **An eastbound District Line train of D stock passes Stamford Brook in February 1998, with what (for a colour light) is a very tall signal. This is for westbound Piccadilly Line trains and the height is due to sighting difficulties.** *Author*

from time to time, especially at weekends. The whole is due to be completed in 2006.

ENGINEERING CLOSURES

The restriction on services such as that outlined above which saw no trains between Baker Street and Aldgate/Aldgate East for a long succession of weekends in 2003 is becoming more prevalent. For instance:

- Bakerloo Line suspended between Piccadilly Circus and Elephant & Castle for Hungerford Bridge works, for seven consecutive two-day weekends in 2000
- Circle Line suspended between High Street Kensington and Gloucester Road for tunnel roof repair, for a continuous period of 10 weeks in 1999
- East London Line, closed totally for a comprehensive upgrade, for the three years 1995 to 1998.
- Northern Line suspended between Moorgate and Kennington for reconditioning works, for a continuous period of nine weeks in 2001
- Victoria Line suspended between Victoria and Brixton for pointwork renewal, for a continuous period of three weeks in 2000

Station works may also cause partial or total closures, with escalator and/or lift renewals being the most common causes.

Underground services may be replaced by bus route(s) laid on for the purpose, or by stepping up the frequency on all or part of existing route(s). The Central Line suspension early in 2003 saw no fewer than ten special bus routes laid on, all but one of which operated daily.

Alternatively, passengers can be left to their own devices.

The scale of work implied by the infrastructure PPPs suggests that such closures will have to become commonplace, and that this will continue for the foreseeable future. The following extract is from a book published in

1862, discussing the Metropolitan Railway a year before the first section opened:

'These works…will give employment to many, and be a nuisance to others, as long as they are being constructed. But when the mess is cleared up and the new channels (of railway) are thrown open, a sense of comfort and relief will be felt throughout the vast general traffic of London.'

OYSTER

The revolution in transport ticketing and revenue collection is represented by the Oyster card (formerly PRESTIGE) project which is now well under way. Worldwide, more and more operators are recognising the benefits of contactless Smartcard technology, and hard practical experience on an increasing scale is now being added to the theoretical case.

This contract was let in 1998 to TranSys Ltd, a consortium consisting of Electronic Data Systems, Cubic Corporation, ICL Enterprises and W. S. Atkins. It requires TranSys to develop a new revenue collection service for London Underground and the buses under the Private Finance Initiative. TranSys finances and provides an operating system throughout the life of the contract. There are many opportunities for expanding the system to other transport (and non-transport) applications. Train Operating Companies are clearly prime candidates, but London taxis and bus operators outside Greater London are also possibilities.

Smartcard is like a credit card that contains a small microchip (a memory) which can process and store electronic data. It is attached to an aerial inside the card; when the card reader reads the card, power flows through the aerial and information moves from the card to the reader and back again. Reading is achieved by the card being 'shown' to the reader, which needs to be within only a few centimetres of the card; the latter does not leave the customer's possession. This is in contrast to the present Underground Ticketing System (UTS). It is anticipated that the passage of customers through the gates will be that much faster, with a reduction in the 'fumble factor'.

To obtain an Oyster card, the holder makes a down payment and the card is given an equivalent value. This is encoded on the card. Each time the card is used, the value remaining is reduced by the amount of the fare charged for the journey. The card can be topped up at any time by the holder making additional payments at a ticket office, and these are also encoded. The card itself thus continues in use for an indefinite period.

STORED VALUE TICKETING

This whole concept is known as Stored Value Ticketing (SVT). Crucial differences from the Travelcard are that the geographical area over which travel may be made is limited only by the scope of the scheme, and that each journey is charged individually. This need not imply that

Above: **A train of A stock in one of the experimental liveries is seen from a tower block on the East London Line, south of Canal Junction and heading for New Cross.** *Author*

the full standard fare will always be the amount charged. Fares can be varied at different times of day, discounts given to frequent users (as in supermarket loyalty cards), and all types of linked promotions can be undertaken.

Some of this is for the future, but it indicates the strength of the business case. From London Transport's point of view, ticket purchase and ticket validation will need less in the way of resources, much more management information will be available, and fraud should be contained more effectively.

The overall aim is:
● to make tickets easier to buy and to use
● to make bus, Underground and rail travel seamless
● to provide a real public transport alternative to the car
● to support the concept of integrated transport

On the hardware side, the installation of new ticket-office and passenger-operated machines is complete, and nearly all stations are gated. The Multifare ticket machines are being replaced by PC menu-driven touch screens, which will offer up to seven languages. Early examples could be seen at the Jubilee Line Extension stations. Press the screen not hard enough and nothing happens; too hard, and it tells you off! A couple of ladies seen experiencing this at Stratford dissolved into laughter; so much for speed of ticket issue!

The responsibility for the design, construction, installation and finance of Oyster rests with TranSys, with selected maintenance, support and operating responsibilities.

At present, three quarters of all Underground journeys are made by Travelcard holders, and Travelcard will remain. The new machines are also capable of issuing a greater range of tickets, and new till technology is being applied to ticket offices.

The technology must be safe, effective and robust but must also allow for further development. There are likely to be two kinds of card:

● transferable card of low value, for single tickets and perhaps a one-day ticket
● personalised card of higher value, for period tickets and used by more regular travellers, replacing season tickets; this will need a photocard

CROXLEY LINK

One of the odder results of past railway construction was the Metropolitan & Great Central Joint Watford branch, which opened in 1925. This never managed to reach Watford proper, as intended, since the route would have taken it through Cassiobury Park. To the south, the London & North Western Railway's branch from Watford Junction ended at its own less-than-satisfactory terminus of Croxley Green.

A scheme to link the two involves the building of 500m of new viaduct, the construction of a new station at Ascot Road, and use of the presently closed Watford West (rebuilt with two platforms), Watford High Street and Watford Junction stations. Metropolitan Line trains would be diverted to terminate there in Platforms 1 and 2, and the present LUL Watford station would be closed. A bid for funding this modest £40m scheme is included in Hertfordshire County Council's Local Transport Plan. If the project goes forward, the earliest possible completion date is around 2008.

TERMINAL 5

The construction of Heathrow Airport's Terminal 5 will add to the daily passenger and staff movement requirements. As part of the overall scheme, London Underground will extend the Piccadilly Line from a new junction to the west of Heathrow Terminals 1, 2, 3, in a double-track formation to T5. The new terminal is to be located 2km away, to the west of the Central Terminal Area.

One possible service pattern would be for all trains to run to Terminals 1, 2, 3. From there, most would continue to T5, with some proceeding in an anticlockwise direction to Terminal 4, and terminate there. All trains would then return via Terminals 1, 2, 3 on their way back to central London. (This would result in the effective abandonment of the Hatton Cross–Terminal 4 link.)

There is of course no need to terminate at T5, and a further projection of the Piccadilly Line to an interchange station on the GW main line could well be feasible.

It might be observed that one of the difficulties associated with the Piccadilly Line generally is the need to interrupt the Heathrow service pattern to offer trains from central London to the Rayners Lane branch. An alternative way of providing for the branch has to be found if an enhanced service is needed for Heathrow.

EAST LONDON LINE EXTENSION

The indicative route and potential route options for this project are Highbury & Islington in the north, with branches to Clapham Junction (and a new station at Brixton) and to West Croydon in the south, with a short stub off the latter to Crystal Palace. The existing line to New Cross remains.

Preliminary works are underway, but there have been a number of problems. The scheme dates from 1985, and was seen as a fully integrated Metro-cum-City Crossrail. This is now a joint Transport *for* London and Strategic Rail Authority project, but its scope in the past was not clearly defined.

The basis has always been clear: use the existing East London Line of the Underground as the in-town section, and extend it at both ends. In the north, this would result in a new station at Bishopsgate (replacing the present Shoreditch), the line then joining the old Broad

Right: **The East London Line Extension will have relatively little trouble with Whitechapel, whose platforms are of adequate length as they stand. However, access and egress is decidedly tight, while the depth (from wall to platform edge) is little more than adequate. What volumes of passengers might be expected?** *Author*

Left: **Shoreditch is the end of the line, and will be closed. The limitations on going further north on this alignment are the Great Eastern main line, immediately beyond the now considerable amount of undergrowth.** *Author*

Below left: **Shoreditch, even with its restrictive opening hours, still sees reasonable flow volumes. This A-stock train has just opened its doors after a morning peak arrival, June 2003.** *Author*

Street-Dalston Junction formation with a new station at Hoxton & Haggerston (replacing that closed in 1940). Trains would then call at a reincarnated Dalston Junction and terminate at Highbury & Islington. To the south, a number of alternatives were pursued. But all would be over tracks of National Railways, where eight-car trains are really the minimum which could be contemplated.

This led to problems at a number of stations, notably at Wapping. The platforms here are of minimal depth, and access includes a substantial flight of stairs. Platforms would also be costly to extend, to the extent that the work needed to accommodate eight-car trains plus making this one station Disability Discrimination Act compliant would cost roundly £100m. Similar difficulties occur elsewhere, but not at Whitechapel which is in a deep cutting. Here the platform lengths, although presently partly disused, can be made sufficient. Was there another way of operating the service?

The inclusion of Whitechapel in Crossrail 1 would make this an important interchange station, with services in five directions by Crossrail as well as the extended East London and the existing District and Hammersmith & City Underground services. It is presently proposed that the East London Line services be divided into two groups – one of eight-car trains for the longer distance services, the other of four cars for the core services.

The estimated capital cost is now £1.3bn, and the scheme meets the Strategic Rail Authority's Value for Money guidelines. Agreement needs to be reached on who would be the infrastructure controller and operator, but this would almost certainly have to be Network Rail. New trains would be required, and possibly a new franchise. This would be a high-density third-rail operation; it would probably be operated by a main-line Train Operating Company, not London Underground.

An opening in 2008 is seen as a realistic target.

CROSSRAIL 1

Indicative route options for Crossrail 1 show Heathrow in the west to Shenfield in the east, with a junction at Whitechapel for a branch to the Isle of Dogs. Stations in central London remain as Paddington, Bond Street, Tottenham Court Road, Farringdon and Liverpool Street. The eastern branch is shown extending beyond the Isle of Dogs in a potential corridor to Ebbsfleet. Watford Junction remains in the frame as a possible second western terminal, but the GW main line to Reading has gone.

The aim is to provide a high-quality service giving access to the key financial nodes of the City and Canary Wharf, and also to Heathrow.

The inclusion of a station at Whitechapel has other benefits too (see below). This will be a fully integrated rail scheme, bigger and better than had been proposed earlier.

Its financing will involve collaboration with the Treasury and the Office of the Deputy Prime Minister. What are the *real* benefits? The aim is to provide transport, but also regeneration, and add to the wellbeing of London. The scheme needs to reflect this, and a bargain basement-type railway is not what is wanted. Crossrail services might amount to 16tph to Shenfield, plus 12tph to the Isle of Dogs and perhaps beyond.

London Underground and British Rail had already spent £120m developing the scheme, and it is now necessary to reconcile the Mayor's aspirations and ministerial views on generation and growth. It will also relieve the Central Line; £154m has been allocated for planning, forming a company, and obtaining the necessary powers.

London Rail and the SRA have set up a joint company, Cross London Rail Links Ltd, to progress both Crossrail 1 and Crossrail 2. Crossrail 1 is the most important scheme for a generation, and route options are still being developed. The target date for completion is 2012, and it will thus increase east-west rail capacity within a decade. This will add 10% to rail/tube capacity in the city centre.

CROSSRAIL 2

The core section of Crossrail 2 remains unchanged as King's Cross St Pancras to Victoria, with an intermediate station at Tottenham Court Road and (probably) Piccadilly Circus. However,

various alternatives to a tube scheme have been proposed, and one recent possibility in the south is three branches. One would take over the present branch of the District Line from Wimbledon as far as Parsons Green where it would enter tunnel. It might then proceed via Chelsea to Victoria. It would be joined by the other branch, which would run south to Clapham Junction, and thence onto Network Rail lines. There are similar novel possibilities for the north, aiming at Hackney Central, and thence to Leytonstone and Epping on the Central Line alignment, or to Stratford International or Stratford itself, where there are more choices.

The earliest possible completion date is 2014.

KEY QUESTIONS

These three schemes have substantial implications for the Underground, though in all cases it might be some other company which operates the rail services. Some of the considerations here are:

- the diameters to which running and station tunnels are constructed
- the train capacities and lengths to be accommodated
- the type of operation – urban, suburban, or what?
- a train design to cope with different passenger journey lengths and purposes
- the electrification system(s) to be used
- joint use and ownership of infrastructure, especially stations
- any requirement for interworking over Underground/Network Rail lines
- availability of rolling-stock depots
- operational control of the system
- roles of the various statutory bodies
- who determines priorities and decides what is to be operated

Above: **The bridge at Kilburn carrying the railway over the A5, which reminds everybody that railway heritage doesn't disappear quickly. The Metropolitan Railway makes sure it is remembered.** *Author*

The other cross-London scheme is of course Thameslink 2000, but this has always been thought of as a National Railways scheme.

THE UNDERGROUND AND NETWORK RAIL

Throughout, the loosening of the informal lines of demarcation between 'heavy' rail and Underground are noticeable. Yes, there are real problems of mixing the two on the same infrastructure, whether they be operational, engineering or technical snags. Any solution must meet the defined safety requirements.

There is much scope for development. If passenger volumes continue to grow, massive investment is unavoidable, the only rail alternative being demand management through fares. With major road building rightly ruled out as a practicable alternative, rail must be the mode to be exploited. After all, the formal function of Transport *for* London is to best meet the transport needs of Greater London.

It is system expansion which seems to cause the most difficulty. Who benefits? Who will pay for it? How much can users be expected to contribute? What can be expected from the private sector – and from government by means of grant?

Transport projects are typified by having initial spare capacity, which is filled only over time. This means long pay-back periods. Then, while revenues are reasonably stable and predictable once the asset is operational, there is considerable uncertainty at the

feasibility and development stages. Also, once built in a location, infrastructure cannot be moved if better opportunities subsequently appear to lie elsewhere.

Finally, transport projects are always up against competition with those from other industry sectors, which may have better cash flows and less risk attached to them. New ideas are needed; perhaps investment finance can be funded from a securitised tax income from enhanced property values?

As matters stand, public cash is needed in the vast majority of cases, justified by the 'free' benefits which are received by the non-users and by London as a whole.

How reliable are the forecasts of employment and activity generally? Over the years, there have been three classic and interlocking mistakes:

- underestimating the future rate of growth
- providing insufficient investment to meet demand
- a lack of foresight on the best way forward

Somehow, the same errors must be avoided in future. When it comes to new Underground railways, the costs are enormous and the time-scale for building is extended, but once complete they are there for ever. The premium which is to be placed on stable policies is incalculable. Underground railways quickly become the unseen but essential parts of the cities which they serve. But their conception, planning, financing and construction are so complex and involve so many different interests that it is a real struggle to bring them into existence. New railways – or extensions to an existing system – are long-term solutions to long-term problems.

And so the development of London's rail transport services continues. Let us not lose sight of the purpose of the system. People congregate in cities because of the greater opportunities which they offer in terms of employment, education and social life. These opportunities can only be grasped if efficient transport is available at a reasonable cost; otherwise the whole purpose of the city is lost. Roads alone can never be the sole solution.

THE CHALLENGE

London's economy is strong; it requires more transport facilities and thus new projects. Current projections are that by 2014 there will be 700,000 additional people living and working in London, with the population of around 7.3 million in 2000 rising to 8.1 million.

Both National Rail and the Underground are vital for the economic health of central London. Demand is increasing steadily, and there is little chance that the present Underground can keep pace, even given planned capacity increases to the system.

The years to come promise great things; let us hope that a combination of political will, managerial excellence and the garnering of political and public support will enable them to be achieved. As a nation, we cannot afford to take London's transport system for granted.

Selected Further Reading

This brief guide can only skim the surface of the available literature, and those looking for a deeper understanding of various parts of the subject matter will have to explore further.

For a general overview of London itself, the series of books by Gavin Weightman and Steve Humphries *The Making of Modern London* (Sidgwick & Jackson, from 1983) is difficult to beat, while the standard work on London Transport is undoubtedly T. C. Barker and Michael Robbins's *A History of London Transport. Volume 1 The Nineteenth Century*, and *Volume 2 The Twentieth Century to 1970*. Both were published by Allen & Unwin, in 1963 and 1974 respectively, although are long out of print. Mike Horne's series of short histories of individual tube lines, published by Douglas Rose, is also excellent, as are the more recent individual line volumes by various authors and published by Capital Transport.

Those interested in the political machinations will find Paul E. Garbutt's *London Transport and the Politicians* (Ian Allan, 1985) of value. For a look at the wider railway scene, H. P. White's *Volume 3 Greater London* in the David & Charles series of *Regional Histories of the Railways of Great Britain* is an excellent historical account, while there are numerous Stationery Office publications, notably the *Central London Rail Study* (1989). The *Annual Report and Accounts of London Transport* (and similar) are a mine of financial and statistical information. A mainly business-based overview will be found in my own *abc London Underground* (Ian Allan Publishing, 1997).

Dealing specifically with the Underground, the technical side of the rolling stock is examined in loving detail by J. Graeme Bruce in three complementary volumes: *Steam to Silver* (Capital Transport, 1983), *The London Underground Tube Stock* (Ian Allan, 1988), and *Workhorses of the London Underground* (Capital Transport, 1987). For what makes it happen, try the present author's *Principles of London Underground Operations* (Ian Allan Publishing, 2000).

Fleet details will be found in Brian Hardy's *London Underground Rolling Stock*, (Capital Transport, 15th edition, 2002). Martin Smith's well-illustrated *Steam on the Underground* (Ian Allan, 1994) provides extensive coverage on that topic.

Of the detailed company histories, few can compare with Alan A. Jackson's *London's Metropolitan Railway* (David & Charles, 1986). A much lighter but more colourful read is my own *Glory Days: Metropolitan Railway* (Ian Allan Publishing, 1998). Also from Alan A. Jackson, in conjunction with Desmond Croome, comes *Rails Through the Clay*, (2nd edition), (Capital Transport, 1994). A quite remarkable treatise on the stations, illustrated by many drawings, is Laurence Menear's *London's Underground Stations: A Social and Architectural Study*, (Midas Books, 1983). For an excursion into the Northern wastes, *By Tube Beyond Edgware* by Tony Beard (Capital Transport, 2002) is a valuable piece of research.

Ken Garland's *Mr Beck's Underground Map* (Capital Transport, 1994) gives a detailed account of how the Journey Planner was developed, but as for establishing 'what opened when', Douglas Rose's splendidly detailed and privately published *The London Underground: A Diagrammatic History*, (6th edition, 1994) has no equal. For detailed line-by-line drawings, the Quail Map Co's *Railway Track Diagrams 5: England South and London Underground* (2nd edition, 2002) is most valuable.

Useful reference material includes the Underground's internal publications when available, such as the line timetables and Rule Book, while *Who Goes Home? – a study of last trains from London* (LRPC, 2000) gives much detail on that topic.

An 'Official' publication presently in print is *London Underground Ltd: An Official Handbook* (5th edition, 2000) published by Capital Transport.

Underground-related articles appear in *Modern Railways* and other magazines from time to time. Finally, *Underground News*, the monthly journal of the London Underground Railway Society, can be recommended as a record of current events.

Appendices

Appendix I: Before the Underground

Some routes were opened to passengers by other than Underground companies, and only later became part of the present day Underground system. This list excludes lines such as that to Upminster, where broadly parallel operation by National Rail remains.

25 March 1843
Thames Tunnel for pedestrian use, Wapping-Rotherhithe

22 August 1856
Eastern Counties Railway, Stratford-Loughton

24 April 1865
Great Eastern Railway, Loughton-Ongar

22 August 1867
Great Northern Railway, (Finsbury Park-) East Finchley-Mill Hill East (-Edgware)

1 January 1869
London & South Western Railway, Ravenscourt Park-Richmond

7 December 1869
East London Railway, Thames Tunnel converted to railway operation; Wapping-New Cross Gate

1 April 1872
Great Northern Railway, Finchley Central-High Barnet

10 April 1876
East London Railway, Wapping-Shoreditch

1 April 1880
East London Railway, Surrey Quays-New Cross

8 August 1898
Waterloo & City Railway, Waterloo-Bank

1 May 1903
Great Eastern Railway, (Ilford-)Newbury Park-Woodford

Appendix II: Chronology of Principal Events on London's Underground Railways

This appendix is in two sections. Part I gives the opening dates of lines, by railway, before the formation of the London Passenger Transport Board on 1 July 1933; Part II records major events across the system from that date.

PART I: Opening Dates of Sections of Railway, by Company

Metropolitan Railway

10 January 1863	Farringdon-Paddington
1 October 1863	Connection to Great Northern Railway at King's Cross
13 June 1864	Paddington-Hammersmith
23 December 1865	Farringdon-Moorgate
13 April 1868	Baker Street-Swiss Cottage
1 October 1868	Paddington-Gloucester Road
24 December 1868	Gloucester Road-South Kensington
1 February 1875	Moorgate-Liverpool Street, connecting with the Great Eastern Railway
12 July 1875	Moorgate-Liverpool Street (Metropolitan)
18 November 1876	Liverpool Street-Aldgate
30 June 1879	Swiss Cottage-West Hampstead
24 November 1879	West Hampstead-Willesden Green
2 August 1880	Willesden Green-Harrow-on-the-Hill
25 September 1882	Aldgate-Tower Hill
6 October 1884	Liverpool Street-Whitechapel
25 May 1885	Harrow-on-the-Hill-Pinner
1 September 1887	Pinner-Rickmansworth
8 July 1889	Rickmansworth-Chesham
1 September 1892	Chalfont & Latimer-Aylesbury (old)
1 January 1894	Stoke Mandeville-Aylesbury
1 April 1894	Aylesbury-Verney Junction (absorbed)
1 December 1899	Quainton Road-Brill (absorbed)
4 July 1904	Harrow-on-the-Hill-Uxbridge
1 January 1905	Electrification, Baker Street-Uxbridge
1 July 1905	First stage of Inner Circle electrification inaugurated
2 November 1925	Moor Park and Rickmansworth-Watford
10 December 1932	Wembley Park-Stanmore

Metropolitan District Railway

1 October 1868	High Street Kensington-Gloucester Road
24 December 1868	Gloucester Road-Westminster
12 April 1869	Gloucester Road-West Brompton
30 May 1870	Westminster-Blackfriars
3 July 1871	Blackfriars-Mansion House and High Street Kensington-Earl's Court
9 September 1874	Earl's Court-Hammersmith
1 June 1877	Hammersmith-Richmond
1 July 1879	Turnham Green-Ealing Broadway
1 March 1880	West Brompton-Putney Bridge
1 May 1883	Acton Town-Hounslow Town
21 July 1884	Osterley-Hounslow West
6 October 1884	Mansion House-Whitechapel. Inner Circle completed and junction made with East London Railway at Whitechapel
3 June 1889	Putney Bridge-Wimbledon
2 June 1902	Whitechapel-Upminster
23 June 1903	Ealing Common-Park Royal
28 June 1903	Park Royal-South Harrow
1 March 1910	South Harrow-Uxbridge
2 June 1932	Through working Barking-Upminster began

East London Railway

1 October 1884	Underground services operated Whitechapel-New Cross and New Cross Gate until 3 December 1906
31 March 1913	Shoreditch-New Cross and New Cross Gate, using electric traction

Great Northern & City Railway

14 February 1904	Finsbury Park-Moorgate

City & South London Railway

18 December 1890	King William Street-Stockwell
25 February 1900	Borough-Moorgate
3 June 1900	Stockwell-Clapham Common
17 November 1901	Moorgate-Angel
12 May 1907	Angel-Euston
20 April 1924	Moorgate-Euston reopened after reconstruction. Through running to Hampstead line via Camden Town
1 December 1924	Moorgate-Clapham Common reopened
13 December 1926	Clapham Common-Morden. Through running via Kennington and Embankment to Hampstead line

Waterloo & City Railway

8 August 1898	Waterloo & City, worked by London & South Western Railway

Central London Railway

30 July 1900	Shepherd's Bush-Bank
14 May 1908	Shepherd's Bush-Wood Lane
28 July 1912	Bank-Liverpool Street
3 August 1920	Wood Lane-Ealing Broadway

Baker Street & Waterloo Railway

10 March 1906	Baker Street-Lambeth North
5 August 1906	Lambeth North-Elephant & Castle
27 March 1907	Baker Street-Marylebone
15 June 1907	Marylebone-Edgware Road
1 December 1913	Edgware Road-Paddington
31 January 1915	Paddington-Kilburn Park
11 February 1915	Kilburn Park-Queen's Park
10 May 1915	Queen's Park-Willesden Junction
16 April 1917	Willesden Junction-Watford Junction

Great Northern, Piccadilly & Brompton Railway

15 December 1906	Hammersmith-Finsbury Park
30 November 1907	Holborn-Aldwych
4 July 1932	Hammersmith-South Harrow
19 September 1932	Finsbury Park-Arnos Grove
9 January 1933	Acton Town-Northfields
13 March 1933	Northfields-Hounslow West and Arnos Grove-Oakwood

Charing Cross, Euston & Hampstead Railway

22 June 1907	Charing Cross-Golders Green and Archway
6 April 1914	Charing Cross-Embankment
19 November 1923	Golders Green-Hendon Central
18 August 1924	Hendon Central-Edgware

PART II: Major Events from 1 July 1933

1 July 1933	Formation of London Passenger Transport Board under the Act of 1933
31 July 1933	Opening, Oakwood-Cockfosters, Piccadilly Line
18 September 1933	Monument-Bank escalator link opened
25 September 1933	Opening of reconstructed Holborn station
23 October 1933	Opening, South Harrow-Uxbridge, Piccadilly Line
5 June 1935	New Works Programme 1935-40 announced
1 November 1937	All steam locomotives and goods rolling stock transferred to London & North Eastern Railway (except service stock)
30 June 1938	1938 tube stock enters revenue-earning service
31 October 1938	Opening of new Aldgate East station
4 December 1938	Opening of new Uxbridge station
3 July 1939	Opening, Archway-East Finchley, Northern Line
1 September 1939	Control of undertaking passed to Government through the Railway Executive Committee
20 November 1939	Opening, Baker Street-Stanmore, Bakerloo Line
14 April 1940	Opening, East Finchley-High Barnet, Northern Line
19 October 1940	Latimer Road-Kensington (Olympia) closed
19 January 1941	Opening of Highgate station, Northern Line
14 March 1941	Opening, Finchley Central-Mill Hill East, Northern Line
4 December 1946	Opening, Liverpool Street-Stratford, Central Line
5 May 1947	Opening, Stratford-Leytonstone, Central Line
30 June 1947	Opening, North Acton-Greenford, Central Line
23 November 1947	Opening of new White City station
14 December 1947	Opening, Leytonstone-Woodford and Newbury Park, Central Line
1 January 1948	Formation of London Transport Executive as a nationalised body under the British Transport Commission, following Transport Act 1947. End of wartime controls
31 May 1948	Opening, Newbury Park-Hainault, Central Line
21 November 1948	Opening, Woodford-Hainault and Loughton; also Greenford-West Ruislip, Central Line
25 September 1949	Opening, Loughton-Epping, Central Line
18 November 1957	Opening, Epping-Ongar, Central Line
26 January 1958	First installation of programme machines for automatic junction signalling at Kennington
28 February 1959	Acton Town-South Acton closed
1 March 1959	Opening of interchange between Central and District/Circle lines at Notting Hill Gate
12 September 1960	Opening of electrification, Rickmansworth-Amersham/Chesham, Metropolitan Line
10 September 1961	Metropolitan Line services north of Amersham withdrawn; end of steam passenger working of Underground services
18 June 1962	Completion of four tracks, Harrow North Junction-Watford South Junction, Metropolitan Line
1 January 1963	Formation of London Transport Board, following Transport Act 1962
10 January 1963	Centenary of first Underground railway
5 January 1964	First automatic ticket barrier installed at Stamford Brook
5 April 1964	Full-scale trials of automatic train operation (ATO) commenced between Woodford and Hainault
3 October 1964	Finsbury Park-Drayton Park closed
9 October 1964	District Line services withdrawn between Acton Town and Hounslow West
5 February 1967	Opening of new Tower Hill station, District and Circle lines
1 September 1968	Opening, Walthamstow-Highbury & Islington, Victoria Line

Above: **The 1992 stock was built primarily for the Central Line, but additional cars were built for the Waterloo & City Line, then part of British Rail's Network SouthEast. The picture shows a Driving Motor car raised on jacks in the maintenance area at Waterloo on 8 August 1998, the centenary of this line.** *Author*

1 December 1968	Opening, Highbury & Islington-Warren Street, Victoria Line
7 March 1969	Opening, Warren Street-Victoria, Victoria Line
1 January 1970	Formation of London Transport Executive under the control of the Greater London Council, following Transport (London) Act 1969
6 June 1971	Steam working of engineers' trains ceases
23 July 1971	Opening, Victoria-Brixton, Victoria Line
14 September 1972	Opening of Pimlico station, Victoria Line
28 September 1975	42 killed and 74 injured in tunnel end wall collision at Moorgate, Northern City Line
19 July 1975	Opening, Hounslow West-Hatton Cross, Piccadilly Line
16 August 1976	British Rail commences services Old Street-Drayton Park
8 November 1976	British Rail commences services Old Street-Moorgate and Drayton Park-Finsbury Park BR station
16 October 1977	Opening, Hatton Cross-Heathrow Central (later renamed Heathrow Terminals 1, 2, 3), Piccadilly Line
1 May 1979	Opening, Baker Street-Charing Cross, and transfer of Baker Street-Stanmore line to new Jubilee Line. Opening of interchange at new Charing Cross station
28 March 1980	Opening, London Transport Museum at Covent Garden
4 October 1981	'Fares Fair' introduced by Greater London Council, reducing fares by 32%

17 December 1981	Law Lords rule 'Fares Fair' unlawful
21 March 1982	Fares increased by 96%
24 September 1982	Bakerloo Line services withdrawn north of Stonebridge Park
22 May 1983	GLC reduces fares by 25%. Zonal fares and Travelcards introduced
1 July 1983	Golden Jubilee of London Transport
26 March 1984	Introduction of one-person operation (OPO), surface lines
4 June 1984	Bakerloo Line services restored between Stonebridge Park and Harrow & Wealdstone
29 June 1984	Formation of London Regional Transport under the control of the Secretary of State for Transport following London Regional Transport Act 1984
1 April 1985	Formation of London Underground Ltd as a subsidiary of London Regional Transport
12 April 1986	Opening, Heathrow Terminal 4 station, Piccadilly Line
31 August 1987	Introduction on tube lines of one-person-operated, conventionally driven trains
18 November 1987	31 killed in fire at King's Cross, Piccadilly Line escalators
1 April 1994	Waterloo & City Line, Kensington (Olympia) line and Putney Bridge–Wimbledon transferred to London Underground Ltd
30 September 1994	Holborn–Aldwych and Epping–Ongar closed
14 May 1999	Opening, Stratford–North Greenwich, Jubilee Line
19 August 1999	Opening, North Greenwich–Waterloo, Jubilee Line (these stations only)
17 September 1999	Opening, Canada Water, Canary Wharf and Bermondsey, Jubilee Line

24 September 1999	Opening, Waterloo, Jubilee Line
7 October 1999	Opening, London Bridge, Jubilee Line
	Opening, Waterloo–Green Park and Southwark station, Jubilee Line
3 July 2000	Creation of Transport *for* London, but without London Underground
25 September 2002	First occasion on which Underground brought to complete standstill by strike (in support of a 10% pay claim)
31 December 2002	Tube Lines signs 30-year PPP maintenance contract for the Jubilee, Northern and Piccadilly (JNP) lines
25 January 2003	Detached traction motor causes derailment of a 1992-stock train at Chancery Lane; minimal injuries. Central and Waterloo & City lines closed
18 February 2003	Waterloo & City Line services restored
12 April 2003	All Central Line stations again served
14 May 2003	Metronet signs 30-year PPP maintenance contracts for Metropolitan, District, Hammersmith & City and East London lines (SSL) and for Bakerloo, Central and Victoria (BCV) lines
15 July 2003	Control of London Underground passes to Transport *for* London
17 October 2003	Derailment of Piccadilly Line train between Hammersmith and Barons Court due to broken rail
19 October 2003	Derailment of Northern Line train as it entered Camden Town High Barnet line northbound platform

---

Notes: Dates shown as 'Openings' refer to the first day of public service. Thus, although Stage 1 of the Jubilee Line was officially opened by HRH The Prince of Wales on 30 April 1979, public services south of Baker Street did not commence until the following day. Sometimes opening dates refer to the first Underground involvement; 14 April 1940 was the first day of electric traction from East Finchley to High Barnet, the Underground having supplanted the previous LNER steam service.

Throughout, present-day names of stations have been used to avoid confusion; the station shown as opening on 25 September 1882 at Tower Hill, for instance, was originally named Tower of London.

Appendix III: Closed Underground Stations

Over the years, stations have closed for a variety of reasons, from relocation to suit new developments or to provide interchange, or service withdrawal due to lack of traffic. The principal changes affecting London Underground and its predecessors are listed here, together with a brief note as to cause. Permanent closures only are noted; those due to what have sometimes amounted to very extended engineering works or what turned out to be only a temporary suspension of services have been ignored. Also omitted are the closure of platforms on adjacent tracks, such as the Metropolitan platforms between Finchley Road and Wembley Park. These stations remain served generally by what are now Jubilee Line trains.

It should perhaps be pointed out that the renaming of stations is another reason why once familiar names disappear. Thus Strand became Charing Cross, and Dover Street became Green Park. Closure was not involved.

'Opened' and 'closed' refer to the first and last dates a station was served under the aegis of the Underground, although even then services and station facilities may be provided by a third party like British Railways or their successors. Stations may have been served previously by another railway, before the Underground.

Bakerloo Line

Bakerloo line Underground services running north of Harrow & Wealdstone to Watford Junction were withdrawn on 24 September 1982, after which services were provided solely by British Railways.

Central Line

Station	Opened	Closed	Notes
Blake Hall	25 September 1949	31 October 1981	Lack of traffic
British Museum	30 July 1900	24 September 1933	Replaced by Holborn
North Weald	25 September 1949	30 September 1994	Ongar branch closure
Ongar	25 September 1949	30 September 1994	Ongar branch closure
Wood Lane	14 May 1908	22 November 1947	Replaced by White City

District Line

Station	Opened	Closed	Notes
Hounslow Town	1 May 1883	1 May 1908	Replaced by Hounslow East
Northfields & Little Ealing	16 April 1908	18 May 1932	Replaced by Northfields on new site
Osterley & Spring Grove	1 May 1883	24 March 1934	Replaced by Osterley on new site

District Line continued

Station	Opened	Closed	Notes
St Mary's Whitechapel Rd	1 October 1884	30 April 1938	) Both replaced by new Aldgate East
Aldgate East	6 October 1884	30 October 1938	)
South Acton	13 June 1905	28 February 1959	Closure of branch from Acton Town
Tower Hill	6 October 1884	4 February 1967	Relocated to old site, used until 1884

Hammersmith & City Line

Station	Opened	Closed	Notes
Hammersmith Grove Rd	1 October 1887	31 December 1906	Service withdrawn
Shepherd's Bush	13 June 1884	31 March 1914	Relocated to new site
Uxbridge Road	1 November 1869	19 October 1940	Service withdrawn following enemy action
White City (H&C)	1 May 1908	24 October 1959	Fire damage, but used only intermittently

Jubilee Line

Station	Opened	Closed	Notes
Charing Cross (Jubilee)	1 May 1979	19 November 1999	Diversion of line to Stratford

Metropolitan Line

Services on the Metropolitan were withdrawn between Quainton Road and Brill on 30 November 1935, and between Aylesbury and Verney Junction on 4 July 1936. Quainton Road remained served by British Railways until 4 March 1963.

Subsequently, Metropolitan Line services were withdrawn between Amersham and Aylesbury on and from 10 September 1961, after which date services beyond Amersham were provided solely by British Railways.

Station	Opened	Closed	Notes
Farringdon Street	10 January 1863	22 December 1865	Replaced by Farringdon
Hillingdon	10 December 1923	5 December 1992	Relocated to new site
King's Cross (Metropolitan)	10 January 1863	9 March 1941	Replaced by new station to the west
Lord's	13 April 1868	19 November 1939	Replaced by St John's Wood Bakerloo Line
Marlborough Road	13 April 1868	19 November 1939	Replaced by St John's Wood Bakerloo Line
Swiss Cottage	13 April 1868	17 August 1940	Replaced by Bakerloo line station
Uxbridge	4 July 1904	3 December 1938	Relocated to new site

Northern Line

Station	Opened	Closed	Notes
City Road	17 November 1901	8 August 1922	Lack of traffic, service acceleration
King William Street	18 December 1890	24 February 1900	Replaced by Monument and Bank and diversion of line to Moorgate
South Kentish Town	22 June 1907	5 June 1924	Lack of traffic, service acceleration

Northern City Line

Services were withdrawn between Drayton Park and Moorgate in September/October 1975 by London Underground. The line was transferred to British Railways and reopened under the Great Northern Suburban electrification scheme in August/November 1976, with a new connection to reach the main-line station at Finsbury Park.

Piccadilly Line

Station	Opened	Closed	Notes
Aldwych	30 September 1907	30 September 1994	Closure of branch from Holborn
Brompton Road	15 December 1906	29 July 1934	Lack of traffic, service acceleration
Down Street	15 March 1907	21 May 1932	Lack of traffic, service acceleration
Park Royal & Twyford Abbey	23 June 2003	5 July 1931	Replaced by Park Royal
South Harrow	28 June 1903	4 July 1935	Relocated to new site
York Road	15 December 1906	17 September 1932	Lack of traffic, service acceleration

Never operated by London Transport

The following LNER stations were all due to become part of the never-completed Northern Line electrification under the 1935-40 New Works Programme:
- Mill Hill, The Hale, Edgware (LNER); passenger services were finally withdrawn by the LNER on 11 September 1939.
- Stroud Green, Crouch End, Highgate (HL), Cranley Gardens, Muswell Hill, Alexandra Palace; passenger services were finally withdrawn by British Railways Eastern Region on 5 July 1954.

Never opened

There have been many others planned but not constructed; for those mentioned here all had the necessary powers obtained, and some site work was undertaken.

North End (or Bull & Bush), Northern Line. Partially constructed with platforms and lower-level stairs c1907, this station below Hampstead Heath would have been the deepest on the system. However, it was judged to have little traffic potential, and work was abandoned.

The Northern Line extensions were to be projected beyond Edgware on a new formation to Brockley Hill, Elstree South and Bushey Heath. Partially constructed before World War 2, work was never resumed subsequently, due mainly to Green Belt legislation and the consequent lack of traffic potential.

A similar fate befell the proposed projection of Central Line services beyond West Ruislip to South Harefield and Denham, parallel to the Great Western & Great Central Joint line. Very little work was undertaken; again, it was not resumed post-World War 2.

Appendix IV: Electrification Systems and Connections between Lines

This appendix lists the various electrification systems which have been used on London's Underground railways. Experimental installations have been omitted. It also shows connections with National Railways and between Underground lines.

All sections of Underground line, except where it operates over other railways

Third and fourth rails at 630V dc, positive rail outside the running rails, negative return in the centre.

Baker Street & Waterloo, 1906

Until the opening of the extension to Watford Junction, 1915-17, the polarity of the conductor rails was reversed. Thus the centre third rail was positive, and the outside fourth rail negative.

City & South London Railway, 1890

Third rail laid between the running rails, 305mm in from one of them and at a slightly lower level. Altered to London Underground standard on reconstruction of the line, 1922-4.

Waterloo & City Railway, 1898

Third rail in centre between running rails and at same level; altered to side-of-track position in October 1940 to conform with Southern Railway standard, and voltage raised from 500V dc to 600V dc. Further reconstructed in 1994 to standard Underground fourth-rail specification.

Central London Railway, 1900

Third rail in centre of track; altered to London Underground standard in April 1940, although the positive rail is in a higher than standard position due to the effect of the shape of the running tunnels.

Great Northern & City, 1904

Third and fourth rails, one on each side of the running rails. Altered to London Underground standard in April 1940. Converted to outside third rail from Drayton Park southwards, with the transfer of this line to the British Railways Board following withdrawal of Underground services in 1975.

Bakerloo Line Queen's Park to Watford Junction; District Line Gunnersbury to Richmond

Third and fourth rail, positive outside the running rails, negative in centre. Converted to third rail in 1970, after which the centre negative rail was retained solely for the benefit of Underground trains and earthed to the running rails. The fourth rail was removed north of Harrow & Wealdstone following cessation of Underground working over this section in 1982. In both cases, present use of the infrastructure is shared between London Underground and Silverlink.

District Line East Putney to Wimbledon

Third and fourth rails, positive outside the running rails, but central negative rail provided solely for the benefit of Underground trains and earthed to the running rails. Use of the track is shared between the District Line and South West Trains empty stock to and from Wimbledon Park sidings.

Hammersmith & City Line Latimer Road to Kensington Olympia and Earl's Court

Third and fourth rails, positive outside the track, negative in centre. Following bomb damage on 18 October 1940, service withdrawn north of Kensington Olympia and never reinstated. De-electrified.

District Line electric services between Earl's Court and Kensington Olympia inaugurated on 20 December 1946, though until 1986 these ran only in conjunction with exhibitions at Olympia. Now electrified on standard London Underground system. Physical connection between London Underground and BR later removed.

West London Line subsequently electrified at standard Southern third rail from Clapham Junction to North Pole Junction, with overlapping 25kV ac overhead electrification extending south from Willesden Junction to A40M Westway overbridge.

Physical connections between London Underground and Network Rail

Apart from those listed above, these are now limited to two locations:
- West Ruislip, between Ruislip depot and the Chiltern line, not used for passenger purposes.
- Harrow South Junction (towards Marylebone) and Mantles Wood, north of Amersham (towards Aylesbury), part of former Great Central/Metropolitan Joint operation.

Physical connections between Underground lines

With the sole exception of the Waterloo & City, which is completely self-contained, all other Underground lines are interconnected. In the past, this facility was provided for access to and from Acton Works, and is now used primarily for the movement of engineering trains.

These routes are often of considerable length, and may require reversal(s). This has implications both for the time taken and for line occupancy. Thus a journey from Lillie Bridge depot (west of Earl's Court, District Line) to (say) Epping requires running via Ealing Broadway and reversal, while to reach Golders Green requires running to Hammersmith (reversal), King's Cross (reversal) and thence direct to destination.

Operation of the sub-surface lines involves much inter-running, with many connections in the vicinity of the Circle Line. However, the availability of a route does not necessarily imply that it is available to all types of stock, and the D stock, for instance, is not permitted to run north of High Street Kensington.

About the Author

John Glover FCILT is a transport professional whose varied career in the transport industry has mostly involved railways. He has a wide and extensive knowledge of the business, with 28 books published on various aspects of the railway industry. A contributor to *Modern Railways*, he has also been a member of the Institute of Logistics and Transport's Strategic Rail Forum since its inception in 1992.

He assumed the authorship of this long-standing history of London Underground in the mid-1980s, and this is the fourth edition to appear under his name. He has always taken an interest in the Underground, which provided the passenger rail services in the area where he lived for the whole of his childhood. Perhaps being born in a nursing home from which, he is told, the sounds of passing trains of 1938 stock could be clearly heard has something to do with it!

Index

Below: **Service stock comes and goes; three Sentinel 0-6-0 diesel hydraulic locomotives built in 1967/68 were bought second hand by the Underground to replace the remaining steam locomotives. This is DL83 in authentic pea green livery and now owned by the Nene Valley Railway.** *Author*

Above: **The way we were; this is the interior od 1959 tube stock DM 1030, which was 'poshed up' in a make believe historical livery to form London Underground's Heritage Train. This and trailer 2044 may now be found at Mangapps Farm Railway where it was photographed in June 2002.** *Author*